LATENT
DESTINIES

NEW AMERICANISTS A Series Edited by Donald E. Pease

LATENT DESTINIES

Cultural Paranoia and Contemporary U.S. Narrative

PATRICK O'DONNELL

Duke University Press   Durham and London   2000

© 2000 Duke University Press
All rights reserved
Printed in the United States of
America on acid-free paper ∞
Typeset in Melior by Tseng
Information Systems, Inc.
Library of Congress Cataloging-
in-Publication Data appear on
the last printed page of this book.

Contents

Preface

■ This book has gone through several crucial transformations over the years of its writing. I began with primarily a thematic approach to paranoia in a large assortment of contemporary fictions. Initially, my attempt was to show the relation between paranoia and postmodernist constructions of identity as one of difference and resistance, particularly within the historical framework of the cold war, but I modified this trajectory considerably when it became clear that the binary I was reconstituting—between paranoia and schizophrenia, between paranoid rigidity and postmodern multiplicity—was reductive of what I now believe to be an often complicitous relation between postmodernity and paranoia. Then, my enthusiasm for the topic flagged with *die Wende* in Germany and the illusory end of the cold war: paranoia was out; paranoia was past; paranoia was boring. Only when I began to read through the sudden proliferation of works by Slavoj Žižek, to regard the complex progression of thought between Fredric Jameson's *The Political Unconscious* and his *Postmodernism,* and to reread Anthony Wilden's monumental *System and Structure,* did it become apparent that I ought to regard what I term "cultural paranoia" in this book symptomatically, and in so doing, see contemporary manifestations of paranoia as occurring within a matrix of cultural pressures and forces that include nationalism, global capitalism, and the formation of identity under postmodernity. This discussion of paranoia thus takes place within an evolving area of study that might be called "cultural pathology," or more precisely—given the epidemic nature of contemporary paranoia—"cultural epidemiology," as do such other recent works (however different in perspective) as Žižek's *The Plague of Fantasies,* Elaine Showalter's *Hysteries: Hysterical Epidemics and Modern Culture,* and Mark Seltzer's *Serial Killers: Death and Life in America's Wound Culture.*

Once paranoia is viewed as a cultural symptom—that is, a manifestation of certain sociosymbolic investments—it becomes evident that it is historically anchored in a much more complex and enlarged sense than can be gathered by exploring its more local materializations in cold war culture. Cultural paranoia must be looked at within the larger, global perspective provided by Jameson's understanding of the intersections of late capitalism and postmodernity, even as the analysis must be vectored (as it is in this book) with specific issues related to nationalism, gender and racial differentiations, criminality, the formation of history, and a host of other lines of flight that one could pursue. Paranoia did not die with the fall of the wall and the liberation of Bucharest. It is in fact thriving, as it always has, in the U.S. cultural imaginary: the *X-Files* craze, survivalism, the new millennialism, the Unabomber, comet cults, the fascination with the alien abject, the proliferation of conspiracy theories to the point of self-parody—all speak to the persistence of cultural paranoia as symptomatic of nation and identity within postmodern circumstances. Because the trope that governs cultural paranoia is metonymy, there is little doubt that by the time the reader views this list, several new incarnations will have appeared. Indeed, as I argue, for the very reason that it is a symptom paranoia will not go away; in its most general aspect, it is the symptom of cultural identities negotiated within and in apposition to "history."

In *Latent Destinies,* I scrutinize several U.S. novels and films written and produced over the last three decades as symptomatic representations of paranoia in contemporary culture. The project I undertake here is to come to terms with paranoia as a political factor—one that is deeply connected to global capitalism, the identificatory formations of self, gender, and nation, the ideology of postmodernism, and the use and abuse of history in postmodernity. Rather than provide what would be a capacious survey or catalog of works that manifest paranoia in one form or another, I have chosen to focus on relatively few in the desire to understand contemporary cultural paranoia as, essentially, a narrative process through which the relation between versions of postmodern identity and history conceived in the afterburn of master narratives is negotiated in a manner that elides historical temporality. Neither I nor the works I examine offer any cure for paranoia or any postparanoid utopian projects, as if one could make it go away through a shift in perspective or change in attitude. In fact, the idea that multiplicity, protean identity, or hermeneutic latitude can be set in mere opposition to paranoia is critiqued in the fictions of cultural paranoia that I discuss. To (badly) paraphrase Žižek (accurately) translating and citing Wagner ("The wound is healed only by the spear that smote you"), symptomatically, the "wound" or dis-ease of cultural paranoia is only (ad)dressed by that which inflicted it in the first place: the commodification of identity in postmodern culture that is, precisely, the *constitution* of identity in postmodern culture.

The discussion is organized around the topics of nationalism, gender, criminality, and the construction of history. None of these is exclusive of other trajectories that might have been pursued: issues of class and race, homophobia (which among others, serves here as a recurring and prevailing symptom of cultural paranoia rather than its fundamental element), the fabrication of aliens and borders—all weave their way through the readings and chapters, though I have not devoted a separate section to them. In particular, it seemed to me as I was developing the book that racial paranoia—which, again, crosses into the focused considerations of paranoia and gender or national paranoia that the reader will find here—is of a sufficiently complex nature and historicity that it deserves a full-length treatment of its own, and certainly one that I did not wish to confine to a single chapter in this study. Indeed, like the texts I explore, the topics that organize this book can be thought of as symptomatic rather than categorical in that they locate the "work" of cultural paranoia on specific sites where, at any given moment, multiple paranoiac trajectories are at play. My goal is to provide a diagnostic versus an encyclopedic assessment of paranoia as it operates on political, psychoanalytical, and epistemological levels in the contemporary cultural imaginary.

The readings begin with an entry into the subject: a consideration of two recent films, *Groundhog Day* and *The Truman Show*. This is followed by a chapter that works through several theoretical positions on the construction of postmodern identity. In this introductory analysis, I arrive at the conclusion that the view of temporality shared by these positions as it informs a conception of rhizomic identity within global capitalism is complicitous with forms of cultural paranoia that see history as conspiracy and the other as a threat to the integrity of the self— even if that self is, contradictorily, multiple and schizophrenic. The readings that constitute the bulk of this study, organized consecutively on the topics of nation, gender, and criminality, attempt to elicit and reconcile this central contradiction as it is negotiated within the fictions of cultural paranoia. Some readers may be dissatisfied—as was a respondent to a précis of this project at an earlier stage—that I do not offer, by means of conclusion, some escape from or alterity to the condition of cultural paranoia that I describe in the book. But as I argue throughout, the manifestations of paranoia in contemporary literature and culture are inextricably bound up with the conceptions of identity and history that are being lived out within the epistemic conditions of—to use the epochal shorthand—late capitalism. To posit a beyond to these conditions, and thus to cultural paranoia, would be to indulge in a false utopianism that complies all too easily with uncritical notions of postmodern identity as fluid, heterogeneous, carnivalesque. Such conceptions, I contend, have a way of abetting cultural paranoia, and we can only get at the problem, and thereby enable the possibility of transformation, by working critically within the political, aesthetic, and epistemological frameworks that delineate our apperception of culture in the first instance. Thus, I conclude with an exit on Don DeLillo's seminal, discordant staging of the cold war imaginary and its aftereffects in *Underworld,* a novel that historicizes the symptom of cultural paranoia, and in so doing, offers a view of history that is other than paranoid.

At one point during this project, a friend asked if spending so much time thinking about paranoia was making me more paranoid. I could only respond with another question: How can the paranoid, beset by conspiracy, tell the difference between real and illusory plots, threats, patterns of significance? In the more infamous expression, spoken by many, but perhaps most tellingly by Henry Kissinger when he was national security advisor to Richard Nixon, "even a paranoid has enemies." The study of cultural paranoia under postmodernity, in other words, cannot take place from some impossibly achieved external perspective that would, in essence, reduplicate the conditions of the paranoia it surveys; this is yet another reason why one cannot provide a cure for cultural paranoia. So, I cannot really ever answer my friend's question, any more than "we" can say, immersed as we are in cultural paranoia, how paranoid we are: by what scale could we measure it, even if we give some credence to those who might wish to argue from the position of a postmodern cynicism that we must know its limits in some sense if it can be so readily recognized and parodied? From such a stance, which informs everything from the inanities of current versions of *Saturday Night Live* and the David Letterman Show to the cool hipness of the *X-Files* and its clones, the more we parody paranoia, the more we combat it; but it can be easily seen the degree to which such parodizations offer an enjoyment of and symbolic investment in the paranoias they hypervisualize and mock. The argument of this book is tilted at another angle: cultural paranoia exists in a historical condition that imaginative work can help us to understand—not simply in order to indulge in the reframings of parody but also to begin to engage in transformations of this condition by perceiving the elements of its construction and the assumptions that inform it. To the extent that *Latent Destinies* contributes to that project, its intentions will have been fulfilled.

In the several years of this book's writing, I have relied on the advice and support of colleagues and friends who took time away from their own work to encourage and critique mine. Lynda Zwinger, Judith Roof, and Tom Byers, as always, offered innumerable insights about contemporary culture both in their own assessments and their responses to my readings; more important, they have been the best of companions through times hard and easy. Ed Dryden generously afforded several occasions for me to present work in progress at the annual *Arizona Quarterly* Symposium in Tucson. Marc Chénetier, our ablest and most capacious reader of contemporary U.S. fiction, arranged crucial venues to share my work with European colleagues as well as the immense benefit of his simpatico understanding of contemporary writing. My longtime friend Heide Ziegler gave me the opportunity to develop aspects of this project on two occasions through the offices of the Stuttgart Seminar in Cultural Studies. My former colleagues in arms at Purdue University, Vince Leitch, Richard Dienst, and Geraldine Friedman brought to this work their own incisive perspectives on postmodern and critical theory. Reynolds Smith at Duke University Press has been the most patient of editors, and I am grateful to the press readers for their valuable suggestions regarding revisions of the manuscript. Portions of previous versions of chapters 3 and 4 have been published in *boundary 2* and *Prospects,* and it is a pleasure to acknowledge the support of, respectively, editors Paul Bové and Jack Saltzman in providing a place for early work on this book. Above all, I am grateful to Don Pease for resuscitating flagging energies at exactly the right time and seeing this project through to the end. Diane, Sean, and Sara O'Donnell have lived with me through another book; they know all too well the tangible cost and intangible rewards of doing so.

The Time of Paranoia

■ In *Groundhog Day,* a 1993 film directed by Harold Ramis and starring Bill Murray, a narcissistic television weatherman is stranded in Punxsutawney, Pennsylvania. He has been sent there to report on the famous annual festival in which Punxsutawney Phil, the resident groundhog, is brought to the town square each February 2 to see whether or not he casts a shadow, thereby predicting the beginning of spring. The fabulistic premise of the film is that Murray's character, Phil Connors, is condemned to wake up each morning to a new February 2 in Punxsutawney until he learns how to overcome his vanity and properly romance the new producer who accompanies him in the field. Ramis's clever, gimmicky film presents us with the spectacle of an endlessly repeatable, diurnal temporality framed within the repetition of an annual event that serves to predict the specific future of the infinitely repeatable cycle of the seasons. Trapped in time, Murray's egotistic enunciator of the news is transformed into a small-town good guy content to live (once he has reentered "normal" temporality) within the ritualistic, rigid confines of Punxsutawney—the entire film employs roughly a half-dozen scenarios revisited with each passing of the same day. Yet this transformation only occurs via the film's paranoid performative, or an identificatory logic in which the centrality of the weatherman's existence is bound up with a magical synchronicity that allows him to perfectly match intention with action such that the plot of the world and the plot of his life become one.

    Groundhog Day is, at bottom, a paranoiac fantasy in which the protagonist becomes the center of a web of diurnal, partial narratives that are always repeated in the same manner, yet always viewed from a different perspective as Phil Connors changes positions in relation to the infinitely rehearsed activities of an average Groundhog Day in Punxsutawney. Within the repeatable time frame of twenty-four hours, Murray's character becomes a virtuoso jazz pianist, an expert ice sculptor, a great lover, a humanitarian renowned in the community for always being exactly in the right place at the right time to catch a child falling out of a tree or perform the Heimlich maneuver on a choking diner—in short, a kind of postmodern god who learns how to deal from anyplace in an always-stacked deck; or as Phil himself puts it, "I am a god, not the God, but a god." What might seem initially to be an inversion of paranoia—Phil observing the inhabitants of Punxsutawney going about their business, rather than they purportedly watching him—becomes a form of divine paranoia through which the film's god intervenes in the construction of daily plots that are all "about" him, even though the townsfolk are blissfully unaware of the fact that they are being watched and manipulated while they focus their attention on the stranger from the city.

Paranoid temporality of the kind embodied in *Groundhog Day* appears to be a pervasive element of any number of post-1970s' Hollywood films, including the *Back to the Future* series with its disjunctive overlaying of decades, "hourglass" films such as *Nick of Time* and *D.O.A.* (the remake of the noir classic) that equate fatedness with the ticking of the clock, and *Contact* (no accident that it is directed by Robert Zemeckis, the director behind the *Back to the Future*s and *Forrest Gump*), in which the future is made over in the pastoral mode. These films enfold within the performative function a succession of fantasies about control and identification founded on temporal simultaneity and synchronicity, or what Gilles Deleuze and Félix Guattari term "haecceity,"

a mode of individuation . . . very different from that of a person, subject, thing, or substance. We reserve the name *haecceity* for it. A season, a winter, a summer, an hour, a date have a perfect individuality lacking nothing, even though this individuality is different from that of a thing or a subject. They are haecceities in the sense that they consist entirely of relations of movement and rest between molecules and particles, capacities to affect and to be affected.[1]

Now it may seem at first glance that Deleuze and Guattari's molecular mode of individuation, based on a proliferation of discrete temporalities, is at odds with the narcissistic subjectivity achieved and sublimated through the paranoid performative that I have ascribed to the protagonist of *Groundhog Day*. Yet it is one of the fundamental arguments of this book that haecceity, or the molecularization of temporality, is precisely what enables the performance of paranoia. The temporality in *Groundhog Day* is one in which there is no past and no future beyond the diurnal present, simply a delinked succession of days whose separability and "perfect individuality lacking nothing" undergird much of the film's comic effect in charting the protagonist's progress. When, for example, Phil Connors begins music lessons anew each day with the local piano teacher, she becomes ever more amazed at the apparently innate skills of her student as the days and lessons accrue, for it may be the thousandth reiteration of Groundhog Day for him, but for her, it is always the first iteration of February 2. The film's formula—simultaneity plus repetition equals mastery—is the recipe for a performative logic that relies on the truncation and erasure of historical time, and its replacement with seriality as the form of temporality that enables identification with the social order.

Waking up to the fact that every new day is the same day—but one in which reality thickens, experience accrues, control increases—is one thing; waking up every day to the same day as if it were different is quite another. As a reflection on reality-as-repetition and simulation, *Groundhog Day* might be seen as the Pollyannaish (or Zemekish) version of *The Truman Show*'s (1998) edgy, mercurial representation of postmodern life. One can begin to address the ideological contrasts between the two films by asking similar questions of both: Who put Phil Connors into an endless time loop? Who took possession of an abandoned infant, named him Truman Burbank, constructed a domed island for him, filled it with a cast of thousands, and made him the unwitting star of a real-time television show that has been on the air continuously for over three decades? In the case of *Groundhog Day*, the implication is that Phil himself is entirely responsible for his location in the fantasy/nightmare of February 2 in Punxsutawney, and as an allegory, the film contends that only by transcending his self-centeredness and insensitivity will Phil be able to reenter historical time. Conversely, in *The Truman Show*, everyone except Truman is initially in on the plot of his life, and the person responsible for his plight is the techno god-artist, Christof, who renders Truman as a real person in a virtual construct.

Identifying who created the world in which the protagonist is trapped suggests that the two films are mirror images of each other. In *Groundhog Day*, the performance of paranoia provides a gateway for full entry into the symbolic order. In *The Truman Show*, the symbolic order is already established; it is a construct—but of course the film is out to make the point that the habitus of all our domed islands is, precisely, a construct; and Truman, in the beginning innocent of paranoia, suddenly becomes aware that he is the subject of the plot to record and consume his life. For Truman, becoming paranoid and confirming the plot that contains him initiates the escape from the symbolic order of the film into the more "real reality" beyond (that of both the imaginary and real audiences of *The Truman Show*), which the film has been at odds to prove is just as constructed, just as virtual as the movie-set world he escapes. Plausibly, *The Truman Show* could be seen as director Peter Weir's reflexive critique of such films as *Groundhog Day* in that it divests itself of the fantasy of some form of historical "real" to which we have access outside or beyond whatever historical, virtual, or simulated constructs we are caught up in, though this depends on reading the film's ending as intentionally offering only the flimsiest of exits to Truman from an increasingly flimsy simulation. Put another way, Weir's version of *Groundhog Day* would be one in which all the inhabitants of Punxsutawney are actors hired to pretend that it is always February 2, all eyes watching Phil Connors figure out his prefigured life, rather than he being the only voyeur in a reality that will only change when he does.

But however canny *The Truman Show* may be in recognizing the constructedness of the symbolic order as it engages in Baudrillardian fatality with all the glib optimism appropriate to the view that the fake and the real are one, it participates in the same temporal logic as the seemingly more naive *Groundhog Day,* and it does so more consequentially as Truman's coming-to-identity is fully bound over to his becoming paranoid. Indeed, *The Truman Show* enscenes the birth of paranoia, and although it is questionable whether Weir had the Schreber case in mind while assembling this *Bildungsspiel* in a bubble, certainly the film bears significant traces of Freud's classic study of a paranoid personality: a son trapped in his father's "womb"; a god-son on whom the world is entirely centered, convinced that he must destroy the world in order to gain ascendancy over it; a son (s-o-n) whose actions cause a change in the movements of the sun (s-u-n), and whose relation to the father is one of bondage and eventual release as he exits out the backdoor (the symbolic asshole) of the world whose purpose he has just sundered at film's end. Truman's signature greeting is "Good morning, and if I don't see you again, good afternoon, good evening, and good night." It is both his entry and exit line, the one he reiterates to his neighbors with each recurrent "new" morning of his life and it registers the ideal temporality of his digitilized world. It is both diurnal, in that the greeting (and all the actions of Truman's life) is ritualistically repeated at the same moment of each day, and contradictorily synchronic, haecceitic: all time on Truman's island is one time; it is all the time of the moment, where all futurity and historicity is compressed into the endlessly rehearsed and repeated present. The reason that viewers are fascinated by Truman's screened life is because it removes them from the implied mundaneness of their own lives taking place in historical time and projects them into the eternal present of communal gathering around the television screen to voyeuristically live out the simulated history of Truman's life. The joke of the film, of course, is that Truman's life is far more boring than those of his viewers could ever be; yet, for the audience, haecceity and repetition are the perennial, contradictory components of so-called real history.

This is the time of paranoia. The manifestations of contemporary cultural paranoia—that is, paranoia as the symptomatic condition of postmodernity in contrast to the name for a personal pathological disorder —reveals haecceitic temporality to be the medium for the formation of paranoid identities and epistemologies.[2] In *The Truman Show*'s canny redoubling of its own constitutive elements, the film stages Truman's escape from this time-world as enabled by his recognition of its spatial and temporal lineaments and his accession to paranoid knowledge. A few technical glitches—a falling klieg light, some radio interference, an overheard unscripted comment—lead Truman to the dawning awareness that he is, indeed, at the center of his universe, and that everyone in it is watching his every move in order to control his actions and contain him. This premise might suggest that Weir (whose films, from *Picnic at Hanging Rock* to *Fearless,* typically mystify origins and consequences, while providing stark clarity to the moment or act that posits those ends) intends *The Truman Show* to be distinctly antiparanoid. For the paranoid scenario is what exists as reality for Truman, and his breaking out of that world—literally, breaking through its shell—along with the demystification of the father/god/Christ Christof as a bumbling autocrat whose power is entirely bureaucratic, might be viewed as a deconstruction of the island simulacrum, along with the paranoid epistemology and temporality that attends it. From this perspective, Truman's escape is not necessarily into a world more real than that of the island on which he has been imprisoned for the first three decades of his life, for again the film promotes the concept that the real and virtual worlds are simply reflections of each other; his escape is simply into a world where the father will not be able to watch him anymore, though necessarily Truman enters a world where he will continue to be watched by others until the end of his days.

It is more useful, however, to see *The Truman Show* not as an anatomy of our paranoid times but as a parodic enactment of pervasive fantasies about cultural identity founded on certain unitary versions of temporality that coincide with cultural paranoia as I shall elicit it from a variety of contemporary novels and films. To pose the question differently, what do the films I have been discussing—along with all the other symptomatic hip excesses of contemporary conspiracy and paranoia—tell us about the current fascination with, or desire for, paranoia? This is to regard fantasy in Žižek's terms as symptomatic of subject-object relations in the symbolic order, full of holes needing ideological plugging:

> The first thing to note is that fantasy does not simply realize a desire in a hallucinatory way; rather, its function is similar to that of Kantian "transcendental schematism": a fantasy constitutes our desire, provides its co-ordinates; that is, it literally "teaches us how to desire." The role of fantasy is thus in a way analogous to that of the ill-fated pineal gland in Descartes's philosophy, this mediator between *res cogitans* and *res extensa:* fantasy mediates between the formal symbolic structure and the positivity of the objects we encounter in reality . . . it provides a "schema" according to which certain positive objects in reality can function as objects of desire, filling in the empty places opened up by the formal symbolic structure. To put it in [other] terms: fantasy does not mean that when I desire a strawberry cake and cannot get it in reality, I fantasize about eating it; the problem is, rather: *how do I know that I desire a strawberry cake in the first place?*[3]

Playing on the title of Žižek's account of fantasy and ideology, *The Plague of Fantasies,* what can explain the current plague of paranoid fantasies, which come in the teeth of historical expectation following the supposed conclusion of a cold war that was the excuse for paranoia? As Eric Santner has suggested, "when one would expect an easing of paranoid anxieties about dangers emanating from the 'evil empire' and its satellites," we instead find that "cold war paranoia may have actually played the role of a collective psychological defense mechanism against a far more disturbing pathology that is only now beginning to find public avenues of expression."[4] In this entry to the discussion of cultural paranoia in contemporary narrative, I will offer some speculation on these questions that may seem to refer to, in a short-term historical sense, a surprising turn of events, but that reveal an ongoing cultural logic operating on the level of cultural fantasies about postmodern identity. Why are we paranoid now? Why is paranoia viewed as the cool, reflexive mode of self-knowledge? Why are we not paranoid about paranoia?

Žižek encourages us to regard fantasy as a clue to cultural identity that is signified through the binding of the desire of the subject to objects, and we might look once more to *The Truman Show* to detect a clue about the nature of certain kinds of postmodern desire that, attached to objects, fills in "the empty places opened up by the formal symbolic structure." First, it is fair to ask, what could Truman possibly desire? Everything he needs is made available to him; indeed the needs themselves have been constructed for him in advance of his desiring. What empty places in the symbolic structure of his universe could possibly exist? In fact, the entire premise of *The Truman Show* as it is conveyed to its worldwide audience is that Truman's universe is replete with objects of desire to which he has immediate access. These are always present to him in his eternal, diurnal present, but for the audience they are commodities that they *should* desire since Truman has them and uses them. Because the show runs twenty-four hours a day and, thus, cannot deploy the usual commercial breaks, it relies on placing before Truman as what he needs and desires (from the cereal he eats to the tires on his car and the lawnmower he uses on the weekend) the brand-name objects being covertly advertised by the actors who surround Truman. The symbolic universe of *The Truman Show,* initially, contains no holes because it *is* the hole, or gap—the place from which desire issues and becomes attached to specific objects—in the symbolic universe of its audience. Consequently, as a whole, it symptomatically reveals the how and what of their desires, or in terms of the film's logic, the virtual origin of and response to desire in the supposedly real world of its audience.

In this sense, the film's function, which admittedly it sets out to subvert, may not immediately seem to tell us much about the cultural paranoia for which (Santner is correct) the cold war was a long-running historical occasion, but certainly not cause or end. Yet something in this function—in the relation between virtual and "real" desire and the relation between the screened objects of Truman's eternal present and the series of relays and delays instituted between real objects and their acquisition—is symptomatic of what might be labeled paranoid desire. That desire, which combines the yearning for absolute centeredness, immediacy, transparency, and control, is built on an internal contradiction. Its pressures, in effect, crack open the closed world of inverted paranoia within which Truman lives—as the subject, not the author, of paranoia — until certain revelations from above disable the mechanisms by which that contradiction is repressed. The nature of the contradiction is entirely temporal, and it may be stated in this manner. The commodity culture that idealizes itself in a spatialization of time where everything is available, where the totality of desired objects is immediately present, depends on a series of temporal and spatial dislocations and molecularizations that separate the object from s/he who desires it. Desire can only be satisfied via a series of capital exchanges that must take place through a series of relays that literally take time: one must watch the show to become aware of desires and objects; one must labor to accumulate capital; one must exchange capital for the object; one must wait for the manufacture and/or delivery of the object; one must go to the place where it is sold, or take the time to log on to the Internet where it can be purchased under the illusion of global immediacy and availability. In Žižek's terms, the fantasy that *The Truman Show* enacts serves both to reveal and repress the mechanism by which that fantasy becomes attached to specific objects.

For Truman, the move from unconsciousness to ideological awareness occurs when he discovers that there are objects or messages in his world that call attention to themselves as nonimmediate, inaccessible in some way, or untranslatable. And it is that foreignness or alienness — when Truman starts to hear voices, when he begins to believe that everyone is watching him, when he first desires to escape from the totality in which he is immersed, when he begins to compare the promise of a multiple self to the reality of a constructed fate — that call to paranoia that instigates both his awareness of self and his desire to escape to another world of bodies and objects to which he does not have immediate access. In this manner, I am suggesting, the film symptomatizes its own fantasy. This is a fantasy of haecceity, of the eternal present of always available objects fulfilling desire before it even knows itself as such, secreted around the kernel of paranoia that bursts open when the spatial and temporal rifts of Truman's utopia manifest themselves. Interestingly enough, these rifts are often glitches of a technology tending evermore toward the virtualization of space and spatialization of time.

For the purposes of scrutinizing the plague of cultural paranoia, the value of films such as *Groundhog Day* or *The Truman Show* is not so much that they are, respectively, celebrations or critiques of postmodernity as they are symptomatic of the fantasies on which a simulated totality roughly approximating a postmodern "world" is founded. As symptoms, then, do they help us comprehend current paranoia fashion, our playful obsession with it, our fetishizing of its historical irruptions? Or more accurately, are these films symptoms of a symptom, since paranoia today in its savvy, hyperkinetic mode itself seems symptomatic of something else going on in postmodern culture that needs explaining? Prefatory to eliciting those explanations, I offer the following speculations as to why we seem beset by paranoia when, as it were, we thought it might be otherwise in the historical incongruity elaborated in the novels and films of cultural paranoia I discuss. While some of these conjectures will be familiar, they all are related to a fundamental temporal contradiction in postmodernity that reveals the paranoia of postmodern identity relative to historical processes.

1. We are paranoid because paranoia is the last refuge of identity so aware of itself as a construct and as constructed by desires assembled for it that it becomes a parody of itself;

2. we are paranoid because we are approaching with increasing rapidity the commodification and virtualization of temporality itself, at which point we will seek the power to reinstantiate a nostalgic past remade to provide a virtual depth to a future that has been brought entirely into the present;

3. paranoia is fun, or pleasurable, because it allows us to perceive what might be called a self-referential depth in the fantasy of the totalized world of available objects, folding back into it a kind of personal history, destiny, and temporality that fantasy itself attempts to erase or revise as immediacy;

4. we are paranoid because, like Truman, we seek escape from the *huit clos* of what Jameson calls the totality of late capitalism, which is at the same time a desire to control it or, to switch theoretical terms, control the interface (our bodies) between libidinal economy and that of our own vestigial selves: this control is precisely what Truman discovers he wants and cannot have (not in "this world") in *The Truman Show;*

5. we seize paranoia in a kind of Nietzschean embrace because, perhaps counterintuitively (given that Schreber thought of himself as a kind of cyborg), we regard paranoia as the last epistemology, the final form of human knowledge before knowledge passes away into information. Paranoia is, at root, a way of knowing ourselves in relation to others as having the capacity to be known, to be seen, to be objects of desire and attention. In this regard, Truman never had it so good, and in the mode of parodic paranoid regression, one can project a more comically sinister ending for the film—one in which Truman, knowing what he knows once he has per-

ceived that he is the star of the show, returns to the island to live out his life; he would, at that point, indeed be in charge of his world.

These five theses about contemporary paranoia only refer to scattered symptoms of what Žižek, Showalter, Seltzer, and others describe as the cultural epidemics that assail us. As we shall see, cultural paranoia in particular has much to do with the anxieties about power, nation, history, technology, knowledge, and identity for which temporality is a kind of recurrent vector. The novels and films that I consider reveal how fantasies about immediacy, multiplicity, and the transparency of desire inform our understanding of paranoia as a condition that enables specific identifications with the social order and through which we experience great pleasure as well as great unease. Coming to terms with this contradiction may offer if not a way out of paranoia, at least a means of comprehending its role in an ongoing history whose temporal reach extends well beyond and before any breaks, posts, eruptions, repetitions, and epochs we may invent to mark it as being somehow for us.

Postmodernity and the Symptom of Paranoia

A paranoid is someone who has possession of all of the facts.
—attributed to William Burroughs

The truth is out there. . . . Trust no one.
—*X-Files*

■ The Symptom of Paranoia

If, as various takes on the subject suggest, fear and panic are the most evident somatic responses to the fragmentations and decenterings of the so-called postmodern condition, then paranoia can be viewed as the reaction-formation par excellence to the schizophrenias of postmodern identity, economy, and aesthetics.[1] Visible in every aspect of late capitalist culture—from the hermeneutic posturings of high postmodernist texts such as Thomas Pynchon's *The Crying of Lot 49*, to the latest episode in the chain of CNN scenarios that unfailingly dramatize the constants of nationalism and individuality in the ongoing historical miniseries—paranoia manifests itself as a mechanism that rearranges chaos into order, the contingent into the determined. As such, it is a means of (re)writing history. Doubly confronted with "the disappearance of *external* standards of public conduct when the social itself becomes the transparent field of cynical power" and "the dissolution of the *internal* foundations of identity . . . when the self is transformed into an empty screen of an exhausted, but hypertechnical, culture," as the *Panic Encyclopedia* puts it,[2] the paranoid subject resurrects these standards and foundations by taking advantage of the very fluidity of relations and contingency of events that mark the postmodern. Through the arbitrations of narrative, the subject restructures the real as the historical; using the very materials, as it were, that cause paranoia, s/he converts the arbitrary and contingent into the determined fatalities of "history" and the stories of the nation.

The evidence of this tautological narrative process at work is (paranoically) omnipresent and painfully obvious. Contrary to projection, our paranoia seems to have intensified in the wake of the cold war's supposed denouement. As the "post" cold war reflections of Eric Santner, Daniel Pipes, and others have demonstrated, it appears that the trilateral paranoia of the cold war is now in the process of being internalized, scattered, localized, and reiterated at a multitude of sites—from Oklahoma City, Waco, and Ruby Ridge, to Bosnia, the White House, and the security fire walls of the Internet—giving rise, as Santner observes, to a perverse nostalgia "for a paranoia in which the persecutor had a more or less recognizable face and a clear geographical location."[3] The narrativizing—the "story"—of contemporary cultural paranoia in the United States reflects the investments and economies of postmodern identity, in Žižek's term, as "*the form of subjectivity that corresponds to late capitalism.*"[4] What can be characterized as the recurrence of variously displaced scenarios indicate that the cold war can now be seen as a sequencing of events and geopolitical relations to be set within the larger framework of the ongoing globalization of capitalism, which for Santner, reveals a "far more disturbing pathology" (x)—one not deflected by the fall of the wall. The critical narratives of paranoia examined in detail here divulge this pathology in the social identifications and historical investitures of deeply conflicted postmodern subjects, who celebrate fluidity, schizophrenia, and deterritorialization—who, as Brian Massumi notes, live off of these as commodified subjects that are "determined . . . through the serial commission of the act of groundless consumption"—yet whose obsession with boundaries and boundary crossing suggests a collective nostalgia for the old binaries, economies, orders, and nations.[5]

Contradictions, of course, underlie the formation of a postmodern identity within various frameworks during a time when identity as such—with the symbolic orderings of gender, race, sexuality, nation, historical epoch—is at odds with the compelling desire to be free of these orders, to live out their alterities. Cultural paranoia can be seen as a symptomatic response to these contradictions, operating through an elision of temporality and a fantasizing of historical centrality in which, for example, self and nation become one. In the identificatory fantasies of cultural paranoia, history becomes the conspiratorial siting of the confluence of destinies where the latent omnipotence of the "individual"—an empowerment underwritten by the availability and flow of capital—becomes storied into the narrative of nation or its displacements in other narratives of identity. As mentioned earlier, I approach the issue of cultural paranoia in this chapter by considering it as a symptom of postmodernity and, specifically, as symptomatic of postmodernist materializations of history and temporality; to elicit its movements and effects, I discuss in ensuing chapters a number of literary and cinematic representations of paranoia in contemporary U.S. culture. The choice of venue is significant, for however variously these works address the "contemporary" historical moment and "American" setting, they commonly regard the United States as the visible site where the incongruities of subjectival fluidity operating within the prefigurative historical order of a national destiny are negotiated in the epoch of late capitalism and the attendant phantasmic remapping of national onto global orders and agendas. In the works I discuss, cultural paranoia is not projected as an existentially specific social dis-ease nor a pathology that subtends a universally conceived "American way of life" but as a certain suturing of individuals to the social imaginary in which crucial differences between agency and national or other identificatory fantasies are collapsed. The representations of interpellation to be found in these works compel us to consider the ways in which cultural paranoia is a problem related to constructions of postmodern identity as symptomatic of late capitalism, its enjoyments and its discontents.

Usually employed as a term for individual and, increasingly, collective psychosis, paranoia commonly refers to the pathological condition of individuals who exhibit a host of familiar symptoms, many of which derive from Freud's classic study of the Saxon supreme court judge Daniel Paul Schreber.[6] These symptoms include megalomania; a sense of impending, apocalyptic doom; racist, homophobic, or gynophobic fear and hatred of those marked out as other deployed as a means of externalizing certain internal conflicts and desires (the scapegoating of otherness thus is essential to the ongoing work of paranoia); delusions of persecution instigated by these others or their agents; feelings of being under constant observation; an obsession with order; and a fantasizing of the reviled, abjected self as at the center of intersecting social and historical plots. When not limited to the symptoms of individual psychopathology, paranoia is often viewed either as a universal personal condition (one available to individual subjects across history, as much to Julius Caesar as to Lee Harvey Oswald) or a mindset that, like a contagion, can temporarily afflict a nation or a people (the United States during the Salem witch trials; Germany during the Third Reich).

In departing from these familiar senses in the present study, I argue that the classic, universalized symptoms of an individual pathological condition can be seen as symptomatic of a collective identity when we regard those contemporary events and narratives that reveal paranoia as a kind of narrative work or operation that articulates the "individual's" relation to the symbolic order: the stories that emerge from this are narratives of identification with the cultural imaginary. Paranoia as manifested in contemporary narrative can be further considered as the multifarious contradiction of a postmodern condition in which the libidinal investment in mutability, in being utterly other, contests with an equally intense investment in the commodification of discrete identities: this contradiction pertains both to the formation of individual subjects and to the national and political bodies into which they are interpellated as collective subjects.[7] The works examined in this book, written and filmed under this condition, are thus representations of identities called to order within the historical framework of late capitalist postmodernity, where desire and capital are knit together and, concomitant with "technological advances," globalized. More specifically, what is being globalized can be viewed as acutely symptomatic of contemporary U.S. culture (postmodernism being our highest-grossing intellectual export), which exhibits the conjunction of any number of conflicting, yet often conflated, pressures and forces: the emergence of new world orders amid recursive obsessing over national identity; the cults of renewed individualism coming in the age of the cyborg and postmodern modularity; the United States as the site of historical centrality in its role as arbiter of a (now global) manifest destiny or the site of historical exceptionalism and a separate peace; the United States as the fount of late capital or, contradictorily, as anachronistic junkyard of a Fordist economy.

To historicize cultural paranoia in this manner is to consider it as conjoining a series of related trajectories: the psychopathology of individual paranoia; the cultural pathology informing the recurrences of social paranoia in the United States; the multiple crises animating postmodern identity formations and deformations under late capitalism; the paranoia of narrative formations per se in their mania for plots and endings. The work of Žižek, which everywhere informs this study, has been crucial to enhancing our understanding of how such personal, collective, and narrative constructions both overlap and offer resistances to each other, and how they can be read symptomatically in order to come to terms with the culturally specific locations of our avoidances and elisions of the "real" of history. Yet, though the work of cultural paranoia evidences the deep contradictions within postmodern identity, I refrain from claiming for it historical certainty or referentiality. To assume that we can know paranoia from the outside, even if we are "in" it, that it is a disease that may have a cure, even if the cure is paranoia itself (as suggested by versions of so-called redemptive paranoia often attributed to writers such as Pynchon), is merely to mirror paranoia.[8] To even begin with the assumption that we *are* paranoid in a nonsymptomatic sense presumes a totalizing, paranoid, critical formation that is characteristic of discussions of paranoia—that it exists, that it is real, that it is obvious and everywhere.[9] To construct a paranoia based on historical certainty is at once to generate a phantasmic secret history whose labyrinthine contingencies and mysteries are known only full by the paranoid. The paranoic condition of what O. K. Werckmeister terms "citadel culture" in his iconoclastic study of postmodernism is such that certainty about the obvious historical conditions of a Manichaean cold war and post–cold war United States vie with critical doubts about the reality of those conditions—doubts generated by the paradoxical reflexivity of cold war culture.[10] This is one of the self-generated contradictions of cultural paranoia: a processing of the real wherein the apprehension of a source or cause of paranoia becomes the means for questioning its existence. Was there, for instance, really a plot to kill Kennedy, or does the insistence on figuring assassination plots around the historical accident called "Lee Harvey Oswald" mark an obsession with historical and political plots as such, regardless of the actualities that are orchestrated through them? If Oswald did not exist, wouldn't we have to invent him as, indeed, it appears we have done according to the Oswald-fictions of Mailer's *Oswald's Tale* (1995) and DeLillo's *Libra* (1988)?

The initial question, then, for the study of cultural paranoia is not "what is paranoia?" or "where is it?" but "who is paranoia for?" Framing it in this way allows us to view paranoia as mediated by postmodernist conceptions of history where "history" as understood under Jean-François Lyotard's "postmodern condition," rather than being seen as the grand narrative of major events or the national story, is an aggregate of minor narratives, each arising from an assemblage of perspectives, experiences, and vested interests.[11] This is to regard paranoia not as an episteme or a hermeneutic—simply one available way of seeing or organizing reality in a pluralistic menu of perspectives—but as a symptom of a detotalized postmodern culture, part and parcel of our suspicion of the overview, the national epic, the official history. Equally, paranoia can be viewed as symptomatic of what Fredric Jameson describes as the spatialization of temporality under postmodernism.[12] For Jameson, the compression of time and space to be observed in the spatial organization of postmodern architecture materializes the repression of the "real" of history in late capitalism.[13] It is a symptom, precisely, in the sense that paranoia is an alibi, a form of accommodation for the loss of those grand narratives along with the temporal depth and sequential ordering that founds a putative collective historical belonging.

Cultural paranoia is a compensatory fiction that binds individual subjects to identificatory collective bodies such as those of the nation, class, gender (when articulated according to the logic of compulsory heterosexuality), and the "human." It operates under the rubric of a postmodern cynicism that, in Peter Sloterdijk's analysis, wavers unevenly between skepticism about Enlightenment values and rationality (even as revised by Jürgen Habermas in "the unfinished project of modernity") and full investiture in the Deleuzian "postsignifying regime" of bodies without organs and deterritorialized subjectivities.[14] For the paranoid, identity, knowledge, and history are validated by what is out there, and only hidden to the eyes of those who cannot see the *formal* relation between dispersed signs and objects. To employ the kind of tautology that typifies paranoia in the works to follow: the signs and objects of the world are dispersed because this, supposedly, is the ruling condition of a decentered and detemporalized postmodern reality. And to indulge in the kind of paradox that is equally typical of paranoia: for the paranoid, the relation between the dispersed manifestations of the real to be woven into narratives of cultural identity is hidden to others because they either have not come to terms with the explosion of the subject under this regime (they are not schizophrenic enough), or they do not retain a belief in the capacity of the now-exploded subject to remap itself onto the real by uncovering the hidden relation between things that have always been there for us to see (they are not paranoid enough). Who is paranoia for? It is for us, as national, corporate, historical subjects in a time when these formations are beset by questions about their cohesion and continuance.

It is within these terms that we consider paranoia as a symptomatology indicative of specific relations between postmodern identity and the formations of history in contemporary U.S. culture. In tracing the genealogy of the concept of "symptom" from the early to late Lacan,

Žižek writes that Lacan's most radical postulation of it was as "sinthome," or "a certain signifying formation penetrated with enjoyment."[15] Žižek elaborates on "the radical ontological status of symptom" viewed in this way:

Symptom, conceived as sinthome, is literally our only substance, the only positive support of our being, the only point that gives consistency to the subject. In other words, symptom is the way we—the subjects—"avoid madness," the way we "choose something" (the symptom-formation) instead of nothing (radical psychotic autism, the destruction of the symbolic universe) through the binding of our enjoyment to a certain signifying, symbolic formation which assures a minimum of consistency to our being-in-the-world. (*Sublime Object,* 75)

The cultural production of paranoia is, for our purposes, a symptom/sinthome: it is a projection—a "signifying, symbolic formation"— that enables the construction of certain versions or representations of identity in which the constituencies of self, body, race, gender, and nation are bound together in the fabrication of the historical subject. As Leo Bersani argues, the relation between paranoia and identity formation is tautological—the manufacturing of replicant bifurcations between self and other, or nonself, or enemy, in the attempt to preserve a unitary identity: "In paranoia, the primary function of the enemy is to provide a definition of the real that makes paranoia necessary. We must therefore begin to suspect the paranoid structure itself as a device by which consciousness maintains the polarity of self and nonself, thus preserving the concept of identity."[16] As we will see, it is the *overidentification* of articulated identities—such as the conflation of gendered, human (as opposed to cyborg or criminal), and national identities as these cohere around certain ideological conjoinments and exclusions— that underwrites cultural paranoia in late capitalist U.S. culture. Žižek notes in the aptly titled essay "Enjoy Your Nation as Yourself" that a "nation *exists* only as long as its specific *enjoyment* continues to be materialized in a set of social practices and transmitted through national myths that structure these practices" (*Tarrying,* 202). I would add that this national enjoyment is intimately linked to the formation of individual subjects within a specific national regime precisely to the extent that they view themselves as citizens of a nation, defined as an assemblage of behaviors, laws, boundaries, and invested historical narratives. In cultural paranoia, the nation's citizens are not just projections of the "good" (patriotic) or "bad" (traitorous) self; these projections continually shift ground so that, for example, the patriotism of survivalists is easily amenable to anti–U.S. government sentiments. The national self is also viewed experientially and historically as symptomatic of the nation as a whole.

Thus, the conflation of national and personal identities is symptomatic of itself: it is its own symptom, in that it is a projection validated, always after the fact, by the self or nation that organizes itself within the symbolic order of a world that "makes sense" as the place where its paranoid fear—the source of its enjoyment—is confirmed.[17] Paranoia is not symptomatic of some other, deeper, hidden cause or meaning. It is, rather, an effect without cause, a post hoc, sliding signifier of identity—hence its reliance on multiplicity—though one of the manifestations of cultural paranoia is the ceaseless search for the determinate source of paranoid anxiety. This is a quest that is always fulfilled in the eradication of specific paranoided objects or persons, and never finished because, according to Freud's conception of paranoia, the other who is the object of paranoia is, in fact, a self-projection, as Paul Smith argues:

In paranoia, the libido is turned upon the ego itself so that, in a loose sense, the paranoiac's object-choice is his/her own ego. Freud suggests that in such a case anything perceived as noxious within the ego (in the interior, as it were) is then projected onto external objects: the "subject" thus endows the external world with what it takes to be its own worst tendencies and qualities.[18]

Even though, and especially after, Freud "introduced the fascinated rejection of the other at the heart of that 'our self' . . . which precisely no longer exists ever since [he showed it] to be a strange land of borders and otherness ceaselessly constructed and deconstructed," as Julia Kristeva observes, paranoia operates as the means by which paranoid identity regains or re-members itself.[19]

Freud's notorious conception of the "dementia praecox" of paranoia in the Schreber case located the "fascinated rejection of the other at the heart" of an anachronistic self as an anxiety pertaining to "homosexual panic." To the extent that paranoia has been seen as a problem of sexuality, it has been associated with the rigidifying of heterosexual, male identity as a means of repressing same-sex desire, of excluding the homosexual and/or feminine self/other: in several of the novels discussed later, we shall see paranoia operating under this sexualized rubric.[20] More broadly, however, the postmodern condition of cultural paranoia I am describing is such that all identity differentials (sexual, gendered, racial, national, etc.) reveal the work of paranoia as that which both polices the boundaries between self and other, and like the border patrol, has more to do the more susceptible those boundaries are to transgression and erasure.[21] In the tautology of paranoia, as long as the paranoid identity (or nation) exists, so will the other race, gender, or country projected by the paranoid. These are the sources of the enjoyment of his/her identity; that is to say, the libidinal investment in a free self—free to the extent that one identifies and attempts to satisfy specific needs within the "loop of enjoyment" that, for Žižek, constitutes the overarching framework of late capitalism as such. As he writes, "Capitalism is caught in a kind of loop, a vicious circle, that was clearly designated already by Marx: producing more than any other socioeconomic formation to satisfy human needs, capitalism nonetheless also produces even more needs to be satisfied" (*Tarrying*, 209). Among many other things, the nation is the political formation that ensures that the distribution of capital will take place in an orderly and continuous fashion by constantly reorganizing itself according to capital flows. In order to stabilize itself within these structural shifts, the nation constructs myths of origin and identification that provide a virtual rigid foundation to its protean shape. As Donald Pease explains, the narratives of nationalism in a late capitalist, "postnational" phase serve as "instruments of psychic governance" that are "best evidenced perhaps in the panic that has accompanied the desymbolization and subversion of national narratives."[22] This "panic," in part, is a result of a symptomatic recognition that the very material on which the nation constitutes its rigid ideologies of order and destiny is continually in flux, as it must be if capital and the libidinal economies associated with it are to run their course in the "free" marketplace. Replicating this contradiction of rigidity beneath fluidity, the paranoid subject identifies with the rigid formation of the nation and its adherent essentialized race, class, and gender categories (or with reciprocal counternational formations such as clans, cults, factions)—an identification that can only occur by virtue of the fluid, postmodern subject's paradoxically voluntary confinement within boundaries that depend on the projection and exclusion of the other, the enemy.

■ Paranoia and History: Latent Destiny

The relation between what I have been describing as the paranoid subject under postmodernism interpellated into collective narratives of nation, identity, and destiny along with the construction of history as a narrative, is central to my discussion. I will begin to unfold its complexity momentarily in looking briefly at an example from narratives of that most wrenching national story, the Kennedy assassination, which will form the focus of the next chapter. Recall that paranoia treated here is not a condition or a collection of symptoms (though we will treat it symptomatically) but a *narrative process* by means of which an individual constructs a historical or cultural identity. To coin an expression, this process relies on the formation of "cultural mnemonics," or Lacanian *points de capiton* (quilting points) that enable the buttoning down—the anchoring—of discrete traumatic events as moments in which cultural identity-narratives reveal their shape and horizon as a kind of destiny.[23] The consequences of such constructed destinies are inevitably forged in the aftermath of the event itself, but as if the event, in its latency, always possessed this meaning and was always being prepared for by history itself. In this sense, history under paranoia is latent destiny, or history spatialized and stripped of its temporality. Such history is constructed through a process of interpretation that compresses contingent events, memories, or traumas into a singular story that manifests the real of self or nation as organized around a central paranoid "truth": that it is always, and has always been, at the focal point of historical processes rather than on their periphery.

History is symptomatically experienced in such narratives as a self-fulfilling prophecy, for the strategies of back-formation and fore-shadowing ensure that whatever happens (whatever acquires memorial status) will be conflated and woven into the paranoid fabrications of self or nation.[24] In the "manifest destiny" of U.S. national narratives as they have evolved in the aftermath of the cold war, history has become something akin to the racist white man's burden: imaginably, now alone at the center of a global history, "we" are responsible for the continuation of methodical historical processes (the formation of the "new world order" of global capitalism); "we" are the means by which the supposed heterogeneity of the so-called Third World is converted—to be sure, in an orderly fashion—into the homogeneity of the First World; "we" have taken on the encumbrances of the historical superego who must define and sublimate or destroy the evil others who would foul up history, and who simply can't understand that their narrative is, in a sense, a historical lie because it does not fit ours. In short, the "we" here, itself a paranoid projection (but one actualized in contemporary events), positions "us" as the schizoid arbiters of history: both its authors (the ones who make history) and readers (the ones who organize its signs into the significant patterns of historical destiny).

The Kennedy assassination is a particularly overdetermined cultural mnemonic in that around an event whose status as event is perpetually in question, there has gathered a host of narratives about national destiny, alternative histories, and tragic turns. Inevitably linked to the assassinations of Martin Luther King Jr. and Robert Kennedy as one in a series of events in which national heroes were murdered, the Kennedy assassination has become the point of departure—the watershed moment—for an entire generation: it is not much of an exaggeration to say that everyone (in 2000) approximately over the age of forty-five remembers where s/he was when s/he heard that President Kennedy had been shot on November 22, 1963. The members of that generation locate themselves in one of the founding moments of a continuously revised history in which new events must be symptomatically linked to the original trauma. Depending on what assumptions about history guide the narrativization of the assassination, the event itself will be constituted *as* event.

In the film *JFK* (1991), director Oliver Stone, who in much of his work foments cultural paranoia by mapping the quest for personal identity onto the formation and destiny of the nation, represents the assassination, in the first instance, as causally linked to the Vietnam War (Kennedy was killed as part of a military coup that ensured the continued dominance of the military and radically enhanced engagement in Vietnam even after the demise of the Eisenhower regime in Nixon's loss to Kennedy) and, in the second instance, as symptomatic of the ongoing oedipal national narrative in which the bad king has killed the good king, who must be resurrected by his loyal sons. For Stone, the cultural mnemonic of the Kennedy assassination is the site where identity is sutured to the symbolic order of history. Why were we in Vietnam? The answer, for Stone, who had already represented the effects of the primal scene of the father's slaying/castration in *Platoon* (1986), is that "we" had to grow up, that boys had to become men in order to restore the good father and wreak revenge on the bad father, but our national tragedy is that "we" had to do it by means of a bad war.[25] What is evident in Stone's narrative of the assassination, as in other versions of this national moment, is that it serves as a point of origin and rupture from which ensues history in the form of fallout: Vietnam, Watergate, Iran-Contra, the Gulf War, etc., can be connected causally and symptomatically to the assassination, as if it had been planned from the beginning, as if it all could not have happened any other way. This clearly paranoid version of history—this positioning of a cultural mnemonic within a narrative that links chronology to, among other things, castration anxiety—depends on a contradiction that allows it to incorporate any divergent histories of the event, including those that would assert that the Kennedy assassination was a historical accident. As in the discrepancy of the postmodern subject that seeks both mutability and order, so Stone's "history" reflects a desire for multiple, alternative histories and a single plot. The contradiction resides in the formation of the assassination in the cultural imaginary as a discrete moment that arbitrarily anchors history while, at the same time, serving as the origin of a chain of events whose significance becomes clear only in the aftermath and in a determined relation to the original event. The elision of temporality evident in such narratives is also a component of crucial versions of postmodern subjectivity that implicitly underwrite the cultural paranoia that informs the narrativization of these subjectivities.

In terms of the narratives that have grown up around it, the Kennedy assassination has taken on the status of what Žižek defines as the Lacanian "Real." On one level, it happened—there is the corpse of the president to prove it. But on another level, its status as real is constantly put into question by the very evidence that establishes it as a historical event. Like the autopsy photos from the Parkland Hospital morgue, the infamous Zapruder film, a home movie intended for personal consumption that "accidentally" became a documentary of a presidential assassination, rather than providing certainty about what happened in Dallas on that day, has served to foster multiple and contradictory conspiracy and anticonspiracy theories. In this way, the assassination has become, in Žižek's words,

the radically contingent element through which . . . symbolic necessity arises [that reveals] the greatest mystery of the symbolic order: how its necessity arises from the shock of a totally contingent encounter of the Real—like the well-known accident in the *Arabian Nights:* the hero, lost in the desert, quite by chance enters a cave; there, he finds three old wise men, awoken by his entry, who say to him: "Finally you have arrived! We have been waiting for you for the last three hundred years." (*Sublime Object,* 185)

This explains, to some extent, why the Zapruder film—reviewed hundreds of time, blownup, reprocessed, looked at from every angle—can still fail to convey the truth of the assassination or the reality of the event. It fails as a representation partly because it has become the "Real" in the narratives constructed about it, the contradictorily determining and radically indeterminate image-event that marks the crossing between utter contingency and historical conspiracy.

As an "entity which must be constructed afterwards so that we can account for the distortions of the symbolic structure" (Žižek, *Sublime*

Object, 162), as a "hole, a gap, an opening in the middle of the symbolic order . . . the lack around which the symbolic order is structured" (ibid., 170), the assassination reveals a paradoxical historical desire evident in a number of contemporary narratives. The paradox is characteristic of a culture and nation that, on the one hand, have accrued revolutionary and posthistorical self-representations, yet, on the other, insist in these representations on being at the center of history, taking place on a destinal site whose topographic details are forever inscribed on the national memory.

The narratives surrounding the Kennedy assassination register the contradiction inherent in representing the historical "real" by dramatizing it as a historical eruption or catastrophe, and then, recontaining it as a critical event in a sequential chronology that demarcates a national destiny. The process through which contingency becomes a key element of destinal logic is equally present in narratives such as Pynchon's *The Crying of Lot 49* or Kathy Acker's *Empire of the Senseless* that variously chart the peregrinations of fluid, postmodern identities operating within increasingly complex and encroaching disciplinary matrices; or, in the enscenements of events such as the Oklahoma City bombing where the site of a chaotic and violent manifestation of paranoid reciprocity is, first, visually framed (by CNN) as a kind of proscenium (the damaged building draped and backlit), and then, metonymically incorporated into a series of narratives involving cults and government agencies reaching back, potentially, to the Civil War. What these narratives symptomatically reveal is an enjoyment of—a desire for—the fantasy of a libidinal free agent operating under the umbrella of a historically determinate social and political economy. This condensation of temporality in paranoid narratives is perfectly complicit with protean conceptions of the postmodern subject. It is this irresolvable contradiction that produces narratives of cultural paranoia that attempt, through a series of narrative figures and strategies, to organize the postmodern subject—to capitalize on its investments and recuperate its losses—within and for an increasingly tenuous, thus increasingly protective, symbolic order.

Complicating this contradiction is the fact that paranoia relies on projected historical orders in which the differential of temporality has been elided, or a synchronous history where identity emerges as molecular or rhizomic. As different as theoretical conceptions of postmodern subjectivity may be, a remarkable number of them engage in the liquefaction of the postmodern subject/body—a fluidity that marks both its supposed freedom and commodification. Whether it is Luce Irigaray's gendered subjectivity as "fluid," Deleuze and Guattari's nomadic "BwO" (body without organs), Lyotard's "great ephemeral skin," Kristeva's "abject," or Haraway's "cyborg," identity in these conceptions is, by turns, amoebic, fractal, mutative, provisional, or multiple. Nor is this view limited to waves of French theorists and philosophers who insist on (and perform) the conflation of the postmodern body, writing, and identity: chaos theory, the new biology, hypertextuality, fuzzy logic, genetics—all seem, implicitly at least, to conspire in placing the fluid postmodern subject/body under the rubric of a radical contingency, as a mutative process whose tracings (whether these be spoor, writing, or genetic material) constitute a history among histories.

Examining the various readings of the microscopic oddities to be found on the Burgess Shale, the evolutionary biologist Stephen Jay Gould maintains that the "essence" of evolutionary history—itself viewed as fluid and nomadic rather than progressively linear—is "contingency." A retrospective scrutiny of the corpses fossilized in the Burgess Shale's graveyard of "wonderful life" reveals the "overwhelming improbability of human evolution" composed, as it is, of "thousands of improbable stages": "Alter any early event, ever so slightly and without apparent importance at the time, and evolution cascades into a radically different channel."[26] In his argument, Gould compresses the elements of body, "writing" (the interpretable traces left by the fossils), and history that shall concern me throughout this study. As his title indicates, he sees the radical contingency often associated with the fluidity of the postmodern subject as a cause for wonder and celebration; yet, the coexistence of "wonderful life" and cultural paranoia in these terms compels a critical reflection on the comparable fluidities of bodies, identities, writing, historicity, and capital. In turning toward theoretical considerations of these compressions, I will work toward one of the central conceptions of this study: that paranoia capitalizes (on) postmodern identity by underwriting its phantasmic reclamation from history.

■ Postmodern Temporalities

The paradox of the fluid and fragmented postmodern subject gaining identity by means of a spatialized history and operating within structurated networks of ever increasing complexity informs the contemporary fictions I consider. These are narratives that, themselves, simulate the contradiction of prevailing conditions as they "contain" noise and excess within exfoliating and unwieldy, but still arguably paranoid, narrative systems.[27] As such, they foment questions about national identity in terms of the relation between self-formation and personal, national, and cultural borders to be resisted or transgressed; they place the burden of these questions on the operations of late capitalism and its effect on the construction of history in U.S. culture. In order to contextualize my analysis of these works more broadly within the framework of theoretical postmodernism and what it can contribute to our understanding of contemporary cultural paranoia, I now consider three versions of (anti)systematicity and the articulation of identity enunciated, respectively, by Deleuze and Guattari, Lyotard, and Jacques Derrida. In focusing on these versions of identity as articulated through the entities of body, event, state, or nation, I position what can be termed the postmodern dominant as represented by Deleuze/Guattari and Lyotard against Derrida's "return to history" in *Spectres of Marx*. Moving across these works, we note that the symptom of paranoia residing in the collusion of identity and capital is implicitly critiqued by Derrida's "hauntology," which insists that a retemporalized history is the wedge to be driven between human identity and the flow of capital. This critical interference, then, serves as a means for historically framing those dominant conceptions of postmodern identity that conflate libidinal fluidities of the body, schizophrenia as the postmodern "structure of feeling," mutabilities of the self, and the free market fluctuations of capital as evidence of a kind of posthistorical freedom that necessitates a concomitant narrative investment in paranoid reorderings and recenterings through an elision of temporality.

Deleuze and Guattari's *A Thousand Plateaus*, the culmination of their mammoth project on "capitalism and schizophrenia," is in many ways a scrapbook of a postmodern (post)subjectivity.[28] Maddening, if not impossible, to read in any linear or sequential fashion (to read it in this manner would constitute a misreading), *A Thousand Plateaus* both describes and serves as a performance of collective assemblages that speak against the national state, monologism, and singularity. In promoting such exotic, if utopian, "nomadisms" as "deterritorialization," the "rhizomic" organization of the real, and the "BwO," Deleuze and Guattari attempt to align the future of subjectivity with the future of capital. Although hardly uncritical of capitalism as such since it operates under state control and subjects bodies into labor even as it subverts territoriality in the form of multinational conglomerates, Deleuze and Guattari see capital as greasing the wheels for combined epistemological and geopolitical "flows" that are transforming bodies, identities, and nations, and have been doing so since the Middle Ages when capitalism (for them) began.

In *A Thousand Plateaus,* Deleuze and Guattari articulate the adaptive version of subjectivity that operates within the "multilinear system" of late capitalism, where "everything happens at once: the line breaks free of the point as origin; the diagonal breaks free of the vertical and the horizontal as coordinates; and the tranversal breaks free of the diagonal as a localizable connection between two points" (297).[29] Characteristically, Deleuze and Guattari may be discussing locally the movements of Berg's *Wozzeck* or lines and blocks of color in a Klee, but these discrete multilinear systems are equally homologous to the global flows and migrations of entire populations, the flow of capital along hemispheric lines, or the flow of desire in a body no longer conceived as a singular system of organic centers. The "mode of individuation" necessitated by the emergence of such interlocking molecular, regional, and global multisystems, as I mentioned in the entry, is that of Deleuzian haecceity, or "a season, a winter, a summer, an hour, a date hav[ing] a perfect individuality lacking nothing," constituted of "relations of movement and rest between molecules and particles, capacities to affect and be affected" (*Plateaus,* 261). With this stroke, Deleuze and Guattari introduce into this articulation of postmodern individuality the matter of temporality. Here, temporality is viewed not as the set of relations and ruptures existing between past, present, and future that constitute history or the aporias of history (as will be seen in Derrida's reading of Marx) but as haecceity—a temporary formation of "relations of movement" that, like weather patterns, are assemblages in which determinate combinations of elements and chance combine to produce discharges of energy. The "relations of movement" of which Deleuze and Guattari speak exist and interact on every plateau of life, from the formation of DNA, to the molecular "spread" of the body, to the shaping of continents and the movements of people in packs, clans, and nations.

Verging on a chaos theory of identity, Deleuze and Guattari write that

you are a longitude and a latitude, a set of speeds and slownesses between unformed particles, a set of nonsubjectified affects. . . . It should not be thought that a haecceity consists simply of a decor or backdrop that situates subjects, or of appendages that hold things and people to the ground. It is the entire assemblage in its individuated aggregate that is a haecceity; it is this assemblage that is defined by a longitude and a latitude, by speeds and affects, independently of forms and subjects, which belong to another plane. . . . The street enters into the composition with the horse, just as the dying rat enters into composition with the air. . . . At most, we may distinguish between assemblage-haecceities (a body considered only as a longitude and latitude) and interassemblage haecceities, which also mark the potentialities of becoming within each assemblage (the milieu of intersection of the longitudes and latitudes). But the two are strictly inseparable. (*Plateaus*, 262–63)

The individual subject as haecceity is thus always in the state of assemblage—of being assembled to itself, and being assembled to other assemblages. The larger sense of the subject in process conveyed in this passage—of self as palimpsest, collage, or pastiche—has been popularized in both postmodern theory and contemporary narrative, but what is notable about Deleuze and Guattari's radicalized version is that it, in effect, detemporalizes subjectivity. A haecceity is, if nothing else, a mobile and temporary arrangement, dependent on available elements for its patterning, but with no past and no future, no history; in its momentariness, it is always becoming something else. Deleuze and Guattari bring home the point in the later discussion of multilinear systems where, again, "everything happens at once." In their philosophy of plateaus, such systems are, of course, perfectly able to exist alongside more traditional "punctual" assemblages and systems, organized chronologically and hierarchically, just as postmodern subjectivities exist alongside (and in assemblage with) humanistically conceived selves. It is simply a matter of what plane one lives on at the moment, though it is not a matter of existentially choosing to do so as all assemblages—from individual to global—spontaneously and paradoxically conspire with each other in infinitely complex patterns. Hence, there is a dividing line that passes between coexisting "punctual 'history-memory' systems and diagonal or multilinear assemblages, which are in no way eternal: they have to do with becoming; they are a bit of becoming in the pure state; they are transhistorical" (*Plateaus*, 296). The multilinear system or assemblage is the desideratum of *A Thousand Plateaus*, is an instance of the Nietzschean "Untimely," "which is another name for haecceity, becoming, the innocence of becoming (in other words, forgetting as opposed to memory, geography as opposed to history, the map as opposed to the tracing, the rhizome as opposed to aborescence)" (ibid.). The continuous instance of becoming that is formulated as the pure state of the postmodern identity-assemblage therefore depends on the elision of temporality and history as punctual elements that operate on some other plateau. Multilinear assemblages are transhistorical for Deleuze and Guattari precisely to the extent that any temporality is hollowed out from them, nullifying their historical content.

In tracing out the versions of postmodern subjectivity enunciated in *A Thousand Plateaus,* we may seem to have drifted far from the question of paranoia. But in their explication of "regimes of signs," Deleuze and Guattari oppose "schizophrenia"—the capacity to contain partial, peripheral, multiple, and contradictory "points of departure" working on many plateaus within one assemblage (the "mindset" of the postmodern subject)—to "paranoia," or the delimiting tendency of the modern subject to think in terms of centers, wholes, solid states, totalities, harmonies (120). In describing the differences between paranoid and schizophrenic signifying regimes (social and cultural system-assemblages that become actuated as epistemologies), Deleuze and Guattari once more manifest their posthistorical agenda:

We are trying, then, to make a distinction between a paranoid, signifying despotic regime of signs and a passional or subjective, postsignifying authoritarian regime [that is, one that works on its own account]. . . . Once again, we are not, of course, doing history: we are not saying that a people invents this regime of signs, only that at a given moment a people effectuates the assemblage that assures the relative dominance of that regime under certain historical conditions (and that regime, that dominance, that assemblage may be assured under other conditions, for example, pathological, literary, romantic, or entirely mundane). We are not saying that a people is possessed by a given type of delusion but that the map of a delusion, its coordinates considered, may coincide with the map of a people. (121–22)

Let us leave aside, for the moment, the fact that in order to describe the schizophrenic regime of signs, Deleuze and Guattari must employ a mechanism obviously borrowed from the paranoid regime so as to set paranoia and schizophrenia in binary opposition to each other. Here, as in the discussion of haecceity, what marks the subjectivity, regime, or assemblage of the future is its compression and elision of temporality (at a given moment). As we shall see, in representations of cultural paranoia that trouble the binary Deleuze and Guattari establish, paranoia is seen as a state of mind in which the paranoid attempts to escape history and elide temporality by converting the contingent into a narrative assemblage of which s/he is the focal point. Past, present, and future are compressed into the now of the always unfolding conspiracy that surrounds the paranoid, or in a more complex sense, the partial and interlocking conspiracies that the paranoid must negotiate in order to signify her or himself as the mobile subject of conspiracies must always be in process in order to sustain a paranoid identity.

True, Deleuze and Guattari argue that the paranoid regime is

defined by an insidious onset and a hidden center bearing witness to endogeneous forces organized around an idea, [while the schizophrenic regime is] "defined by a decisive external occurrence . . . by a limited constellation operating in a single sector; by a 'postulate' or 'concise formula' serving as the point of departure for a linear series or proceeding that runs its course, at which point a new proceeding begins. (120)

Effectively, they critique the universalism of the paranoid system in setting up the paranoid/schizoid binary as operative at the level of individual projects as well as dominant ideologies. But in doing so, particularly in associating the schizoid regime of signs with multilinear systems and haecceity, they only succeed in recuperating schizophrenia for paranoia. For as much as the paranoid depends on a central plot, a hermeneutic center that in varying degrees s/he approaches and evades, s/he also relies on the segmentation that characterizes the schizoid regime and the atemporality that distinguishes haecceity. The work of paranoia is, precisely, to convert contingent, segmented pieces of the real into an observable and interpretable pattern of conspiracy. Paranoia, in this sense, absolutely depends on a schizoid regime of signs with its single sectors, serialities, and points of departure that provide the material for paranoid activity. Equally, the work of paranoia is sustained by the simultaneity of haecceity and the ahistoricity of multilinear systems. For the paranoid awaits those unexpected, detemporalized instances of revelation when patterns magically converge into full-blown assemblages ripped from historical context that present the conspiracy not merely as symptomatic of the real but as an offshoot of it, a peripheral yet determinate part of the compression of personal, national, and global historical destinies.

Even if we view *A Thousand Plateaus* as merely descriptive of the postmodern condition rather than proscribing a schizophrenic utopia, it becomes clear that the very circumstances of this condition provide the grounds for paranoia. Above all, paranoia is founded on the evacuation of temporality and segmenting of the real that characterizes, for Deleuze and Guattari, the schizophrenia of postmodern identity, elsewhere put in terms of fluidity, cybernicity, or multiplicity. To move up a level, what Deleuze and Guattari posit as a "diagonal," contingent relation between the paranoid state apparatus (which imposes the plot of nation on its subjects) and those schizophrenic, nomadic assemblages that resist it, is equally a relation of dialectical complicity, particularly when we keep in mind that capital is the medium of exchange between these parties, even as the boundaries of nations and states of identity are continually being renegotiated. Capital is one of many "flows" in Deleuze and Guattari. It is the means by which one gains purchase from the state apparatus the right to become a player in the negotiation that continually takes place between the nation (moving on a sliding scale from despotic regime to late capitalist democracy) and self (moving by degrees from paranoid enjoying symptomatic identification with the nation by embodying it to schizophrenic enjoying the symptomatic identification with the nation by resisting it). This comprises the finite set of identificatory negotiations between subject and state assemblages manifested in those narratives of postmodern paranoia that offer critiques of an identity thriving under the sign of multiplicity.

Lyotard's *Libidinal Economy* radicalizes the desire that, for Deleuze and Guattari, runs the assemblage of body and nation. This early work is, according to Steven Best and Douglas Kellner, along with Lyotard's *"Anti-Oedipus* the most striking example of the micropolitics of desire," and one that "almost everyone, including Lyotard himself, found . . . to be a theoretical dead end, trapping its author in a series of untenable positions."[30] Like many other theorists in 1970s who, in contradiction, were attempting to map out the "before" and "after" of identity in its prelinguistic and symbolic states, Lyotard in *Libidinal Economy* (published in France in 1974) is interested in subjective processes as they are informed by his investments in Marx. Here, Lyotard poses the "real" as consisting of infinitely numbered, singular energies flowing across the "libidinal band" over against their inevitable structuration into every formation ranging from the self who economizes desire to the global political economy of capitalism. For Lyotard at this time, there is the great libidinal "skin," a vitalistic metaphor for pure libidinal "impulsions" that have always existed as long as there have been bodies and desire, and there is the channeling of these energies into *"dispositifs,"* or the orders and economies by which libidinal energy is directed at specific objects, thus resulting in the social organizations of class, nation, and the histories that narrate their articulation:

In libidinal economy, there is nothing but skin on the inside and the outside, there is only one monoface surface, the libidinal body is a Moebius strip, and a *dispositif* like that of the *méson* [in particle physics, a primary grouping of quarks and antiquarks; here, used by Lyotard to stand for "the empty center of the ancient Greek collective"] is not an underground machinery beneath the plateau of the stage or the wings, quite the contrary, it commands certain instantiations of libidinal impulsions on the body-band, the blockage and exclusion of other regions.[31]

These "instantiations" are sites—bodies (Lyotard deploys the image of the prostitute to stand for the body in society), public spaces, nations, political economies—where libidinal energies are negotiated and exchanged: "This 'exchange' is the passage of intensities running from one proper name to another, from one initial to another . . . without which there can be no instance, structure . . . no Memory, to register the energies expended here and amassed there" (*Libidinal,* 92).

In this manner, Lyotard locates any social formation—including the construction of identity—as at the end of a process whereby raw libidinal energy is converted into unitary selves, political systems, language, writing, national bodies, memory. Through this conversion process, the body, for example, "is annulled as the immense crumpled band, and instituted as the bag of organs" (187); the city and nation are simply larger "organic" units "made . . . from completely working over the 'bodies' which enter it, from a squaring-off by which they are reduced to a few useful organs, all other organs banished, all vaginas, all foreign tongues" (159). While they serve as sites where "the libido's investment and its flowing towards discharge are strictly restricted" (159), these have as their indeterminate and arbitrary origin the "nothing" of libidinal desire before it is directed at an object or made a vehicle for the exchange of objects.

Though Lyotard's particular investments in marxism compel him to diverge significantly from Deleuze and Guattari by insisting that libidinal economy is linked to specific modes of production, the Nietzschean antimetaphysic that informs *Libidinal Economy* as well as *A Thousand Plateaus* can be contested from a number of positions; again, Lyotard has emphatically distanced himself from what he later referred to as "his evil book."[32] Yet it is useful to consider to what extent the symptomatic conception of identity in such works, especially when linked to notions of capital and temporality, reveals the contradictions underlying the triangulations of the cold war, late capitalism, and postmodernity that inform the inscriptions of paranoia in contemporary U.S. culture.[33] These contradictions can be viewed in terms of a desire that has suffered the conversion process from pure libidinality to specific investments in the social symbolic order: the desire for subject mobility and the rigidification of the social world; the desire to escape history and to be at the center of historical conspiracy. Though Lyotard in particular and theory in general may have moved on from the late 1960s and 1970s' rhapsodic investments in the presubjectival, as symptom, *Libidinal Economy* in linking time, capital, and desire to the formation of identity, has much to tell us about a cultural paranoia brought to the fore in contemporary narrative and consonant with the historical contradictions of the present time that haunt late capitalism.

Libidinal Economy is a detailed theatricalization of the channeling or "inhibition" of the Dionysian flow of libidinal energy resulting in all forms of social organization, all modes of production: in this respect, it is an extension and conflation of Nietzsche's *Birth of Tragedy* and Freud's *Civilization and Its Discontents*. For Lyotard, on the one hand, there is no specific set of contingencies that dictates how these negotiations pursue their course since they, in effect, constitute a void or indeterminate gap between the libidinal band and its fallout in history:

This void is that of the mediator alienating the subject . . . and the object . . . it is that of inhibition, which leads desire away from its primary object towards the *means* of its realization; it is that of capital, which loves production rather than the product. . . . [T]his void is that in which the mechanisms of power are constructed; but it is also the *supple* viscosity of capitalism as fragments of the body, as connected-disconnected singularities, as amnesia, decentered and anarchic, as harlequinade, as metamorphosis without inscription, as the undoing of totalities and totalizations, as ephemeral groupings of unforeseen affirmations. (*Libidinal*, 103)

Yet, as both the example of capitalism that Lyotard chooses and the elaboration on its libidinal potential suggest, these exchanges proliferate and intensify in the movement that Lyotard traces from the *dispositifs* of Greek mercantilist to modern capitalist societies. While Lyotard does not endorse capitalism, he does see it as an advanced stage in the progression toward a revolutionary discourse and economy where there exists "not even the dissimulation of the assimilable and the inexchangeability of the exchangeable; but singularities. Not 'innovations' (deducible from a body of axioms), but unprecedented things" (255).

Implicitly, then, the postmodern subject that Lyotard describes in the passage above is, without naming it as such, conflated with capital: decentered, fragmented, protean, multiply linked other subjectivities, and performative (emphasizing the production rather than the product)—for Lyotard, this version of identity and its dissolution in the future are inextricably connected to the sinuosity of capital flows. Throughout *Libidinal Economy,* capital is figured as an erotic fluid that lubricates the processes of exchange taking place between discrete but increasingly fragmented and multiple bodies and nations. Nor is this merely an analogy for Lyotard: he clearly wishes to suggest that sexual fluids, the flow of capital, the flow of ink from a pen—all are manifestations of libidinal energy disposed into variously eroticized, yet not completely uninhibited systems of exchange. And the desideratum of libidinal economy—what comes after capitalism—is "dissimulation," a posited state that Lyotard admits is based fully on a capitalism that has reached its limits and spread to every sphere of life, the only difference between now and then being that the conduction of intensities "would be able to take place on *all* pieces of the social 'body,' without *exception*" (254). *Libidinal Economy* is thus a description of a present moment in which we are very close to a future that portends the end of history, where the void that separates the libidinal band from dispositions in time and space will have collapsed, and where the social body has become the site for the manifestation of multiple "singularities" or "inventions" (bodies without organs, schizoid identities, ephemeral social groupings) arising freely and spontaneously, not linked by any system of necessities or contingencies.

The fantasy that *Libidinal Economy* articulates is symptomatic of a postmodernity that both lives off of capitalism yet seeks as the end of its desire the consonant dissolution of capital, the poly-"morphing" of the body, the end of time and history.[34] Lyotard does not overlook the obvious paradox of this "postmodern condition," which he would later regulate and legislate in the book of that title: the vehicle (capitalism) that portends the fragmentation of identity at the same time depends on the shoring up of the unitary identity of the consumer by disguising mass desire as the desire of the individual. As for Deleuze and Guattari, for Lyotard an investment in this paradoxical postmodernity (desire seeking the end of desire; capital seeking the end of capitalism; identity seeking its memorial) necessitates the evacuation of temporality and the compression of space and time under the aegis of capitalism.

Lyotard calls capitalism "the great concentrator," which when conceived negatively in terms of an outworn marxist view of production and exchange, seeks "stable circuits, equal cycles, predictable repetitions, untroubled accountability" (*Libidinal,* 215), but when conceived "affirmatively" in terms of speculation and credit, thrives on the contradictions of managed chaos and unpredictable iterability. In the chapter titled "Capital," Lyotard links temporality to the inhibition of libidinal energies that capitalism, viewed "nihilistically" (as a semiotic/economic system of equivalent and differential exchanges), administers and channels as "power":

> The inhibition [of the force of desire, on which monetary exchanges depend,] coincide[s] with the introduction of temporality. . . . For, in the postponing of its fulfillment . . . it would create a reserve or a reservoir of energy at the same time as a lack, awaiting the hour of its suppression. This waiting would open up an interval of the future, and become swollen with the inhibited energy and open up a cumulative process of retention; in this way the second chronological order would be constituted. As in the army, the reserve is something which can serve again: it has already served without being exhausted . . . and it can enter into a process of use in order to start this task again or continue it. It is from the past, it has proved itself, it *can* do so again, it is therefore of the future; but of course that future which is identical to the past, repetitive of the same. (219)

The process of inhibition and retention that Lyotard describes here can be assimilated to a form of capitalism that constitutes a system of exchanges and libidinal investments where temporal delays between the instigation and satisfaction of desire are used to manage desire itself in order to serve the accumulative ends of the powerful few. This is an older capitalism of stable systems, centers of power, and unitary identities, though for Lyotard, capitalism is always moving toward the ultimate dissimulation of its own structures. Lyotard argues that a false or inauthentic temporality underlies this system because the past and future, which appear to constitute the difference between the reserve of desires already partially satisfied and the promise of some new need awaiting fulfillment in an inexhaustible plenitude are, in fact, identical. What is crucial in this passage is the view of temporality it articulates. Here, temporality is the means of registering the conversion of libidinal energy into an economy. The difference between past and future that could constitute a historical relation is reduced to an identification between the states of desire always held in reserve and desire ever awaiting fulfillment: here capital becomes the means by which the illusory difference between the past and future of desire are purchased. From this concept of a recursive temporality underlying a nihilistic version of capitalism, Lyotard will project a "progressive" stance that depends on an embracing of credit and haecceity as the critical economic and temporal elements of a libidinal futurity.

This nihilistic capitalism is a modernist structuration of a libidinal economy that can seek its investments elsewhere once capital, time, and subjectivity have changed, as it appears they have for Lyotard in the ongoing condition where the credit reigns. Credit, Lyotard writes, is the "major deregulator of all capitalist circuits" (224); it is "the advance of wealth which does not exist, made in order that it come to exist" (225), an "*advance of nothing* if we think in terms of commodities; it is just an advance, that is, a credit of time" (225). The "credit of time . . . is only a process of expansive regulation, an arbitrary act by which a power to include new energies is delivered" (225). Thus, credit capital introduces speculation, virtuality, novelty, and uncertainty into a libidinal economy that might otherwise have been relatively ordered and closed; libidinally, it eventuates a "positive delirium, putting authorities and traditional institutions to death, active decrepitude of beliefs and securities, Frankensteinian surgeon of the cities, of imagination, of bodies" (254). In terms of temporality, credit unleashes "intensities [that] have no precise permanence that would permit the fixing of moments and places to them by recourse to a common referentiality" (254). Lyotard fetishizes credit as the random element in an open system that allows for the emergence of, among other things, a form of identity that is "disorganized" (the "bag of organs" dismembered), schizophrenic, and outside temporality: "As for the temporality at work in this advance [of credit], it is the time of reproduction, which is . . . basically atemporal" (226). Credit allows for an advance over time because it collapses the system of temporal delays between desire instigated and desire satisfied on which an older capitalism was based. Using credit, postmodern identity can be purchased because there is a decreasing distance between the libidinal band and what might be called the reification of desire in the (now conflated) libidinal and political economies of body and nation: if one has credit, one can be all he or she wants to be. Lyotard thereby helps us to see the extent to which the libidinal economy of postmodern identity (with its desiderata of fragmentation, mutability, deterritorialization) is linked to the progressions of a specific economic system and the attendant desire to escape from history into immediacy, or "atemporality."[35]

It is not my intention here to critique Lyotard (this Lyotard) for positing the "delirium" of capital as paving the way for the utter freedom of "dissimulation" without taking into account the geopolitical actualities that attend the system he describes. It is all too clear, at this point, that the universal extension of credit in postindustrial societies and the increasing impoverishment and indebtedness of the Third World are interlinked, whatever promise credit may hold for transformations in various political economies. For the purposes of understanding the operations of cultural paranoia, like *A Thousand Plateaus*, *Libidinal Economy* is a theoretical narrative that symptomatizes the contradiction of postmodern identity that, as I have suggested, desires and embodies both the deconstruction and reconstitution of the subject in all of its identificatory postures. Lyotard locates this contradiction in the right place. In his discussion of Freud's famous paranoid, Schreber, Lyotard posits against the referential signs of semiotic systems what he terms the "tensor." The tensor, Lyotard's translator Iain Hamilton Grant explains, is a means of reintroducing "into the sign a tension that prevents it from having either a unitary designation, meaning or calculable series of such designations or meanings" (*Libidinal,* xiv). The tensor is equally an "intensity" that represents Lyotard's desire to "block th[e] movement of referral and remain as faithful as possible to the incompossible intensities informing and exceeding the sign" (ibid.). As such, notes Grant, it does not portend "a move 'beyond' re-presentation, the creation of an elsewhere outside the sign" (ibid.), but (like credit in the system of capital) introduces a random element or energy that can lead to new syntaxes and social formations. The "tensor sign" (the energy of the tensor rendered as a sign) thus embodies a similar contradiction to that of the postmodern subject. Both inside and outside the social order, it exists *as* sign, within representation, yet it is also the form of singularity—the primary element of "the discourse of dissimulation"—that unfixes reference.

Credit is a tensor sign for Lyotard, as is Paul Emil Flechsig, the doctor who treated Schreber for paranoid psychosis: this is the treatment on which Schreber would base the autobiographical account that Freud used to define the basis of paranoia as the "primary narcissism" evidenced in homoerotic desire. As Grant points out, Flechsig is "an exemplary case of the tensor sign" because in Schreber's account of his own treatment,

Flechsig's name is no longer a depositing site for the stock-piled remnants of an identity, but functions as an unstable and unpredictable intense sign whose aleatory whirl traces labyrinthine paths into Judge Schreber's multi-sexed body, drawing, along with jurisprudential, psychiatric and theological phrases, even a libidinal-somatic semiotics, into its wake. (xix)

Lyotard contends that Flechsig and Schreber form a pair roughly approximating the relation of the "organic" to the "libidinal" body, that is, between the "functional assemblage," the "montage of montages," and an entity that "appears to have no established channels for the circulation and discharge of impulsions" (58). As opposed to the Freudian model according to which transferences take place in a semiotic system where the analyst is transformed into the patient's object of desire through a metonymic series of substitutions, the transference between Schreber and Flechsig is one in which the paranoid locates in the analyst the "incandescent vertigo" of his own repressed libidinality, which forces him to take sides in the struggle "between hetero- and homosexuality, between virility and femininity" (59). Lyotard ventriloquizes Schreber in depicting Flechsig as the site of ultimate indeterminacy:

I make you, doctor, not into a piece of the paranoiac's game, as you think, but into an unpredictable scrap of the immense band where anonymous influxes circulate. Your name is the guarantee of anonymity, the guarantee that these pulsions *belong to no one,* that no one, not even the "doctor," is sheltered from their course and their investment. That is why you fear me and you lock me up. What is woven under the name of Flechsig is not then just the wise polysemia found in the most anodyne of statements, it is the incandescence of a piece of the body which can have no further assignations, for it invests both the for and against to other libidinal regions. . . . [The] body is undone and its pieces are project[ed] across libidinal, mingling with other pieces in an inextricable patchwork. (60)

In this fantasy, Lyotard casts Flechsig as a fragmented, fetishistic, and virtual "investment" in a libidinal system of circulation whose specific movements are located in a capitalism where credit, like Flechsig, has become a tensor sign that "opens up" an "ephemeral time" and a "labyrinthine evanescent space" (237).

What is notable in this complex and reflexive fantasy of transference (Lyotard reading Freud reading Schreber reading "himself" as transferred onto Flechsig) is that it takes place wholly within the terms of the dyadic relation figured between Flechsig and Schreber. As a theatricalization of postmodern identity, "Flechsig" comes about as the dispersal of the formerly organic body into libidinal fragments, but it must necessarily posit this unitary body—just as capitalism must posit the allegedly organic entities of the marketplace, the consumer—as its origin and end in the globalization of the libidinal band that will now contain all of these dispersed and rhizomic energies. This reveals, once again, the contradiction at the heart of cultural paranoia—the symptom of its desire—which for identity, is the desire to be a bodily fragment on the libidinal band wholly given over to the discharge of fully eroticized corporeal and economic pulsions, yet still at the center of the plot, the receiver of credit, at the discursive origin of the process of transference and countertransference that generates Flechsig from Schreber and Schreber from Flechsig. In short, it takes a paranoid to project the libidinal fantasy.

Analogously, it may be said, the global capitalism under which such identities would be ideally produced rests on the contradictory fantasy of fragmentation (the dissemination of capital and credit to every locality) and differentiation (the fetishizing of the consumer item, available in endless variety and novelty in the free libidinal marketplace, each speaking to the individuality of the consumer). And, as the narratives of paranoia will tell us, globalization in these terms is founded on paradoxical reinvestments in individual subjects who are at once, by virtue of these investments, national subjects. In these narratives, we observe a continuous negotiation between the deconstruction and reconstitution of identities that intersects with the relation between constructed global and national politics. Jameson illuminates this contradiction in terms of a "cultural paradox" that is "the equivalence between an unparalleled rate of change on all levels of social life and an unparalleled standardization of everything—feelings along with consumer goods, language along with built space—that would seem incompatible with just such mutability." [36] The modular social identity-formation consonant with this contradiction is mapped out on the phantasmic coordinates of ephemeral time and evanescent space: a virtual spatio-temporality that signifies the negation of the gap between desire and its objects, portending an escape from history and the historical narrative that frames cultural paranoia under postmodernity. With Derrida, we return by a circuitous route to history as that which haunts these fantasies of postmodern subjectivity and offers for it another end.

In *Spectres of Marx,* a work regarded by some as already too late, Derrida figures a disjointed temporality in this time of global capitalism that bodes for economists such as Francis Fukuyama the "end of history," the end of war and class struggle and world unification under a single economy. As I have regarded *A Thousand Plateaus* and *Libidinal Economy* as symptomatic, so I wish to see *Spectres*—appearing at the moment of the (supposed) conclusion of the cold war, the (supposed) disappearance of socialism and communism as viable political formations, and the (supposed) triumph of global capitalism—as a diagnosis of the postmodern chimera of identity outside, or beyond, history. *Spectres* might be said to appear at the far end of the trajectory that had reached its apogee in the 1970s with the work of Lyotard, Deleuze and Guattari, and the Derrida of *L'ecriture et la différence* (1967) and *La dissémination* (1972). More precisely, *Spectres* implicitly "deconstructs" this trajectory by showing the extent to which the "ideological fantasy" of eternal presence and the exchange of commodities are haunted by the twinned specters of temporality and historical experience, the "residue" or "surplus" of history that, in fact, comprises "the very condition" of this fantasy, and thus the historical condition of postmodernity as such (Žižek, *Sublime Object,* 43).

In his reading of the first "ghost" scene from *Hamlet,* Derrida posits a view of time "out of joint," of temporality as *"the non-contemporaneity with itself of the living present."* [37] Without this disjointure there would be no past and no future: without "justice," without recognition of and response to "those who *are not there,* of those who are no longer or who are not yet *present and living,* what sense would there be to ask the question 'where?' 'where tomorrow?' 'whither?' " (*Spectres,* xix). Promoting "a politics of memory," Derrida argues that the "other" exists only in terms of "justification"—a coming to terms with the irreducibility of the present as always haunted by (disjointed in relation to; bearing the residue of) the past:

Beyond right, and still more beyond juridicism, beyond morality, and still more beyond moralism, does not justice as relation to the other suppose on the contrary some irreducible excess of a disjointure or an anachrony, some *Un-Fuge,* some "out of joint" dislocation in Being and in time itself, a disjointure that, in always risking the evil, appropriation, and injustice (*adikia*) against which there is no calculable insurance, would alone be able to *do justice* or to *render justice* to the other as other? (27)

Relying on Heideggerian notions of temporality, yet implicitly rejecting the idealism of a metaphysical system that points "beyond" time, Derrida maintains that the disjoining of the present—the contradictory disavowal of a past that continues to haunt the present moment—is *differánce* per se, which in part constitutes for him identity, thought, experience.[38]

Spectres, therefore, redefines "event" or "event-ness" beyond the purely performative, as something that cannot even be "thought" (not conceived or enacted)

as long as one relies on the simple . . . opposition of the real presence of the real present or the living present to its ghostly simulacrum, the opposition of the effective or actual (*wirklich*) to the non-effective, inactual . . . as long as one relies on a general temporality or an historical temporality made up of the *successive* linking of presents identical to themselves and contemporary with themselves. (70)

Apropos a Deleuzian haecceity or Lyotardian dissimulation, Derrida posits the experience of temporality as differential: not as identity dissolved into a present identical with itself but as a temporal dislocation within identity by which the present, as such, is noncontemporaneous and sedimented. For Derrida, the present is a site where the past *remains* as remnant not to be forgotten in the mere opposition of present to past, or actual to inactual, but as a residue that can be either repressed in identificatory fantasies attached to bodies (gendered, human, national) that depend on temporal elisions comprising what Homi Bhabha terms "national time," or justified as the other or before of the present that actually constitutes it.[39] In this regard, Derrida might be said to agree with the primary Lacanian notion that language foregrounds the condition on which the subject "seek[s] its being beyond that which its image presents to it; it causes the subject always to find in its image something lacking."[40] The Derridean "*non-contemporaneity with itself of the living present*" temporalizes the Lacanian principle, where the present is doubly seen as the time-space in which the past asserts itself as thought, recalled, remaindered as an event-experience that marks its passing ("this happened"), *and* as the condition of identity split between the presencing of its own image and the recognition that there is something missing from the picture. This missing piece is at once the lack inherent in the impossible desire (which I have framed as the desire of postmodernity) for identity's haecceious presence-to-itself, and the nonfulfillment of that desire in the historical experience that disincorporates identity from its other, marking the nonovercoming and noncommodifying of difference—an experience that, for Derrida, we have yet to do justice.

Reading *Capital,* Derrida links the experience of time to the status of commodities as objects of exchange; thus, as we have seen in Deleuze/Guattari and Lyotard, Derrida connects temporality to capitalism, though his understanding of this linkage effects a reversal of those versions that conflate the compression of time and space, the fluidity of identity, and the flow of capital. In *Given Time 1: Counterfeit Money,* Derrida had argued that the exchange of gifts necessarily involves temporal displacements and delays that constitute the "thing" of the gift and the desire for "gift/countergift" as bound in time: "This demand of the thing, this demand for term and temporization, would be the very structure of the thing. The thing would demand limit and time, at once the mark of the margin—that is, the measure that sets a boundary—and temporality."[41] Extending this principle to the exchange of commodities in *Spectres,* Derrida maintains that, like the "present," commodity-things are not contemporaneous with or present to themselves but articulated within a temporalized system of iteration and spectralization. They are reproduced, but as reproductions; they are haunted by an "excess"—that which exceeds their "use-value," their posited origin, "by a promise of gift beyond exchange" (*Spectres,* 160). The very form of the "thing" caught up in capitalism—and it should be clear that "thing" can stand for any formation, including those of self or nation, that gains identity within the symbolic order of exchange—invokes time. Its production and exchange calls up both the temporality of desire that motors capitalism (the system of time delays between the initiation of desire and its ever partial satisfaction via acquisition of the object) and the "pastness" of the object itself, always an iteration of its "first" appearance in the present tense of its origin, always removed from and haunted by that posited origin that is deconstructed by its very nature *as* object. Even if the object is capital itself—even if commodities are virtualized as information or surplus value exchanged for its own sake—temporality still underlies the *operation* of the exchange that determines the nature of the object.

The phenomenology of the object that Derrida here constructs leads him to a description of the *socius* of capitalism that is neither transcendent nor subject to the kinds of sublimation that we have observed in Lyotard:

This *socius,* then, binds "men" who are first of all experiences of time, existences determined by this relation to time which itself would not be possible without surviving and returning, without that being "out-of-joint" that dislocates the self-presence of the living present and installs thereby the relation to the other. The same socius, the same "social form" of the relation binds, on the other hand, commodity-things to each other. *On the other hand,* but how? And how is what takes place *on the one hand* among men, in their apprehension of time, explained by what takes place *on the other hand* among those spectres that are commodities? How do those whom one calls "men," living men, temporal and finite existences, become subjected, in their social relations, to these spectres that are relations, *equally social* relations, among commodities? (154)

This remarkable passage, in which the temporal existence of humans and objects are joined, poses questions that are not answered in *Spectres;* rather, they are questions for capitalism, and for our lives under capitalism, as a temporalized economic system whose future (like the future of the human race) will take place in time. By locating temporality within the heart of capital exchange, Derrida effectively frames the conflated, postmodern fantasies of fluid identity and haecceity as symptoms produced within capitalism as a condition that always seeks to forget its own history.

For Derrida, this forgetting is both endemic and unjustified: it is what causes the present to be out of joint. Crucially, for the discussion of cultural paranoia, one of the manifestations of forgetting—which is to repress the temporality of the Derridean socius that "installs . . . the relation to the other"—is the projection of the essential "differance" of the self or ego onto the "not-self" in order to exorcise the specter of noncontemporaneity with itself that constitutes bodies and objects in time:

Whatever is not the body but belongs to it comes back to it: prosthesis and delegation, repetition, differance. The living ego is auto-immune. . . . To protect its life . . . to relate, as the same, to itself, it is necessarily led to welcome the other within (so many figures of death: differance of the technical apparatus, iterability, non-uniqueness, prosthesis, synthetic image, simulacrum, all of which begins with language, before language), it must therefore take the immune defenses apparently meant for the non-ego, the enemy, the opposite, the adversary and direct them once *for itself and against itself*. (141)

In this figure that Derrida generates as the mode of identity temporalized under capitalism, it is precisely a kind of schizophrenia (the embracing of the "other within") that provides the strategy—the "immune defense"—for the protection of "the living ego," or the unitary identity that seeks to repress its location within the spatiotemporal matrix of production and exchange. In the paradox of identity that Derrida articulates, schizophrenia, rather than being a deterritorialization of the self, symptomatically reveals the operations of a paranoia that reinstantiates "the living ego" and projects it over against the other, which in turn, is to project it over against itself. This is a historical condition not to be escaped. There is no solution to our being situated within time or economy, and all fantasies to the contrary merely serve as symptomatic revelations of a process of social identity-formation that operates to suppress its own temporality and is inevitably haunted by it. For Derrida, this is the postmodern condition at the present time, and only by doing justice to it—by recognizing what relation to the other it enfolds or negates, by coming to terms with the history of its historical repressions—can we hope to transform it.

In the narratives of cultural paranoia previewed in Stone's rendering of the Kennedy assassination, postmodern identity is posited as a form of historical crisis in which deep anxieties about subjectival identifications in time and space percolate. Such anxieties are theatricalized in contemporary U.S. culture on a daily basis, and while "we" may not be exceptional in this regard, it may fairly be said that the conflations of postmodern identity-formation and contemporary historical experience in the United States lend a certain specificity and intensity to these anxieties that subtend everyday social and political life in this country. In other words, in the representations of historical identity in crisis that I will be scrutinizing forthwith, theory meets history. Thus, I have staged in this chapter an internal debate between Deleuze/Guattari and Lyotard, on the one hand, and Derrida, on the other, that is critically joined in contemporary narratives of cultural paranoia. These narratives inevitably convey representations of identity in history that, most often, reinforce paranoia; yet, they also work to limn cultural paranoia not just as another version of identity in history in a pluralistic menu but as symptomatic of the contradictory state of postmodernity under late capitalism in a nation and culture that continues to be obsessed with questions of national destiny and identity. In this contradiction, charted as the desire of identity for its other in fluidity and fragmentation, countered by the reaction formations of identity in an ascending series of ego, national, and global orders that are narrativized as history, what is elided or what constitutes the "hole" in the symbolic order is temporality, the materiality of historical experience. It remains to draw out this contradiction in the narratives of cultural paranoia, and to query the desire subtending it that forms "the binding of our enjoyment to a certain signifying, symbolic formation which assures a minimum of consistency to our being in the world" (Žižek, *Sublime Object,* 75). In coming to terms with temporality as the "sinthome" of postmodernity, we have the opportunity, through these narratives, to address the historical repressions that, even when secreted, reveal us as being within rather than beyond history.

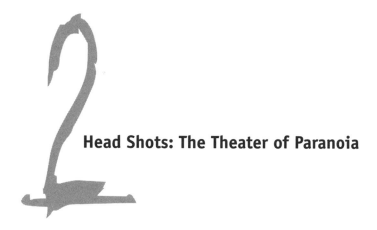

Head Shots: The Theater of Paranoia

It is the magic of nationalism to turn chance into destiny.
—Benedict Anderson, *Imagined Communities*

■ For nearly four decades, the Kennedy assassination has served as
the site of a national trauma in the United States—a stroke in the cultural imaginary—that insists on repeating itself in the aftermath of the
interpretive narratives spun out of the original event. The head shot
that killed the President has been repeatedly viewed and reviewed via
the offices of the Zapruder "home movie"—its individual frames blown
up, enhanced, and magnified—as if it were possible to derive the truth
of the event from the sheer iterability of its mediations. In the same
vein, taken as a headless project that bears an amazing consistency in
terms of its implicit desires and goals, the seemingly unlimited flood
of information about and historical reinterpretations of the assassination and the events leading up to it seek to pin down the logic of presidential murder. Whether one accepts, at one explanatory extreme, the
"lone gunman" theory of the assassination, or a mega-conspiracy at the
other in which the Mafia, the CIA, the FBI, Lyndon Johnson, and/or pro-
and anti-Castro extremists intentionally or accidentally cooperated to
derail the national destiny, all of the renarrativizations and re-viewings
of the symptomatic event suggest that what is unacceptable to the interpellated general public is that there is no final sacramental relic of the
"real" to be gained by researching the photos and archives, no ultimate

exegetical logic to an episode that threatens to undermine the orderly progress of history and destiny.

Because such elisions are unthinkable, we return obsessively through the reruns and revised scenarios to that still point in time, the caught moment of pigeons flying up from the Texas Book Depository at the report of gunshots and the image of the president's wife reaching for the portion of her husband's scalp blown onto the rear deck of the Lincoln Continental by the fatal head shot. In the national memory of the assassination fueled both by official investigation and fictive speculation, the material elements and sites of the event have been made over into fetishes—the grassy knoll, Jackie Kennedy's pink pillbox hat and dress, the Zapruder film, the umbrella man, Oswald's torn sweater, the Carousel Club, Parkland General Hospital, the doubled date of 11/22—each arranged and invested with fatal significance. As the critical narrative enactments of the enchained circumstances of the assassination and its personages indicate, we seem to desire—even enjoy—the multiple theatricalizations and investitures of the event because they somehow both offer the promise of the truth behind Kennedy's murder (whether the product of a conspiracy or an isolated incident) and yet withhold a total explanation that would close the books on the matter.

This form of traumatic enjoyment with its attendant remappings, symbolic investments, and fetishizations is, for Žižek, indicative of the work of the superego operating on a collective level, which seeks to organize into a form of knowledge or necessity that to which, paradoxically, we must remain blind: "Where one doesn't (want to) know, in the blanks of one's symbolic universe, one enjoys."[1] The Kennedy assassination is just such a blank in the symbolic universe of national recollection. It is one we fill in with artifacts and narratives that both proffer historical revelation and conceal as mystery or conspiracy what we don't want to know: that this anchoring point of a country's destiny (and thus, our identities as national subjects) is possibly founded on sheer contingency, portending an entropic history in which the Kennedy assassination is an accident, a kernel of the real that cannot be woven into narratives of character, fate, or nation. The narratives I shall consider—Don DeLillo's *Libra,* Oliver Stone's *JFK,* and Norman Mailer's *Oswald's Tale: An American Mystery*—compel us to view the assassination as a "quilting point" in the federal story where the suturing of individuals to history takes place at the same time that the very foundations of identity are threatened by the nature of an event that cannot be reconciled with any logic or narrative that would explain it.[2] This then, too, is a story of cultural paranoia, in which the desire for the historically determinate order of events and the manifest relation of self to historical plot—the successful completion of the operation accomplished by the binding of the individual to national destiny and the healing of the wound caused by that operation—is at odds with the desire for an ongoing, open-ended narrative that offers further possibilities for connection, enjoyment, and the proliferation of identities awaiting integration into future permutations of the public story. The moment of the assassination—this time out of joint—made over into narrative, thus offers us the opportunity for critical reflection on the condition of national and historical subjects in postmodernity, and paranoia as a response to that condition.

■ Branch-Work: *Libra*

No one reading the multiple, dispersed narratives of the Kennedy assassination and the cast of characters involved in the various historical puncta that lead toward and away from the event can fail to note the extent to which these accounts reflexively focus on narrativity itself as proffering a logic of return—a reason or motive for going back to the fatal 5.6 seconds of Kennedy's murder in search of explanations.[3] The narrative may be that of the twenty-six-volume Warren Commission Report, which DeLillo has characterized as "the novel in which nothing is left out," and which Nicholas Branch, the detective-hermeneut of *Libra,* terms "the megaton novel James Joyce would have written if he'd moved to Iowa City and lived to be a hundred."[4] It may be the latest "documentary" plumping for Oswald the lone gunman, Oswald the CIA puppet, Oswald the failed revolutionary, or as *Libra* is often viewed, high postmodern fiction reveling in the indeterminacies of the event and artifices of plot, or factual "tale" as Mailer packages his speculation on Oswald's life. What all of these works share in common is the sense that a renarration of the assassination and its related events and characters will somehow allow us to get closer to the materiality of a historical trauma whose scars, remnants, and debris seem to obscure its "reality" the more they proliferate.

DeLillo has remarked that in writing *Libra,* he was interested in "finding rhythms and symmetries" not available in the sheer mass of material on the assassination, thereby providing a kind of clarity, not in order to answer the question "Who killed Kennedy?" but to elucidate the historicity of the event as an articulation, a convergence of chance, circumstance, and intent. "Fiction rescues history from its confusions," comments DeLillo.[5] Indeed, it is this redemptive or healing quality that accompanies many of the narrative theatricalizations of the assassination, as if by going over the details repeatedly and speculating on the connections between the far-flung trajectories of the scattered facts, events, and personalities, narrative could hope to recoup what has been lost in that hyper-represented, but still blank moment in Dallas.

But DeLillo's rescue operation is of a particular kind, for what he attempts to salvage from the historical debris of the assassination is a clear articulation of the desire for conflated multiplicities of the self and a re-destined national historical identity that depends on this loss. For DeLillo, what has been lost is "the sense of a coherent reality" as such ("American Blood," 22); the Kennedy assassination then conceivably serves as the point of origin for the fragmentation of reality under postmodernity. In terms of the nation's story, the assassination narratives tell of the loss of a coherent narrative founded on a confidence in the nation's ability to authorize and control the fabrications of its own political and historical plots that occurs with the annihilation of the head of state—a figural loss that has its eerie physiological counterpart with the disappearance of Kennedy's autopsied brain from the National Archives. It is, precisely, the collapsing of the loss of the head of state into the felt loss of a coherent reality that underlies the identificatory logic (realized in the question "Where were you when Kennedy was shot?") that DeLillo unknots in *Libra*.

Broadly, what has been lost at the moment of the president's death is history itself, or that narrative sense of history as a series of logical connections between discrete moments ordered in time in the unfolding scheme of the individual or the nation's special destiny.[6] In *Libra*'s intensive reflection on the collision between narrative plots and the contingencies of actuality, what replaces this lost sense of a coherent reality are the hermeneutic productions of cultural paranoia. Whether they bear the code names of "conspiracy," "fate," or "coincidence," these productions lead to a "historical" reinscription that secretes the real beneath a simulated history productive of nations and citizens. For DeLillo, narratively speaking, the wound of the assassination is continuously reopened and healed, in what Žižek calls "the loop of enjoyment," by means of "the symbolic order's [recovery of] its own constitutive debt."[7] The "enjoyment" *Libra* scores and critiques resides in the incessant restitution of a conflated national identity in the paranoid plots leading to and following from the assassination—plots that in the mind of one of *Libra*'s conspirators, "carry their own logic" that "move toward death" (DeLillo, *Libra*, 221) and that are traversed by protean agents whose access to conspiracy is enabled by their multiplicity. In *Libra*, we are compelled to consider to what extent the killing of a president scandalously offers prolific opportunities for remaking ourselves.

In his revealing essay on *Libra* as a critique of postmodernity, Frank Lentricchia claims that the novel is a "double narrative" in which a form of determinacy (narrative plot) incorporates radical indeterminacy (Lee Harvey Oswald):

What [DeLillo] has done . . . is given us one perfectly shaped, intention-driven narrative while folding within it, every other chapter, a second narrative, his imagined biography of Oswald, a plotless tale of an aimless life propelled by the agonies of inconsistent and contradictory motivation, a life without coherent form except for the form inspired by the book's title: Oswald is a negative Libran, somewhat unsteady and impulsive.[8]

In Lentricchia's view, *Libra* theatricalizes an encounter between a version of postmodern identity—the protean and fragmented Oswald—and a paranoid version of history as "intention-driven narrative."[9] Like a filing to a magnet, Oswald is drawn to the linearities of the half-formed, coincidentally intersecting plots that surround him, and his insertion into the symbolic order of narrative generates further narratives that accumulate to form the secret history of the Kennedy assassination. *Libra*'s thesis, if it can be called that, is that there were mismanaged, ill-conceived plots behind the assassination initiated by renegade elements of the FBI and CIA who, disgruntled with the failure of the Bay of Pigs and what they perceived to be Kennedy's cozening up to Castro, constructed a scheme in which Kennedy would be shot at and missed in a trip to Miami; pro-Castro elements would be blamed for the attempt, and Kennedy would be moved to take a harder line toward Cuba. But this plot falters when crossed by other stray plots initiated by the Mafia and other ex-CIA cells that take in the equally stray element of Oswald, who is multiply available to any number of these contingent conspiracies. He is finally taken in by a small coterie of anti-Castro conspirators who intend to actually kill Kennedy and set Oswald up as the patsy for the Dallas assassination. DeLillo's critique lies in his exposing the narrative process whereby random agency is consumed by plotting intention constituting "a new arena of action in which first-person agents of desire seek self-annihilation and fulfillment in the magical third" of historical determinacy.[10]

This compelling account of *Libra*'s double narrative places emphasis on two of the novel's triangulated interests: the protean nature of postmodern identity and its collision with historical intention. The third—

the formation of the disciplinary subject in the processing of information under the rubric of a paranoid hermeneutic—is represented in the novel by the work of Nicholas Branch, a "retired senior analyst of the Central Intelligence Agency, hired on contract to write the secret history of the assassination of President Kennedy" (DeLillo, *Libra*, 15). The novel's "branch-work" is a hermeneutic process that allows Branch, the reader, fellow-conspirators, and Oswald to assemble from fragments "theories that gleam like jade idols, intriguing systems of assumption, four-fold, graceful" (ibid.), and to construct Oswald himself as a historical back-formation whose "future" is a determinate relation to a simulated past. It is in this third cusp of the novel's intersecting lines of agency and intention that we can observe one of the primary operations of cultural paranoia: to generate the subject as detected or known by inserting him or her into any number of intersecting plots and disciplinary matrices, thus conferring on him or her historical subjectivity. And it is under the code name of "coincidence" that we can see how Lee Harvey Oswald merges with a secret history (which becomes the open secret of national destiny) that necessarily depends for its construction on the fluidity of identity and rhizomic connectivity of the archival traces it leaves in the wake of its formation.

Like the assassination itself, Oswald in *Libra* is represented as a symptomatic quilting point, though one constantly in motion: a construction site that exhibits a continuous process of dispersal and return, fragmentation and gathering. As DeLillo portrays him, Oswald is a hermeneutic fabrication put together, in prospect, by those such as Win Everett, who orchestrates the near miss of Kennedy in the Miami conspiracy and envisions "teams of linguists, photo analysts, fingerprint experts, handwriting experts, experts in hair and fibers, smudges and blurs. Investigators building up chronologies. He would give them the makings of deep chronos, lead them to basement rooms in windy industrial slums, to the lost towns in the Tropics" (*Libra*, 78). By leaving the disciplinary traces of a patsy to be constructed only in the aftermath of the assassination, Everett provides the material for deep interpretation to those who, like Branch, will refabricate in retrospect an assassin from these simulated remnants. Everett wishes to infuse into the never-to-be-fully-disclosed secret history of the assassination the historical materality of temporality or "deep chronos" that confers on trace and coincidence the feel of actual history as a process consonant with achieved intentions and acts. By means of temporal inversions, he projects a subjectivity to be derived from an analysis of fragments of a past scattered about in the present of conspiracy and alibi's making, a recursive formation of subjectivity that simulates historical chronology, but collapses temporality into those instances of revelation when connections are joined and Oswald is sutured to the plot. Everett, in short, desires to generate the kind of clarification of actuality's confusions that DeLillo indicates fiction should accomplish in "rescuing" history, though for DeLillo, the clarity resides in knowing the difference between the construction of plots and the "real" of history that plots always miss.

In his jail cell, only a matter of pages before he will be fatally shot by Jack Ruby and at the end of the wayward process Everett has initiated, Oswald echoes Everett in considering his future as Kennedy's assassin:

Lee Harvey Oswald is awake in his cell. It was beginning to occur to him that he had found his life's work. After the crime comes the reconstruction. He will have motives to analyze, the whole rich question of truth and guilt. Time to reflect, time to turn this thing in his mind. Here is a crime that clearly yields material for deep interpretation. He will be able to bend the light of that heightened moment, shadows fixed on the lawn, the limousine shimmering and still. Time to grow in self-knowledge, to explore the meaning of what he's done. He will vary the act a hundred ways, speed it up and slow it down, sift emphasis, find shadings, see his whole life change.

This was the true beginning.

They will give him writing paper and books. He will fill his cell with books about the case. He will have time to educate himself in criminal law, ballistics, acoustics, photography. Whatever pertains to the case he will examine and consume. People will come to see him, the lawyers first, then psychologists, historians, biographers. His life had a single clear subject now, called Lee Harvey Oswald. (DeLillo, *Libra,* 434–35)

In effect, commencing Branch's work and that of the Warren Commission in the "true beginning" of his self-formation, Oswald, as if in direct response to Everett's mandate, plans a future in which he will piece himself together as an interdisciplinary subject available to multiple interpretations. As an identity, his "clarity" depends on his discursive dispersal, or to use Deleuze and Guattari's vocabulary, the transcoding of his "deterritorializations," his rhizomic capacity *as constructed* to move across discursive "strata," "gradients," and "thresholds of intensity," only to be "reterritorialized" as the one at the center of converging historical and disciplinary plots.[11] In his represented thoughts, Oswald connects temporality with this hermeneutic work of dispersal and gathering that vital to his formation as paranoid, for it is "in time" that he will "grow to self-knowledge," thus conferring Everett's "deep chronos" on the investigation of his case—yet this temporality will be (as the reader well knows) dramatically foreshortened by actuality. When Ruby shoots him, Oswald's projected identity, slowly unfolding in the leisure of a seemingly infinite autodidactic future, is annihilated as the (now) abbreviated aftertime is collapsed into an equally curtailed past that would have become proleptically known had things turned out as he had planned, as opposed to how they have been planned by someone else. In this manner, DeLillo stages a confrontation between the formation of the disciplinary, paranoid subject and "real history"; between the simulations of "deep chronos," the ligatures of "deep interpretation"; and the catastrophic turn of events—itself, perhaps, a plot in which Ruby is implicated—that obliterates Oswald's projected identity. The destruction of this "Oswald project" is consonant with the collapsing temporality that frames him as one assembled from the remnants of an implanted past and the discursive trajectories of a disciplinary future.

The attempt to plot agency and history, DeLillo clearly suggests, is neither under the control of novelists nor conspirators, and it is in the very manufacturing of Oswald himself, as well as in the futile efforts of those such as Branch to put everything back together again from the fallout of the assassination, that the lie is given to simulated deep chronos resulting in history. In *Libra*, Oswald is fabricated from the combined effects of forging coincidence and extending a logic of identification to many entities in the novel, including its author. As the novel's plots and constructions evolve, Oswald becomes the embodiment of "coincidences" that paradoxically conspire with and work against any attempts to finish him off, to finally locate him as the disciplinary subject at the center of the story, whether it be as co-conspirator, patsy, or lone gunman. "Coincidence" is the slippery code word for chance in *Libra*, but it is not the chance of pure randomness or stray accident; rather, the fabrication of Oswald by many parties whose intentions are at odds might be thought of as a fractal equation: something that, empty in itself—a mere cipher—gathers to itself seemingly random elements reconstituted into fluid patterns typified by the phrase "orderly disorder."[12] At one point, Oswald is described as "living at the center of an emptiness. He wants to sense a structure that includes him, a definition clear enough to specify where he belongs. But the system floats right through him, through everything, even the revolution. He is a zero in the system" (DeLillo, *Libra*, 357). As the cipher of the plot, Oswald—alias Hidell, Alek, Leon, Drictal, O. H. Lee, William Bobo, and numerous other self-conferred or imposed names—is the nomadic subject adrift in a realm of total simulacra that DeLillo's readers have described him to be.[13] But he is also the paranoid subject at the center of the plot available both to himself and those who fabricate him as the receptacle of hermeneutic value, potentially full of meaning as the one to his own zero—he is at the window of the Texas Book Depository on that fateful day for a reason; he is part of the larger plan of things, whether political or astrological—if only the merging of his identity with historical outcome can be achieved.

As an aspect of the ambiguity that DeLillo claims informs his enterprise, the entrance into the symbolic order of history that the novel's various Oswald constructions seek to effect might be said to succeed as certain kinds of postmodern fiction while they fail as attempts to ordain history.[14] There is an anxiety that underlies all the plots and edifices of the novel related to its fabrication of coincidence and extended logic of identification—a panic induced by the possibility that all the patterns of coincidence, detected conspiracies, and gleaming theories constructed from the planted and gathered information may add up to much less or much more than control over reality or the restoration of its coherence. Much less, in the sense that possibly "history"—more precisely, an orderly fulfillment of national destiny—really is out of control, that identity really is only a cipher, and that all efforts to reign in the spiral toward apocalypse or entropy are only remarkable for their artificiality; much more, in that larger, hidden forces are always at work behind the partial plots and conspiracies detected by the Nicholas Branches and Warren Commissions. Behind these fears stands, perhaps, the greatest of all: that at some point in time, the hermeneutic riches of the assassination will be exhausted, exposing the gap between knowledge and truth that the assassination symptomatizes. The paranoid dichotomies underlying such fears are evident in Libra in the multiple attempts to systematize Oswald, bring him within disciplinary constraint, and convert coincidence into a kind of parataxis that one would normally seek in a work of intrigue.

All agents in the novel partake of these labors, but perhaps no one more fervently than Oswald himself, who thus becomes a site where self-construction and construction-by-others conspire. Nearing the moment in which he will leave his wife and home in New Orleans for the eventual assignation in Dallas, Oswald reflects on the intensifying patterns of coincidence:

Coincidence. He learned in the bayous, from Raymo, that Castro's guerrilla name was Alex, derived from his middle name, Alejandro. Lee used to be known as Alek.

Coincidence. Bannister was trying to find him, not knowing what city or state he was in, and he walked in the door at 544 and asked for an undercover job.

Coincidence. He ordered the revolver and the carbine six weeks apart. They arrived on the same day.

Coincidence. Lee was always reading two or three books, like Kennedy. Did military service in the Pacific, like Kennedy. Poor handwriting, terrible speller, like Kennedy. Wives pregnant at the same time. Brothers named Robert. (De-Lillo, *Libra,* 336)

In this comically anxious litany, Oswald reveals the logic of identification underlying coincidence in *Libra* as he affiliates himself with Castro, Kennedy, and Guy Bannister, one of the ex-FBI agents who promotes the Dallas assassination plot. Here, the crossing of names, personal idiosyncrasies, and relationships is erected into a kind of paranoid kinship system or historical contagion in which a vast, interwoven set of circumstances all identify Oswald as the agent of history, the man who will have something to do with Kennedy, to the extent that the United Postal Service seems to be in on the plot. The discursive nature of these connections is revealed in Oswald's earlier thoughts about his similarities with Kennedy: "He read somewhere that the President liked James Bond novels. He went to the branch library on Napoleon Avenue . . . and took out some Bond novels. . . . He got a biography of the President which said that Kennedy had read *The White Nile.* He went to the library to get *The White Nile* but it was out. He took *The Blue Nile* instead" (318). To play on the puns DeLillo typically incorporates in such flat descriptions, through this "branch" work of duplicated readings and fated "misreadings" ("He took *The Blue Nile* instead"), Oswald fabricates a skein of literary and historical identifications with the same/other of Kennedy.

Coincidence in this reflection is the means of naming the underlying connections of a secret history with Oswald at its center precisely because as contradictory cipher and repository of meaning, he is eminently available for any form of identification with character or event that merges him further into an ongoing plot whose every manifestation is a sign of its reality. This is a process that works dialectically in several ways. As Oswald identifies with Kennedy and Castro, and in his jail reflections, implicitly with Everett and Branch, so DeLillo's Ruby identifies with Oswald, as does DeLillo himself: in an interview, DeLillo comments that part of his fascination with Oswald derives from the fact that they grew up within a few blocks of each other in the Bronx, and that they both have a sense of what it means to be "an outsider in this society."[15] At the same time that this logic dictates a collapsing of self into other, Oswald into Kennedy, author into character, it also redraws the boundaries between these entities, for the mirroring of coincidence can only occur if there remains in place the crucial, if erased difference between parties: poor handwriting, bad spelling, *like* Kennedy; a proximity to Oswald based on a near distance.

But the novel's logic of identification is more pervasive than scatterings of these manufactured and real coincidences. The projection of Oswald's hermeneutic future as disciplinary investigator of his own identity, while foreshortened, is mirrored in the activities of the conspirators at cross-purposes who "make up" Oswald, in the interpretive labors of *Libra*'s readers who are invited to become, as Joseph Kronick puts it, "the co-inventor of the text,"[16] even in DeLillo's own efforts as an author to construct scenarios, simulate conversations, and register coincidences for Oswald. In a kind of Schreberian carnival, "Oswald" in *Libra* thus becomes the means to forge a series of identifications and differentiations between historical agents, invented characters, readers, the author, and the national history that enfolds them in a discourse proceeding from the rupture produced by the assassination.

In this manner, *Libra* stages the identificatory logic of cultural paranoia in which a figure of multiplicity—Oswald—is the vehicle deployed to fuse the confusions of history into the plot affecting the nation's destiny. For one of the novel's true-life characters, David Ferrie, a New Orleans colleague of Bannister's, the unfolding of this logic is mystified as a transcendental process that will result not in Oswald's merging with history but with his escape from it. Conversing with Oswald about the amazing series of coincidences that have brought him into the Dallas assassination plot as its main character, Ferrie remarks:

"You see what this means. How it shows what you've got to do. We didn't arrange your job in that building or set up the motorcade route. We don't have that kind of reach or power. There's something else generating this event. A pattern outside experience. Something that *jerks* you out of the spin of history. I think you've had it backwards all the time. You wanted to enter history. Wrong approach, Leon. What you really want is out. Get out. Jump out. Find your place and your name on another level." (DeLillo, *Libra*, 384)

Earlier, Ferrie had opined that "'there's a pattern in things. Something in us has an effect on independent events. We make things happen. . . . We extend into time'" (330), but as the plot has advanced, he has revised his position to argue that the extension into time is at once a projection out of it. Ferrie makes clear the paradoxes of Oswald's identity-formation as historical subject in a paranoid plot that, in every way, misses history even as it traverses it: he will escape history by becoming inextricably involved in its constructions. The desire for historical agency represented in *Libra*'s Oswald is, in fact, a desire for a determinate order that negates temporality ("'A pattern outside experience'"; "'You've had it backwards all the time'") while enabling a sublimation of that plot in order to read it continuously and become the ever deferred subject-in-process of this reading.

The embodiment of paranoid identity, Oswald is portrayed in the novel as a romantic who yearns for confirmation of himself as the focal point of any number of intersecting plots; yet he is simultaneously the deterritorialized, nomadic subject of postmodernity, and it is this contradiction that DeLillo deploys in *Libra* to represent the repression of the historical and the "crisis of investiture" that attends the multiple failures to insert Oswald into the symbolic order.[17] While the former may appear to be a centripetal version of identity and the latter a centrifugal one, these opposites meet at the coincidental site of the assassination. The double valence of that site—the scene of an accident, the scene of conspiracy's fulfillment—like the Libran nature of Oswald's identity, enables a double interpretation that allows the believer in plots to view Oswald as the transcendent subject around which all plots cohere, while it allows the believer in chaos to disown the contingency of events, that is, to disavow history altogether. The contradiction that DeLillo locates in the same subject opens up a gap to be filled by the hermeneutic "branch-work" resulting in a version of historical pluralism that sustains cultural paranoia in the form of knowledge (ever) yet to be gained about history. Once again, Oswald offers the quintessential rendition of this project as he weighs his options:

He could play it either way, depending upon what they could prove or couldn't prove. He wasn't on the sixth floor after all. He was in the lunch room eating his lunch. The victim of a total frame. They'd been rigging it for years, watching him, using him, creating a chain of evidence with the innocent facts of his life. Or he could say he was only partly guilty, set up to take the blame for the real conspirators. Okay, he fired some shots from the window. But he didn't kill anyone. He never meant to fire the fatal shot. It was never his intention to cause an actual fatality. . . . They fixed it so he would be the lone gunman. They superimposed his head on someone else's body. Forged his name on documents. Made him a dupe of history. (DeLillo, *Libra,* 418)

Later, in his cell, Oswald considers that "there was a third way he could play it. He could tell them he was the lone gunman. He did it on his own. . . . He did it to protest the anti-Castro aims of the government. . . . He had no help. It was his plan, his weapon. Three shots. All struck home. He was an expert shot with a rifle" (428). In these multiple constructions of identity and plot, the relation between narcissistic intentionality, paranoia, a pluralistic hermeneutic, and the "need to know" is forged. This construction, whatever one wishes to make of it, is cast in *Libra* as the dupe (the double) of history, a para-history that substitutes for the actuality it misses the making of plots and forging of identificatory connections across history.

Through its conflation of epistemology, the logic of identification, and representations of postmodern identity, *Libra* shows to what extent the trauma of the assassination generates multiple narratives that, working under the sign of history, elide the very temporality that constitutes it in the formation of mediated, historical subjects caught in images that seem snatched "out of time," "outside history": Oswald on the sixth floor; Kennedy lurching forward in the limousine; Oswald in his torn sweater, clutching his stomach after Ruby shoots him. In the historical imagination that *Libra* explicates, the wound of the assassination is healed by the narratives that re-create it and that always just miss the reality of the event no matter how many variations of it they depict. Yet again, as DeLillo repeatedly makes clear, we are compelled to proliferate these near misses of history in order to continue in the mode of a misrecognition through which we constitute ourselves as "in" history. Perhaps this provides some accounting for the incessant onslaught of assassination narratives, from the Warren Commission Report to more recent phenomena such as the CD-ROM *J.F.K. Assassination: A Visual Investigation,* which allows for a hypertextual reading of many of these narratives and reconstruction from multiple vantage points of bullet trajectories, or the interactive computer simulation, *Re-Elect JFK!,* which permits a player to stage the reelection of Kennedy after a near miss in Dallas. The polysemy of the assassination lends itself to the commodification of Oswald and projection of history as replayable "sim." Under late capitalism, this form of varied iterability replaces any sense of contextualized movement through history—the ludic narrative of historical free play, then, both replacing the older evolutionary models of historical progress and displacing any emergent models of conflict and contingency not bound over to the binary of conspiracy/chaos. Such branch-work, DeLillo suggests in *Libra,* will continue as long as reconstructing the assassination, its characters and contingencies, allows us to shuttle between utter indeterminacy and utter certainty in search of the history that will contain us as paranoid subjects of knowledge, called to order in the national story.

■ Stone's Oedipus: *JFK*

As an assemblage of images from scattered realms brought under the umbrella of the Kennedy assassination, Oliver Stone's *JFK* (1991) appears at first glance to produce cinematically what *Libra* effects verbally: the generation of multiple scenarios that provide the materials for the construction of plots. In the frenetic style that has become Stone's signature, *JFK* is spliced together from hundreds of fragments and images whose alterations and seam work are so obvious that it causes the viewer to wonder if Stone is not consciously engaging in the kind of postmodern pastiche Jameson characterizes as "a neutral practice of . . . mimicry, without any of parody's ulterior motives, amputated of the satiric impulse, devoid of laughter and of any conviction that . . . some healthy linguistic normality still exists. Pastiche is thus blank parody, a statue with blind eyeballs." [18] In fact, as Jameson makes clear, it is in the nature of postmodern pastiche conceived in these terms to lend itself to any agenda with which the author/assembler wishes to imbue it. In the film assemblage of *JFK,* the agenda is concentric and totalizing: here, as elsewhere, we can observe postmodern means put to paranoid ends. In any number of sequences in *JFK,* such as that depicting the progress of Kennedy's motorcade through Dallas and the aftermath of the assassination, autopsy photographs, film clips, shots of newspaper headlines, and bits of contemporary television broadcasts—all of the visual archival materials that adhere to the assassination—are merged with reenactments of the event shot from various reconstructed vantage points. The ostensible effect is that everything—every point of view, piece of evidence, random gesture—is finally part of the plot, and that reality for Stone is the sum total of its mediations centered not around the paranoid protagonist but focused on and radiating from the event itself. There is no "outside" to this construct in which all differentials, particularly those separating the narrational and the real, have become irrelevant to the work of theatricalizing the assassination.

Viewing *JFK* as an assemblage comprised of stitched mediations coheres with Stone's remarks in an interview regarding the nature of history:

What is history? Some people say it's a bunch of gossip made up by soldiers who passed it around a campfire. They say such and such happened. They create it, they make it bigger, they make it better. I knew guys in combat who made up stuff. I'm sure the cowboys did the same. The nature of human being is that they exaggerate. So what is history? Who the fuck knows.[19]

Yet, contradicting such laissez-faire reasoning in which history is converted into the discursive spread of gossip among combatants, one of the well-publicized intentions behind the making of *JFK* was to compel the U.S. government to "open up the archives" so that the truth behind the assassination could at last be established.[20] Equally contradictory is the visibly, even parodically simulated, deterritorialized composition of this example of "reflexive paranoia"[21] that in its construction of an oedipal narrative, represents Kennedy as a fallen king and "us," as national subjects, his procrastinating sons called on to restore his legacy and historical order. Unlike DeLillo, who employs the effects of simulation to scrutinize the hermeneutics of cultural paranoia, these contradictions reveal Stone engaging in a form of hyper-mediation that is, in essence, a paranoid disavowal of the historical. The particular type of historical renunciation theatricalized in *JFK* is manifested in the self-proclaimed capacity to reconstruct from the ruins of history and fallout of conspiracy a total event that locates the director as a Hamlet on whom the truth of history waits.

The historical assumptions that underlie *JFK* become apparent when the crucial differences between DeLillo's novel and Stone's film are considered. The dissimilarities between *Libra* and *JFK* are numerous, but they are most evident in how the concept of plot itself is handled in these two works about the plotting of an assassination. For DeLillo, the indeterminate totality of the assassination is comprised of half-formed, coincidentally intersecting plots bearing contradictory intentions. For Stone, it appears that a number of major government agencies tied into the "military-industrial complex"—a term that President Eisenhower coined in his farewell address—were stumbling all over each other with a singular purpose in mind: to kill Kennedy, not only because his anti-Castro stance had weakened following the failed Bay of Pigs invasion but also because he was going to pull out of the Vietnam War and, by implication, any number of confrontational engagements directly or via proxy with "communist" aggression as represented by the Soviet Union and China. This singularity of purpose and multiplicity of agency (extending to the Mafia and even the vice president) subtends the primary argument of the film that history is a scenario composed of fragments that coalesce into a totality when brought under the scrutiny of those "few good men," Stone included, who have a grasp on history's deep conspiratorial logic.

The underlying historical contention promoted by the materiality of the film as assemblage allows Stone to conduct the double business of creating connections between *JFK* and earlier films such as *Salvador, Platoon, Born on the Fourth of July*, and *Heaven and Earth*, and representing the cold war epoch as of a piece, a single totality with a singular history in which 1950s' anticommunist paranoia, the string of political assassinations in the 1960s, and foreign policy in the 1970s and 1980s are linked as part of a narrative that has concluded. Stone's *Nixon* bears out the trajectory of a logic in which the national destiny and the director's career as teller of the national political story are conflated, for as a kind of bookend to *JFK, Nixon* enables Stone to resuscitate the dead father who eventually succeeded the slain king. Just as Stone's call at the end of *JFK* for an opening up of all the secret archives so that we can finally know the whole truth about Kennedy may be seen as an apocalyptic gesture—a cry for a final revelation—that marks for him the end of the cold war, so his partially sympathetic portrait of the paranoid and conspiratorial Nixon serves as a parallel "conclusion" to the cold war in which the ghost of Nixon (the impotent specter of Kennedy's phallus) is laid to rest. And thus, the conflicted sons of *Salvador, Platoon, Born on the Fourth of July*, and *Heaven and Earth* are also laid to rest in the ongoing paternal drama that Stone has mapped onto the national imaginary as the key aspect of his directorial project. If we place *JFK* intertextually among Stone's other films in this manner (something we are especially encouraged to do in light of his flagrant auteurism), the relation between nation and author is forged and collapsed: the national story becomes that narrative sequenced through a series of films, each providing yet another piece of the tale that is both concluded (as the apocalypticism of *JFK* and nostalgia of *Nixon* make clear), entire unto itself, yet potentially ongoing as the director adds other segments in order to fill out a plot foreshadowed and foreknown.

The identification of a directorial career with the national story evident in the succession of Stone's films, and the attendant visibility of the singular, "real" history of the cold war reliant on the successful deployment of personal vision (getting at the truth of our history thus depends on Stone's success at the box office), are symptomatic of a cultural paranoia informed by the central story around which the assemblage of *JFK* coheres. This is the story of Jim Garrison, the New Orleans district attorney who investigates connections between the mob, the

FBI, CIA fellow travelers, and the assassination, and who Stone heroicizes as a fellow visionary of "true" history's conspiratorial processes. Garrison, played by Kevin Costner, is a virtual stand-in for Stone (the real Garrison plays Chief Justice Earl Warren), and in the courtroom sequences of the Clay Shaw trial where all the scattered evidence of the assassination is gathered as he redirects the event using models and simulations, Garrison constructs Kennedy as a tragic, mythic figure whose murderers must be caught lest our national destiny become permanently derailed and our national identity deformed.

To be sure, the political assassinations of the 1960s were consequential events of the first order that have incurred disastrous effects. But Kennedy, who as Alexander Cockburn reminds us, "backed a military coup in Guatemala to keep out Arévalo, denied the Dominican Republic the possibility of land reform, helped promote a devastating cycle of Latin American history, including the anticipatory motions of a coup in Brazil, and backed a Baathist coup in Iraq that set up a certain native of Tikrit on the path to power,"[22] is identified as the nation's father and king in Garrison's closing arguments at the trial in a speech manufactured by Stone and Zachary Sklar for the purposes of the film. (In fact, Garrison had one of his assistant district attorneys deliver the closing argument for the state and was not present for the verdict). Stone's Garrison asserts that "we have all become Hamlets in our country—children of a slain father-leader whose children still possess the throne. The ghost of John F. Kennedy confronts us with the secret murder at the heart of the American dream."[23] The blatant oedipality of Garrison's comments reveals the conflation of protagonist, director, and nation in *JFK*: if Kennedy is the slain king, then the Hamlets are Garrison and Stone, attempting to wake the nation up to what has happened, and thus, take back the land lost to that other, dark father—the military-industrial complex.

In the film, Stone plays on the sense of "time out of joint" inculcated by the assassination, or the break in the temporal order unfolding in a history that should be progressing in an orderly manner toward the fulfillment of the national destiny.[24] The difference between this time out of joint, and that which Derrida refers to in *Spectres* as a temporal differential that generates a complex relation between present and past, is that Stone's dislocated temporality is entirely dependent on the restoration of a national historical order—a single chain of cause and effect evolving toward a foreclosed destiny—in which any aporias can be annealed if the oedipal truth of the narrative can be acknowledged. In this manner, for Stone, the erasure of temporality (time out of joint

as projected through his rewriting of *Hamlet*) and the projection of causality as the foundation of a national historical order are fully consonant. The paranoid tale Stone tells through Garrison is an identity story
in which, at once, the nation is restored, the historical/temporal order
is redeemed, and Stone/Garrison/Hamlet acquire historical agency in
overthrowing the dark fathers of conspiracy—if only we will listen in
a commodified process of avowal that involves the marketing and distribution of the truth via the film. In what must be one of the most
overbearing examples of transformation of the political into the personal in U.S. film history, Stone thus converts the history of the cold
war into the singular narrative of a quest for "manhood" and nation-
hood, a quest compounded in the film with what Michael Rogin has
registered as its "demonization of a homosexual band" in linking conspiracy and the closeting of secrets with the gay identities of Ferrie and
Shaw.[25] For Stone, the restitution of history becomes the fulfilling of an
oedipal identity as the sons assume their "proper," homophobic roles
as men who uncover the truth.

We must look once again, more carefully, at the ways in which Stone
achieves these oedipal conversions through the materiality of the film
—its seemingly paradoxical construction as Deleuzian media assemblage. The film is as much a pastiche generically as it is in terms of
the materials it employs. In comparing *JFK*'s opening sequences tracing the progress of the Kennedy motorcade in Dallas, an introduction
posited as a live report, to the focalized courtroom sequence, a climax
falling completely within the generic confines of the dramatized trial
scene, we can see the extent to which Stone dexterously deploys postmodern techniques to paranoid ends. In "recording" Kennedy's route,
Stone combines actual newsreel footage, documentary photographs,
clips from the Zapruder film, and re-creations in order to provide a coherent narrative of the event. Here, Stone appears to foreground with
intent the palimpsestic nature of the sequence, deliberately mixing up
obviously re-created images with actual footage by shooting some of the
former in black-and-white vérité style (the simulation coded as being
closer to the "real" of the event), not even bothering to disguise the fact
that he is using doubles for the Kennedys. On the one hand, it would
seem that Stone is compiling the cinematic bits and pieces in order to
assist the viewer to relive the whole event of the Kennedy assassination; on the other, he is flagrantly gesturing, almost self-parodically and
in a reflexive manner characteristic of "historiographic metafiction,"[26]
toward the fact that this historical narrative of necessity exists in fragments—pieces that only the heroic director or district attorney can put

back together again, filling in the gaps as he goes. The tautology of the assumptions underlying this unique version of parodic intentionality is manifest in the hyper-constructedness of the motorcade sequence: *cinematically,* the kingdom is in ruins, requiring Stone to redeem it and giving him a purpose, an identity; the kingdom was once whole and will be whole again—a fact evidenced by its current fragmented state—providing him (and the nation) with a destiny, an ontology.

Stone ups the ante in the film's climactic sequence. In the scenes depicting Garrison's fictionalized closing arguments at the Shaw trial, where we are exposed to a lengthy explication of his theories about the assassination that would never be permitted in a real courtroom (this, however, is consistent with the generic characteristics of such scenes), we view a re-creation within the re-creation of the assassination sequence represented in the film's opening. A model of Dealy Plaza to which Garrison gestures as he narrates the assassination sequence for the jury, morphs into a scene of the life-size real actors who stand for the actual people who witnessed the execution. Once again, there is rapid movement between color and black-and-white photography to convey the impression of realism, and the aporias of the opening scenes are filled in with the fabricated photograph of a second gunman, a view of Zapruder shooting the very film that is used for part of this sequence, and a snapshot—as if taken by Kennedy himself at the moment of death—of a woman standing next to the car who has just seen him shot. Stone accentuates the Baudrillardian, simulated nature of postmodern history making in *JFK* while maintaining, in Garrison's voice-over as the camera moves from Disneyland model to full-screen head shot, a hold on the central "truth" toward which all of the fragments, re-creations, and simulations point: that we all killed Kennedy (such is the range of the identificatory logic Stone promotes), and that we are all responsible for restoring the national and historical order, the loss of which is compellingly evidenced by these simulacra.

What is symptomatized in *JFK,* and thus the source of its enjoyment, is the desire for the continual reenactment of the event, which in Stone's hands provides the occasion for reformulating the conflation of personal and national identities that "constructedness" itself underwrites. While DeLillo offers a critique of the paranoid process in which history is oedipalized, Stone "democratizes" this process by arguing in the pastiche of *JFK* that what will make us good citizens, good national subjects—even good consumers of the truth—will come about through the disclosure of all the secrets surrounding assassination. Opening up the archives, Stone suggests, will restore our true history, and that restoration can only come about if each individual accepts his or her responsibility for pressuring the government (that is, the very military-industrial complex that maintains its ascendancy as both the repository of secrecy and medium of revelation) to deliver the truth of the assassination. In the film, actor Donald Sutherland, as an ex-CIA official who serves as Garrison's deep throat, inculcates this schizophrenic function of governmental power, which involves securing a trade balance between secrecy and revelation. The paternal logic that Stone deploys to figure the process of becoming citizens stipulates that we "sons," we Hamlets, must regain the phallus/signifier of truth that was stolen and hidden by the dark "uncle" of governmental conspiracy; each one of us must avow secrecy and pursue the paranoid quest for the real of presidential murder if we are to recover "America."

This pursuit, in the film's logic, is entirely performative, as the repeated screening of frames from the Zapruder film before the Clay Shaw jury indicates. It is not that we, as viewers and citizens, must interpret whatever revelations proceed from the film or the opening of the archives; rather, we must literally *subject* ourselves to the deluge of information in order to acknowledge how overwhelming the conspiracy is and how we are all implicated in it. In the cinematic rhetoric of *JFK*, the very fragmented, pastiche-like nature of the central event around which all else coheres provides evidence that before this punctum—to which, looking across Stone's films, all cold war history leads and from which it falls—there was a unified, totalized reality that can be reconstituted if only we will reconstitute ourselves as questers for the truth and directors of the scattered mediations through which it is refracted. The assassination and its fallout, in other words, offer rich opportunities for the reformation of the subject and the nation. Ultimately, *JFK* is a film about the making of the paranoid citizen subject to knowledge rendered as the assemblage of information in a late capitalist democracy. In this state, where the commodification and exchange of secrets between enemies has come home to roost, the democratic individual beyond history evolves in the ever deferred future of the archives' opening and the true commencement of branch work.

■ Performing Character: *Oswald's Tale*

In contrast to DeLillo's depiction of Oswald as cipher, Mailer's portrayal of Oswald as an "American mystery" depends on the author's formidable rhetorical skills in constructing the accused assassin as a tragic "character." *Oswald's Tale* is Mailer's meticulous rendition of Oswald's life from the inception of his decision to go to the Soviet Union to his death at the hands of Jack Ruby. Relying on the techniques he had developed for the narration of condemned killer Gary Gilmore's "true-life story" in *The Executioner's Song*, in *Oswald's Tale*, Mailer builds up the persona of his protagonist through a prodigious accumulation of facts, interviews, and documents. In sharp contrast, however, to the systematic excision of reportage in *The Executioner's Song*, Mailer scatters a number of narrational commentaries across the tale as he traces Oswald's movements from Minsk to Dallas; these "speculations," as they are termed by the narrator/reporter/assembler of the novel (referred to as "the Author" at several points), are so inflected with reflexivity about their hypothetical qualities that the tone in which they are conveyed becomes, at times, Jamesian:

Oswald was a protagonist, a prime mover, a man who made things happen— in short, a figure larger than others would credit him for being. Indeed, this point of view has by now taken hold to a point where the writer would not like to relinquish it for too little. *There* is the danger! Hypotheses commence as our servant—they enable us to keep our facts in order while we attempt to learn more about a partially obscured subject. Once the profits of such a method accumulate, however, one is morally obliged (like a man who has just grown rich) to be scrupulously on guard against one's own corruption. Otherwise, the hitherto useful hypothesis will insist on prevailing over everything that comes in and so will take over the integrity of the project.[27]

It may be that Mailer has more consciously at stake in fabricating Oswald as a tragic character, a "figure larger than others would credit him for being," than he did in the Gilmore story, where, as I will discuss in chapter 4, the elision of the narrator's presence serves as a screen for the author's manipulation of personality and event. As is the case with Stone in *JFK*, the wager Mailer places in building Oswald's character for the purposes of *Oswald's Tale* is performative. If Oswald can be seen not as absurd—not as a cipher à la DeLillo, a random element caught up in the chaos of events—but as tragic agent, then history, which in the wake of the Kennedy assassination becomes either indecipherable or unnarratable, can be restored to its human proportion as a tale with its existential protagonists, traceable plots and subplots, and hermeneutic richness: "We have come at last to the philosophical crux of our inquiry. It would state that the sudden death of a man as large in his possibilities as John Fitzgerald Kennedy is more tolerable if we can perceive his killer as tragic rather than absurd" (Mailer, *Oswald's Tale*, 198). *Oswald's Tale* might be seen as a modernist response to a postmodern event, and thus, an inversion of *JFK,* which is arguably a postmodernist response to an event that signals the collapse of nation and history conceived in modernistic terms. Certainly, a reading of this work proclaimed as "a form of its own somewhere between fiction and non-fiction" (353) along these lines would be in accord with the familiar renderings of Mailer as an existentialist. But it is precisely within the construction and conceptualization of character in this, "our own largest American mystery" (353), that combines the "author's musings" (353) with factual material where we can detect its paranoid logic: a logic in which the authentication of personality—its historical literacy or readability—comes to rest on a figure of history as tragedy that offers the restoration of national form and destiny.

Mailer is visibly concerned with the concept of character in *Oswald's Tale,* and anxious to convince the reader that character building is successfully taking place in this nonfictional bildungsroman that conflates the formation of Oswald as foreign/national subject and his self-construction as a player in the evolution of a global destiny. The device of the narrator in the novel sustains a number of roles: reporter, reference librarian, cultural historian, philosopher. But more than any of these, the narrational presence in *Oswald's Tale* speculates in hypotheses about the motives behind the possible involvement of "the partially obscured subject" in the assassination and the conclusion toward which all the contradictory conjectures about the "*object* (to use the KGB's word for a person under scrutiny) as he tumbles through the prisms of a kaleidoscope" (198) inevitably lead. Arguably, the general project of *Oswald's Tale* involves a collapsing of the subject into the object, for while he capitalizes on the surplus of information that accrues as the tale gets told, Mailer is interested in constructing a historical figure who has multiple, subjectival choices at every turn, and therefore, is indeterminate, obscured.[28] Oswald's opacity predominates until the very end of the story, when he is transformed into the singular, tragic lone gunman of the theory the narrator proffers as the one that most likely follows when the facts are combined with knowledge of Oswald's character: "It is . . . difficult not to believe that he pulled the trigger. . . . If one's personal inclinations would find Oswald innocent, or at least part of a conspiracy, one's gloomy verdict, nonetheless, is that Lee had the character to kill Kennedy, and that he probably did it alone" (Mailer, *Oswald's Tale,* 778).[29] Mailer's "probably" reflects his historicist sense that there is no end to speculation about history, or to the "fact that there are no facts—only the mode of our approach to what we call the facts" (Mailer, *Oswald's Tale,* 516), but in such formulations we can observe a familiar complicitous contradiction between hermeneutic means and performative ends. The double valence of the word *character* is crucial at this point in the narrator's concluding remarks, for throughout this encyclopedic narrative bloated with detail, Mailer is at odds to establish Oswald *as* character—a manly entity who emerges full-blown out of the cross-hatchings of fact, motive, and interpretation. At the same time, Oswald must be articulated as *having* character: not the mere plaything of historical coincidence or conspiratorial design but an existential presence who has entered history by making the choice to attempt the murder of a president.

Implicitly, Mailer's success as an author, and our success as his auditors (hence, Mailer's success as an imaginative historian of the national tragedy, and our success as readers/citizens who must come to terms with it), depends on the efficacy of the performative construction of Oswald's character in the novel. If somehow, beyond the transcripts of dozens of taped interviews, the distended recountings of Oswald's daily routine in Russia, the rhizomic side trips into the lives of those whose relation to Oswald was one of merest contingency, there emerges the "mystery" of Oswald, "our First Ghost" (784), who is both opaque in his subjectivity and transparent as the determinate agent of destiny, then the work of narrative that is "an exploration into the possibilities of . . . character" (513) will have been accomplished. This offers some explanation of why Mailer tracks Oswald from the period just prior to and during his peregrinations in Russia, back to his childhood, and then forward again to his return to the United States and the events surrounding the assassination, as if the narrator, Columbo-like, was ferreting out via flashback and flash forward the scattered parts of a mystery whose solution is already known to the audience and "the Author." Thus, we are offered alternative versions of Oswald and the unfolding plot at several points in the novel, which infers a subject and his implication in ongoing historical developments as aspects of the dialectic Mailer wishes to establish between Oswald the free agent and historical consequence.[30]

Declaring himself to be merely a "literary usher" (Mailer, *Oswald's Tale,* 352) at the point when Oswald is about to return to the United States (the land of opportunity!), the narrator attests, in a structuralist version of branch-work, that we must now comprehend Oswald as multiple, "a man who might have been travelling along any one of . . . three tracks" (456): either spy, closeted homosexual, or alienated political radical who identifies at once with Marx and Hitler. Like his alter ego, the rich political gadfly George De Mohrenschildt who befriends

Oswald in Texas and "delight[s] in presenting himself as right-wing, left-wing, a moralist, an immoralist, an aristocrat, a nihilist, a snob, an atheist, a Republican, a Kennedy lover, a desegregationist, an intimate of oil tycoons, a bohemian, and a socialite, plus a quondam Nazi apologist once a year" (458), Mailer's Oswald is a figure kept in play throughout much of *Oswald's Tale* so that the formation and determination of his character will appear to be something that actually occurs in the telling of his story. While Oswald and everything associated with the assassination may have been wholly commodified over the last thirty-five years, in Mailer's view, he is not to be treated as the mere recipient of socioeconomic investments if he is to be perceived as an epochal agent. Through this process, a temporarily postmodern Oswald is established as a historical character, as opposed to an "ideological" figure: "De Mohrenschildt could hardly have failed to see that there was a profound divide between Oswald's ideology and his character: Absolute freedom for all was the core of his political vision, yet he treated [his wife] Marina as if he were a Nazi corporal shaping up a recruit" (458). Ideological in this eccentric sense (which as we shall see, is aligned with Mailer's concept of plot) implies the repression of subjective freedom that is consonant with the placement of the subject in time, economy, and history, on one of those tracks, and thus the closing down of the author's performative function in the novel's implicit contract with the reader to present an Oswald fully constituted through an authentically historical narrative process.

It is here, however, that Mailer's desire to perform Oswald's character—a desire founded on paranoid identificatory assumptions and anxieties that I will examine momentarily—comes up against the linguistic constraints of constructing identity in narrative. As J. Hillis Miller argues, the self represented by character in narrative "is never present. It is always over there, somewhere else, pointed to by characters (signposts) that cannot be followed to reach an unmediated access to what they indicate."[31] For Miller, reading Nietzsche, character is wholly a figure of speech, a form of metalepsis that reveals the demolition of linear cause and effect relations whenever character is established in narrative since the consciousness of the constructed subject is predicated on a fictitious cause which is posited as prior to thought but which then becomes its effect: "An effect of which we are not yet conscious becomes the cause of an imaginary cause, and that imaginary cause then generates belatedly the effect that fits the imaginary cause" (Miller, 43). This complex equation defines the abysmal performative nature of character-building in narrative, which depends on the collapsing of temporality that we have noted is consonant with cultural paranoia. But because he wants to convert the performative into a constative, Oswald as existentialist manqué into Oswald as destinal figure, Mailer feels compelled to establish a relation of clear priority between the Oswald as subject-in-process and the plot that contains him. In setting up Oswald as the hermeneutic object of scrutiny ("We must not only look at Oswald from many points of view—first Russian and soon American—but even try to perceive him through bureaucratic lenses" [198]), "the Author" argues for the usefulness of a "method of approach" that "search[es] for the nature of the man before we decide on the plot" (198). Mailer's strategy is to posit a polysemous Oswald before locating him within the pattern of events that seals his fate and reveals the truth of his nature, even though, from the perspective of "the Author" and the readers of *Oswald's Tale,* these events have already taken place: the plot in the genre of the historical mystery that Mailer invents is always prior to character. Through this paradoxical method, Mailer hopes to both explain and instantiate Oswald's presence, however ghostly, within history.

But as Miller suggests, the illusion of linearity that Mailer produces —the detected nature of his leading character being the cause that leads directly to the effect of the assassination—occludes the infinite reversability of a process in which it is equally possible to view Oswald as the tragic effect of an overdetermined cause: "the sudden death of a man as large in his possibilities as John Fitzgerald Kennedy." Indeed, in Mailer's circular logic, it is only because the catastrophe of the assassination is so great that we must seek its causal origins in the actions of a tragic, rather than absurd, character, so that the national trauma will accrue historical density as an element of destiny rather than sheer contingency. In *Oswald's Tale,* Mailer is at odds to stabilize the relation between cause and effect, origin and end, even if he is quite aware that the mercurial nature of that relation is integral to the performative method through which he hopes to produce Oswald.

At one point, "the Author" makes a remarkable comment on a snippet from the Warren Commission transcripts in which a witness testifies that "Lee started to bring [into being some of the] events he had just described":

The essence of magic is to exist in a state of consciousness where past and future seem interchangeable. Classical Hebrew, for example, has only two tenses: There is the present, and then there is another tense which barely distinguishes between past and future. . . . A primitive sense of existence is suggested—one that would transgress our modern separation between the real and the imaginary. In such an ancient grammar, yesterday's events are not seen as facts which have already occurred so much as intimations of the future, that is, omens received from dreams. In that primitive world, the events of yesterday mix in one's memory with portents of last night's dream. To say, therefore, that you have done something which you have not yet done becomes the first and essential step in shaping the future. Out of omens come events. It is as if the future cannot exist without an *a priori* delineation of it. (569)

Mailer tries to have it both ways as he constructs an Oswald who is "ancient" in that what he imagines results simultaneously in the determinate real of historical occurrence as character merges with actuality, yet who is also "modern" (that is, tragic) in the attempted establishment of a fully temporalized relation between Oswald's nature and the sequence of contingencies that leads to the assassination. In stark contrast to the statement that character must come before plot, the narrator, drawing the relation between Oswald's being terminated from a job and his posing with firearms for a famous photograph, speculates on

how essential chronology is to motive. For if Oswald was fired on March 29, he might have reacted by asking Marina to take the photographs of himself with rifle and revolver on March 31, whereas if he was given notice on Monday, April 1, the two events are considerably less connected, and we can all assume that there was a glint in Oswald's eye while he was listening to Graef [firing him]. (503)

Mailer thus sets Oswald astride the contradiction inherent in the difference between "ancient" temporality, which Benedict Anderson, paraphrasing Walter Benjamin, refers to as "messianic time, a simultaneity of past and future in an instantaneous present," and the "modern" temporality of the "national imagination," a " 'homogenous, empty time,' in which simultaneity is, as it were, transverse, cross-time, marked . . . by temporal coincidence and measured by clock and calendar." [32] Pursuing a course between DeLillo's hermeneutics of suspicion and Stone's oedipal causality, Mailer figures Oswald as the chiasmus of chance and destiny, the place where one turns into the other. Only by negotiating the contradiction in which the "primitive" Oswald is inserted into modern orders of causality—only through a performative magic that, as we will see shortly, is consonant with the magic of nationalism in Anderson's terms—can Mailer complete the task of fabricating Oswald as the historical agent of a national narrative.

In positing Oswald as both agent and victim of circumstance, Mailer advances a contradiction. "When kings and political leaders of great nations appear in public on charged occasions," the narrator speculates in reference to the overwhelming ballistic evidence that suggests there was more than one shooter at the assassination, "we can anticipate a special property of the cosmos—coincidences accumulate: All variety of happenings race toward the event. It is not inconceivable that two gunmen with wholly separate purposes both fired in the same few lacerated seconds of time" (Mailer, *Oswald's Tale,* 779). Yet, because "delineation of character, not exposition of sound-wave charts, is the aim of this work!" the narrator is compelled to declare that "every insight we have gained of [Oswald] suggests the solitary nature of his act" (ibid.). Having effectually painted himself into a corner where both the solitary nature and cosmic, destinal importance of Oswald's act must be asserted in order for his character to be fully established, Mailer must rhetorically throw up his hands and declare the entire confabulation a mystery, the depths of which cannot be fully gauged, an existential tragedy in which intention and fate, choice and circumstance inexplicably merge. Within this contradiction that conceals a narrative anxiety about the success of performing and differentiating Oswald's character, we can observe the cultural paranoia that attends Mailer's propounding of an "American mystery."

Oswald's Tale is an anxious narrative in several senses. As Oswald is portrayed having anxieties about the establishment of his place in history, so the narrator of his tale is at odds to frame and excuse in terms of 1950s' ideology Oswald's uneasy pursuit of "manhood," earned through "brave acts, the honoring of one's private code, . . . fierce attachment to one's finest habits" (369). As Oswald appears obsessed with his historical potency, so the narrator seems overly concerned with defusing the charge of homosexuality brought against Oswald in the historical aftermath by referring to it as an "enigma," a "paradox" shrouded in the obscurity of recollection (539). As Oswald agonizes over the possibility that he might be marginal to the unfolding of major events, so the narrator worries that instead of being viewed as a fully tragic figure, Oswald will only be seen as a lone paranoid, a "twisted pathetic killer who happened to be in a position to kill a potentially great President," in which case "America is cursed with an absurdity": there is "no logic to the event and no sense of balance in the universe," and "historical absurdity (like the war in Vietnam), breeds social disease" (606).

As we might expect, the larger narrative anxiety underlying these instances is performative, for Mailer is concerned that if Oswald cannot be brought off as a tragic character, then he is merely a random element of an absurdist drama that symptomatically reveals the spread of the "social disease" of paranoia, which for Mailer is an illness of the imagination. More precisely, in Mailer's terms, it is *the* illness of the contemporary "American" imagination, which having run out of space to realize itself in actuality, must now turn inward, inventing "scenarios" filled with imaginary enemies and apocalyptic outcomes.

Still, to say that Americans are somewhat enamored of paranoia requires at least this much explanation: Our country was built on the expansive imaginations of people who kept dreaming about the lands to the west—many Americans moved into the wild with no more personal wealth than the strength of their imaginations. When the frontier was finally closed, imagination inevitably turned into paranoia (which can be described, after all, as the enforced enclosure of the imagination—its artistic form is a scenario) and, lo, there where the westward expansion stopped on the shores of the Pacific grew Hollywood. It would send its reels of film back to the rest of America, where imagination, now landlocked, had need of scenarios. By the late Fifties and early Sixties, a good many of these scenarios had chosen anti-Communism for their theme—the American imagination saw a Red menace under every bed including Marina Oswald's. (722–23)

This forceful indictment of cold war paranoia, forging a parallel between the closing of the frontier and the inward turn of the "American" imagination, echoes Kennedy's speeches that urged, as a counter to the acceptance of these conditions, the opening of a "New Frontier" of "unknown opportunities and perils . . . a set of challenges" that confront a reenergized U.S. imagination ready to go to work on social, as opposed to territorial, issues.[33] But as John McClure has argued, Kennedy's New Frontier speeches can be placed in the genre of "late imperial romance," which begins with Joseph Conrad, where the desire for social change and existential agency is founded on the same premises—territorial expansion, historical centrism, the control of nature—that underlie colonialism and, for Mailer, the enclosure of the imagination once imperialism has done its work.[34] So, too, in *Oswald's Tale,* the cure to a national ailment takes the form of a disease, for the performance of Oswald's character—the articulation of this tragic as opposed to absurd figure—relies on certain contradictions that reinscribe the conditions of cultural paranoia critiqued in DeLillo and disseminated in *JFK.* In turning, finally, to this process of reinscription in *Oswald's Tale,* we can observe the conditions under which Mailer enscenes the performance of an identity that becomes national and historical only to the degree that these scenarios are hedged by "the enforced enclosure of the imagination."

Mailer's Oswald, like DeLillo's, is a figure of multiplicity, but with agency added; he is a figure of identification and difference, but his differentiation in *Oswald's Tale* is a matter of the author's keeping in play as many alternative Oswalds as possible rather than portraying him as a nomadic cipher ever available to the semiotic regime of the moment. For Mailer, Oswald may have been caught up in any number of the scenarios that signify the paranoid, inward turn of the U.S. cultural imagination. But the tragic Oswald that he wishes to construct and locate transcends the limitations of scenario—a fabrication in which all the characters behave according to foreseeable logical patterns—because it is necessary for us, as citizens of a body whose head has been removed ("It had become [Oswald's] fate to decapitate the American political process" [Mailer, *Oswald's Tale*, 782]), to continue to believe in the coherency of an ongoing national narrative with determinable origins and a past of limitless potential given over to a contained, encumbered future. Hence, the narrator explains,

it can hardly be difficult for the reader to understand why it is more agreeable to keep one's developing concept of Oswald as a protagonist, a man to whom, grudgingly, we must give a bit of stature when we take into account the modesty of his origins. . . . If a figure as large as Kennedy is cheated abruptly of life, we feel better, inexplicably better, if his killer is also not without size. Then, to some degree, we can also mourn the loss of possibility in the man who did the deed. Tragedy is vastly preferable to absurdity. (606–7)

Absurdity and the paranoia of the closed territorial imagination lie outside this rationalization of Oswald because they do not allow us to properly "mourn the loss of possibility," the multiplicity and promise that is lost the instant that Oswald pulls the trigger and becomes the lone gunman of history, for once he does so, he can never be anything more than the man who probably shot Kennedy.

In Mailer's logic, if the absurdist reading of Oswald were to hold sway, then the national story that it symptomizes would lose its tragic and exceptionalist power as the narrative of an expansive people for whom the earth is not large enough to allow the full extension of the "American imagination." Beset by the enemies of limited space and passing time, this continental energy has been driven inward and turned paranoid. For Mailer, Oswald's tragedy must be aligned with this tragedy of the imagination if the peripeteia of a national destiny represented by the assassination is to make any sense. In this conflation of character and nation, as a character runs out of choices once the plot is finally laid, so the nation runs out of imaginative space once its territorial limits are reached; what saves both from absurdity, then, is the sustaining of the mystery (the expansive imagination rechanneled through possible Oswalds or alternative futures as chance is transformed into destiny) within the frame of the tale. Oswald is ultimately, in Mailer's conception, a stand-in for "America" itself, part of the tragic manifest destiny of a nation that was replete with possibility, in the past, but now, having run out of the time, territory, and purpose derailed at the site of the assassination, must reconstitute "possibility" as the mystery of loss or succumb to paranoia.

To this extent, *Oswald's Tale* is a work of mourning that may be viewed as countering paranoia—at least the paranoia of the landlocked imagination that Mailer articulates—with tragedy, absurdity with the performance of character. Yet the odd construction of postmodern identity that Mailer fabricates in Oswald, who is an unwieldy assemblage of nomadic, outlaw desire and existentialist intentionality, reinforces the connections between cultural paranoia and national identity that we have observed operating in *Libra* and *JFK*. In *Oswald's Tale,* the historical and existential authenticity of "Oswald" and "America" is dependent on their merging. "Our country," to repeat the key phrase from the passage cited above, "was built on the expansive imaginations of people who kept dreaming about the lands to the west." Like the imaginary Oswald of lost possibility, the imaginary national landscape that Mailer refers to here and throughout his work is a back-formation founded on the need to link the determinacy of events (destiny) with the extrapolation of desire (dreaming) in such a way that the linkage itself provides a historical explanation of how pluralistic means lead to singular, "tragic" ends. In this manner, the assassination, the colonization of the West, the cold war—all of our national tragic turns—are offered up as the destined effects of the exercise of the national character, which is to be expansive in terms of the imagination. To pursue the novel's logic, it is only because this expansiveness has been contained and lost that a national narrative with a destinal plot can be construed, that the United States as a nation can *have* a history and still always be immersed in an unfolding historical process with elastic, yet determinate ends. Mailer's self-assumed task in *Oswald's Tale* is to connect this work of the national imagination with "our" subjectival work as a people of expansive imaginations, to forge the connection between the nation and identity in the act of mourning the loss of the very thing that constitutes their bond and "our" place in history.

This project, as it is marshaled in *Oswald's Tale,* depends on assumptions about the utter historical centricity of the assassination, the exceptional destiny of the United States as the geographic space territorialized by the "expansive imaginations" of its citizens, and the symbolizing of the assassination as the site-event of national loss, along with the "enjoyment" that mourning it brings. These are symptomatic of the cultural paranoia that underlies Mailer's articulation of the U.S. historical imagination even as he protests its paranoid turn in the attempted performance of Oswald's character. The contradiction lies most revealingly in the detemporalizing of Oswald in the wake of the assassination, as if the character whose motives have been so subject to chronology becomes synchronic once he has turned possibility into act and entered history. As David Ferrie suggests to Oswald in *Libra,* so the narrator of *Oswald's Tale* suggests to the reader that in becoming a leading figure of history, Oswald is now beyond it:

If one supposes that he did shoot Kennedy . . . [then] he had passed through the mightiest of the psychic barriers—he had killed the king. It was equal psychologically to breaking through the sound barrier. All the controls were reversed. . . . If he is the killer, then we know enough about him to understand that he has been living with a spiritual caul all morning. . . . Stationed within himself, he has now descended to those depths where one waits for final judgment. (678)

The postassassination Oswald, like the nation that has reached its territorial limits, is now turned in on himself, fully positioned and newly born in an eschatological temporality where final judgment is at hand. This apocalyptic time out of history where cause and effect are reversed is at once Oswald's time at the instant that he has entered history and the national time, now that the liminal contours of its manifest destiny have been shadowed.

Oswald's time after the assassination is the time of paranoia in which a kind of identificatory collapse occurs: here, nation, self, possibility, and destiny are merged in a "future" that "would pre-empt the present" (Mailer, *Oswald's Tale,* 782). This is, precisely, the site of the expansive imagination's fullest extension that takes place outside history, in the preemptive future that is identical to the contingent past made available for conversion into destiny. Mailer's canny awareness of the trajectories of the "American" imagination, homogenized as the machine of national destiny, is matched by his pathological investment in tragic awareness as the cure for cultural paranoia in a time of contraction, for tragedy in his view has the advantage of supplying a national destiny with a bathetic purpose. But Mailer's prescription is homeopathic. As the narratives of assassination I have discussed suggest in common, cultural paranoia is a tautological condition in which subjectival and national fantasies—the one nation, the many selves—converge. At the heart of these convergent destinal fantasies lies the chief contradiction on which they are built: their deployment through historiographic narratives inevitably results in mystifications of self and nation elevated above history. Whether through hermeneutic adventuring, oedipal redemptionism, or tragic ressentiment, these narratives of the assassination figure a paranoid imaginary whose effects through the "magic of nationalism" become leading causes in the formation of subjects and nations.

At different points in these narratives of the Kennedy assassination, the matter of Oswald's purported homosexuality comes to the fore, as if sexuality and sexual preference could serve as an explanation for secrecy, conspiracy, or terrorism. Since Freud's rending of the Schreber case, of course, the bond between paranoia and homosexuality has been explicated generally within the framework of psychoanalytic theory in terms of repressed homoeroticism (love of the same) converted into homophobia (hatred of difference). In *Libra,* alternative sexualities lose their alterity as all energies become incorporated into the intersecting schemes of frayed conspiracies; in *JFK,* the interplay between repressed homoeroticism and homophobia is folded into the oedipal drama that Stone imposes on cold war history; in *Oswald's Tale,* Oswald's homosexuality is incorporated as simply one more "possibility" that the character-in-progress might pursue. As I have suggested in this chapter, the interchange of sameness and difference, multiplicity and singularity, becomes reduced and assimilated in the narratives of cultural paranoia that forge the iron bond between national destiny and national identity. In the next chapter, I consider three novels that manifest the relation between paranoia and gender in terms of sameness and difference, inside and outside, which bear striking similarity to those employed in the assassination narratives. These works enable us to add another layer to the story of cultural paranoia—one in which the relation between sexual identity and the projections of paranoia, which lies at the origins of the study of modern paranoia, is expressed.

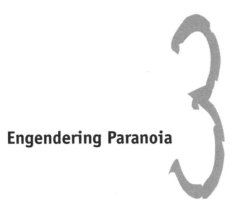

Engendering Paranoia

In the ego's era, symbolic time is stolen, and the "symbolic" function of making connections suffers. . . . If one asks what the ego stands to lose in the face of making consistent connections, one can begin by noting that the ego desires to dominate and control, and that a means to domination and control is the fragmentation and disconnection of everything outside the ego, the reduction of everything different or other than itself to a scale the ego can manage, to a grey background of sameness—in order that the ego can stand out, in order that it does not disappear in the movement of living history, a temporal process where it might be able to identify itself by saying "*that is I,*" but where it cannot say "*it is me.*"
—Teresa Brennan, *History after Lacan*

■ The prevalence of works by male authors in a book on paranoia and contemporary narrative suggests that paranoia—as it has been characterized from Schreber on—is something that occurs "between men." We recall Freud's classic description of paranoia: a fear generated within and among men, as in the Schreber case with its "outburst of homosexual libido," the "object" of which "was probably from the very first [Schreber's] physician, Flechsig"; the "struggles against this libidinal impulse produced the conflict which gave rise to the pathological phenomena."[1] In Freud's view, Schreber's contradictory desire to be a woman and to be a man by destroying the woman within him comes about as a result of an overdetermined relation to another male, his father. This overidentification is a form of castration where the boundary established between male and male is erased: "normally," that boundary is kept in place between males by the trafficking in women ("here is the (m)other lacking the phallus that we do not lack; take her, in the form of an other, as the sign of your discreet identity"), reinforced by the prohibition against incest. As Luce Irigaray writes:

The use and traffic in women subtend and uphold the reign of masculine hom(m)o-sexuality in speculations, mirror games, identifications, and more or less rivalrous appropriations, which defer its real practice. Reigning everywhere, although prohibited in practice, hom(m)o-sexuality is played out through the bodies of women, matter, or sign, and heterosexuality has been up to now just an alibi for the smooth workings of man's relation to himself, of relations among men." [2]

In Irigaray's argument, what is between men is a narcissistic relation that excludes by repressing and abjecting the feminine, a double process of internalization and exteriorization that erects a double, mirroring boundary between the self that is male and the other that is female, and between the self that is male and the other that is male displaced onto the female.

For Freud, the collapse of boundaries between self and other engendered through the process of oedipal disavowal produces the homosexual panic he labels paranoia. The universe of the Freudian paranoid is an all-encompassing mirror of the narcissistic ego, whose imperialism is only matched by the repressed anxiety that it has been invaded by the woman, the other; but this alterity is, in fact, merely a displacement of the selfsame identity who both dreads and desires this invasion. As Eve Kosofsky Sedgwick has put it in her historicist revision of the Freudian paradigm, "Paranoia in men results from the repression of their homosexual desire," which "has nothing to do with a classification of the paranoid . . . in terms of 'latent' or 'overt' 'homosexual' 'types,' but everything to do with the foregrounding . . . of intense male homosocial desire as at once the most compulsory and the most prohibited of social bonds." [3] Sedgwick is discussing here the "paranoid Gothic" as indicative of a modern epoch in which male bonding of a certain kind is institutionally authorized (in schools, fraternities, business organizations) while sexual bonding between men is criminalized under the dominion of compulsory heterosexuality. In both Freud's model and in Irigaray and Sedgwick's revisionary views of male paranoia, women are constituted as ciphers: they become the guarantors in a modern civilization under the rule of heterosexuality that what takes place between men is legitimate as long as they, the women, stand in for other men as the proper receptacles and mediators of desire.

One might maintain, facilely, that things have changed since the novels of the "paranoid Gothic" and Henry James were written, and that under postmodernism, with its endorsements of fluid identities, multiple subject positions, and gender performances, the relation between paranoia and homosociality should have disappeared. This might well be the case (or could be the case, if the utopian tendencies we have seen in certain construals of postmodern identity ever fully evolved) if cultural paranoia were simply something "between men." To some extent, it is precisely because the bond between heterosexuality and specific social formations such as the family or the state has become less determining and determinate, and because the marketplace in which women are trafficked has been affected by transformations in the nature of capital and commodities, that we can observe everywhere today paranoid reactions to the recognized fragility of male identity. This reaction formation is enacted at a number of sites, but perhaps most visibly, and comically, in the frantic bolstering of heterosexually predatory, unitary, male subjects in such films as *The Terminator,* despite its cybernetic updating of subjectivity, and *Lethal Weapon,* with its sanctioning of a "safe" interracial homoeroticism.[4]

Yet, as the novels I examine in this chapter reveal, there is much more to the story than this. As Teresa Brennan has contended, while cultural paranoia often finds specific representation as a contradictory relation of desire and distance between men in which women are excluded by virtue of their inclusion as mediators of desire, it is more generally a condition produced by what she calls the "ego's era" that began with the onset of capitalism. In this epoch produced by the collision of infantile aggression with the production of commodities, the permanent, "omnipotent fantasy about controlling the other" and "the objectification of knowledge . . . based on a need for control" runs up against the "resistances" offered by commodities themselves, which exist as objects of desire that take up a certain amount of space, take a certain amount of time to make, and fixate a certain amount of energy.[5] In Brennan's view, the ego aggressively wants to control the source of its desire—originally, the mother, or rather the absence of her body, which causes the desire for it—displaced onto commodities. The ego wants instant gratification in the merging of the self with what it desires, thus eliminating the temporal and spatial distance between the self and other objects. But because these objects are commodities, they can only proliferate desire and amplify the anxiety induced by the recognition that there is always more to want of objects that can never be fully incorporated into the self. In the current circumstance of late capitalism, when temporality has actually slowed down as it has become spatialized and as energy has flowed into the proliferation of commodity objects, Brennan maintains that the "ego's need to speed things up, its anxiety, its splitting, its need for control, its 'cutting up' in the urge to know, its spoiling of living nature, and its general aggression toward the other" is ever increasing, even as "the ego, by these processes, only accelerates the production of the conditions that produce its fears" ("Age of Paranoia," 39). As Brennan implies, and as we have seen in the previous chapter, it is the very multiplication of the ego under postmodernity (often coded as Deleuzian schizophrenia) that "accelerates the production" of paranoia.

Brennan's complex sense of contemporary paranoia, founded on her bringing together of Lacanian and marxist theories, enlarges both the libidinal and epistemological reach of cultural paranoia beyond something that occurs between men. Yet, Brennan also "engenders" paranoia by showing how desire originates in the mother's body, or rather, in the lack of control over the mother's body that the child experiences when that body is removed—a loss that eventuates in the marking of the maternal body as contradictorily material and indeterminate. The aggression manifested toward the lost material and maternal body is culturally directed toward whatever can be located as alterities to the self, often identified as women, or aliens, or racial others.[6] For the purposes of the discussion of cultural paranoia in contemporary narrative, and particularly for those works that articulate the relation between knowledge, control, and the engendering of identity, Brennan's model is apt.

In the novels I consider in detail here—Thomas Pynchon's *The Crying of Lot 49,* Diane Johnson's *The Shadow Knows,* and Kathy Acker's *Empire of the Senseless*—the multiplicity of identity, the proliferation of commodities, and the desire to purchase some control over an entropic universe of increasing information and decreasing order are elements of a paranoid scenario in which the objectification of knowledge and bodies holds out the delusory promise of stabilization. Each of these novels focuses on the question of knowing and the relation between paranoid surmise and the real. In each instance, whether by means of Pynchon's mapping of oedipal knowledge, Johnson's dramatization of the alienation of interiority, or Acker's critique of cultural reproduction, what induces paranoid anxiety is the absence of a semiotic origin or mat(t)er that everywhere is segmented and disseminated in commodities, the constructions of the body, and the productions of knowledge. What lies at the bottom of paranoia in these works is not a repressed homoerotic relation between men but a displaced relation to the maternal that manifests itself as desire for semiotic wholeness ("the Truth"). This desire is variously evidenced as a need for dominion over the scattered simulacra of postmodernity, a merging with interiority that presumes a split between "inside" and "outside" aligned with "female" and "male," or a projection of libidinality that results in a reinscription of the gendered logic of reproduction. Pynchon's female quester, Johnson's female paranoid, and Acker's nomadic interlocutors incisively establish the relation between constrictive performances or constructions of gender and the manifestation of cultural paranoia as the desire to name and control the real. In these novels, as in the fictions of paranoia and nationalism, the multifarious projections of selves and others, subjects and objects, serve as symptomatic compensations for a capital loss secreted within an identificatory fantasy of separation and control.

■ The Point of the Cry: *The Crying of Lot 49*

The *point of the cry* in a cinematographic fiction . . . is defined . . . as something which gushes forth, generally from the mouth of a woman, something which is not, moreover, inevitably heard, but which above all must fall at a *named point,* explode at a precise moment, at the cross-roads of convergent lines, at the conclusion of an often alembic and disproportionate path: the film functions, then, like those big animating machines, full of gears and connecting rods, of chains of actions and reactions, here a machine made in order to deliver a cry. . . . The point of the cry is an unthinkable point at the interior of thought, an inexpressible [point] at the interior of enunciation, an unrepresentable point at the interior of representation. . . . This cry incarnates a fantasm of absolute sonorousness.—Michel Chion, *La voix au cinéma*

But then she wondered if the gemlike "clues" were only some kind of compensation. To make up for her having lost the direct, epileptic Word, the cry that might abolish the night.—Thomas Pynchon, *The Crying of Lot 49*

The "big animating machine" of *The Crying of Lot 49* teems with connections, red herrings, semiotic chains, systems, metaphors of "God knew how many parts," and "actions and reactions" of every kind. Pynchon's second, slim novel attempts—like Chion's "cinematographic fiction"—to deliver up a "cry that might abolish the night" of indeterminacy, loss, and death through which the protagonist Oedipa Maas wanders. So full of hermeneutic potential is *The Crying of Lot 49,* so replete with interpretive seductions operating under what John Johnston elucidates as a paranoid "semiotic regime," that a large volume of criticism that well exceeds the sum total of Pynchon's collective work has been written in an effort to explain the partial revelations of Oedipa's quest.[7] As Frank Kermode has suggested, the novel "is crammed with disappointed promises of significance, with ambiguous invitations to paradigmatic construction, and this is precisely Oedipa's problem. Is there a structure *au fond,* or only deceptive galaxies of signifiers?"[8] Pynchon's readers, moving between states of hermeneutic arousal and detumescence, have repeatedly recapitulated Oedipa's journey through a wilderness of signs, seeking the revelation—epiphany, message, cry— as to what lies at the bottom of the novel's furious textual activity, even if there is no bottom. Oedipa, "engaged in exploring the riddle of her own identity,"[9] is thus conflated with the reader, who like her, seeks to audit the "point of the cry," the "unrepresentable point at the interior of representation" that would, paradoxically, deliver up the final word regarding this text, even while accompanied by the "secular" recognition that such desires are founded on the logocentric fantasies that Pynchon seemingly subverts.

In becoming executor to the estate of her former lover, the megalomaniacal Pierce Inverarity—hence, responsible for proper enactment of his paternal will and intention—Oedipa finds herself caught up in a convergence of plots that are at once autobiographical, historical, and metafictional. Seeking knowledge about the scattered interests of Inverarity's empire, Oedipa stumbles onto a secret history (at once her own and that of the "world") that reveals that either conspiratorial design or sheer randomness governs the progress of "History" and the formation of nations; both, Oedipa finds, are mirrored in the secret histories and countercultures that proliferate in the novel, just as official and subversive discursive systems in *The Crying of Lot 49* replicate while contending with each other. As the plots of the novel unfold— as the cabals involving secret postal systems, anarchist conspiracies, right-wing cults, and far-flung corporate transactions overlap or collide—Oedipa comes under increasing pressure to respond to two, interrelated questions posed to her by the sheer experience of navigating "the hieroglyphic streets" of San Narciso, "like walking among the matrices of a great digital computer, the zeroes and ones twinned above, hanging like balanced mobiles right and left, ahead, thick, maybe endless."[10] The questions are: What intentionality, if any, lies behind this binary realm of either semiotic plenitude or reality "degree zero"? and, Does this intentionality operate according to any discernible principle of order?

Earlier, after a Walpurgisnacht of revelations, Oedipa had divided the binary issue (either "transcendent meaning, or only the earth" [Pynchon, 181]) into a "symmetrical four" alternatives (171). Wandering through the streets of San Narciso in search of clues about a proliferating historical conspiracy that appears to reach back to the sixteenth century and forward to the next millennium, Oedipa sees in every marginalized entity she encounters the sign of the "Trystero," the mark of an underground system of communication and community that unites the disinherited of the earth in the legacy of power and control represented by Inverarity's capitalist empire. Beset by the kind of hyper-reflexive hermeneutic suspicion that the intentionality called "Pynchon" seems to instill in his readers even as his protagonist formulates the crucial questions regarding intentionality in a novel where the real is represented as a series of maps, matrices, or circuit boards, Oedipa considers four possibilities:

Either you have stumbled indeed, without the aid of LSD or other indole alkaloids, onto a secret richness and concealed density of dream; onto a network by which X number of Americans are truly communicating whilst reserving their lies, recitations of routine, arid betrayals of spiritual poverty, for the official government delivery system; maybe even onto a real alternative to the exitlessness, to the absence of surprise to life. . . . Or you are hallucinating it. Or a plot has been mounted against you . . . so labyrinthine that it must have meaning beyond just a practical joke. Or you are fantasying some such plot, in which case you are a nut, Oedipa, out of your skull. (170–71)

Recognizing that all the plots of the world she has encountered structurally reduplicate each other, and that all projections are identical as attempts gain ascendancy and control over the messiness of the real, Oedipa reduces these four—historical conspiracy, hallucination, personalized conspiracy, and paranoia—to the binary "symmetry of choices" (181) that remain intact as the novel concludes. She is fated to experience either the order of revelation or the chaos of meaninglessness; either the revelation of will or intention within a comprehensive plot, or a semiotic collapse as the hermeneutic carapace of the novel shatters into myriad fragments with the recognition that the plot is a simulation manufactured as a joke on the paranoid, oedipal reader looking for malevolent intentions; either a secret United States or a hodgepodge of nomadic individuals and groups connected by contingency.

As a textual entity, Oedipa awaits the auctioning of Inverarity's postage stamp collection in the novel's final scene ("the crying of lot 49") and the appearance of a secret bidder who may be the orchestrator of the plot that enfolds her. Ultimately, she is interminably suspended in the matrix on the near side of intentionality, before the hearing of the "cry that might abolish the night." Similarly, Pynchon's reader, awash in semiosis, is seemingly compelled to accept the textuality of this novel that insists that all intention lies in the ongoing negotiation between the proliferation of signs and the partiality of significance.[11]

The account I have given of *The Crying of Lot 49* is in accord with its characterization as exemplar of the high metafiction of the 1970s and 1980s, usually written by white, male authors, concordant with the emergence of various deconstructionist and poststructuralist theories of that era, and primarily invested in semiotic play as (falsely) opposed to social processes.[12] In this view, Pynchon's novel is a carnival of paranoia—the marijuana-induced paranoia of the 1960s, the paranoia of reading, "American" national paranoia with its long history running from the Salem witch trials to the cold war—that mocks its own status as a discursive system that mediates between intention and interpretation. To be sure, Oedipa is a child of her times, a "cold war subject" raised under the paranoid, watchful eyes of "Secretaries James and Foster and Senator Joseph, those dear daft numina who'd mothered over Oedipa's so temperate youth," and who "had managed to turn the young Oedipa into a rare creature indeed, unfit perhaps for marches and sit-ins, but just a whiz at pursuing strange words in Jacobean texts" (Pynchon, 104). *The Crying of Lot 49* is ostensibly Pynchon's conflated parodic reflection on the 1950s, the specious depoliticizations of New Criticism, corporate America, and its own status as text. Yet, this is to overlook how the novel historicizes, in a different sense, its own reflexivity—a historicizing that registers the repressed "bad shit" of "excluded middles" (181) underlying the cultural paranoia that has its engendering in the production of signs and their fallout in the history of subjectivity.

The textualized world Oedipa enters as she drives into San Narciso and becomes entrapped in multiple plots is one in which there is an overload of information and a paucity of resources to process it. Initially, San Narciso appears to be a typical L.A. suburb: "Like many named places in California it was less an identifiable city than a grouping of concepts—census tracts, special purpose bond-issue districts, shopping nuclei, all overlaid with access roads to its own freeway" (24). To Oedipa, Los Angeles represents at first glance a constellation of order with its "vast sprawl of houses which had grown up all together, like a well-tended crop . . . and she thought of the time she'd opened a transistor radio to replace a battery and seen her first printed circuit. The ordered swirl of houses and streets, from this high angle, sprang at her now with the same unexpected, astonishing clarity as the circuit card had" (24). Soon, however, what appears to be an orderly social system undergirded by an efficient mechanism for the processing of information becomes a veneer disguising the presence of a rhizomic network of paranoid cults and secret communications systems that everywhere proliferate signs that are legible to insiders, but unreadable to outsiders. San Narciso, then, is the site of entropy, one of Pynchon's key (and most overread) metaphors, deployed in his fiction to suggest that the universe is running down as it suffers heat loss according to the second law of thermodynamics and as it becomes overcrowded with bodies, commodities, and redundant information. Paradoxically, entropy in Pynchon can be a creative process in which the sheer glut of information and static of communication can lead to new connections, messages, and discursive communities.[13] Thus Oedipa, encountering the semiotic complexity of San Narciso, feels overwhelmed by the deadly weight of conspiratorial affiliations, yet on the verge of some radically different historical revelation arising from conspiracy.

The familiar double sense of entropy in Pynchon as a process inculcating redundancy and alterity is enhanced by Brennan's sense that the paranoia of the "ego's era" is a form of aggression that seeks to control through objectification and commodification, which entropically binds energy and slows temporality, everything that is "other" than the self. Such aggression is prevalent in *The Crying of Lot 49* in those modes of transformation that are utterly dependent on the fluid exchange of capital, bodies, material, and signs that at once demarcate and incorporate what is other. While Pynchon will go on in *Gravity's Rainbow* to expand on the schematic that *The Crying of Lot 49* offers, in the earlier novel he charts the course of paranoia in the ego's era across the transformations enacted by cultural plots and counterplots, as well as what they elide or suppress.

To trace one such route of transformation and exchange that, typically, operates by virtue of Inverarity's ability to articulate the "plots" of his various interests: one of Inverarity's innumerable firms hold many of the contracts for the construction of southern California's vast freeway system, but in digging up the land in order to build the roads, his workers are also forced to dig up cemeteries and remove skeletal remains; these, in turn, are smuggled to Inverarity's cigarette factory,

where they are ground up for use in the "bone charcoal" filters of Bea-
consfield cigarettes. The process by which remnants of the dead are
converted into devices to spuriously protect the living from the harm-
ful effects of nicotine (repeated in the story of American World War II
G.I.s whose bones have been transported from their resting place in
an Italian lake as part of Inverarity's dealings with the Mafia) is one in
which bodies are commodified, the memorial is transmogrified into the
ephemeral (literally, going up in smoke), and death is placed at the service of pleasure. We can view this bizarre example of almagamatory
capitalism as a metaphor for the cultural order depicted in the novel
that everywhere works to assimilate dispersed cultural productions and
remains into interlinked systems of transformation and exchange that
feed desire. Even the scattered elements of the novel's second world—
the underground cults, unofficial systems of communication, and marginalized entities that constitute a nomadicy—operate according to an
assimilatory rubric in which the stray message and wandering soul are
incorporated into the singular conspiracy of the oppressed mirroring
the singular conspiracy of the powerful. In this regard, the paranoia of
The Crying of Lot 49, as the many references to Narcissus and narcissism imply, is that of the mirror: every element of the novel—all of its
multiple sites, stories, messages, puns, identities, and scenarios—reflect the positioning of all the others in the welter of overlapping plots
and discourses. What emerges from the cross-hatchings of conspiracy
in *The Crying of Lot 49* is a monolithic, silvered image of the symbolic
order as Pynchon perceives it operating in the articulation of economies, histories, and narratives.

Arguably, Pynchon is simply holding up a mirror to the ego's era,
which in his hands, becomes more precisely the era of narcissistic
paranoia in which the global distribution of aggression by means of objectification and commodification, lubricated by the flow of capital, is
paralleled to an epistemological need "to bring the estate into pulsing
stelliferous Meaning" (Pynchon, 82). In offering a critique of the politics
of epistemology, *The Crying of Lot 49* does operate as a reflexively overdetermined diagnosis of cultural paranoia, but beyond this it mutely, if
disingenuously, records a cry, "the unrepresentable point at the interior
of representation" that is anterior to paranoia. This is the "named point"
that the representational regime of the novel includes and attempts to
digest as part of the work of its machinery, and thus marks as loss.

We can approach the "point of the cry" in the novel by attending to
one element in the "hum" of *The Crying of Lot 49:* the network of audi-

tory puns that comprises its background noise. At the conclusion of her odyssey through the San Narciso underground and realm of the disinherited, Oedipa comes to rest momentarily at a rooming house where she encounters another voyager, an old sailor in the last stages of alcoholism whom she comforts: "Exhausted, hardly knowing what she was doing, she came the last three steps and sat, took the man in her arms, actually held him. . . . She felt wetness against her breast and saw that he was crying again" (126). Glancing around his paltry quarters, she reflects on the sailor's unknown history:

What voices overheard, flinders of luminiscent gods glimpsed among the wallpaper's stained foliage, candlestubs lit to rotate in the air over him prefiguring the cigarette he or a friend must fall asleep someday smoking, thus to end among the flaming, secret salts held all those years by the insatiable stuffing of the mattress that could keep vestiges of every nightmare sweat, helpless overflowing bladder, viciously, tearfully consummated wet dream, like the memory bank to a computer of the lost? (126)

The image of the sailor's mattress, compared in this scene of paranoia with its prefigurations and "luminiscent gods" to "the memory bank to a computer of the lost" as it records the excrescences of the material body and desire, resonates with the sound of the "matrices" of the "great digital computer, the zeroes and ones twinned above" within which Oedipa feels she is entrapped. As we shall see momentarily, the auditory connection reveals the extremities of the novel's representational regime in corporeal loss and information overload.

Continuing her reflection, Oedipa contemplates:

the stored, coded years of uselessness . . . the set of all the men who had slept on it . . . [who] would truly cease to be, forever, when the mattress burned. She stared at it in wonder. It was as if she had just discovered the irreversible process. It astonished her to think that so much could be lost, even the quantity of hallucination belonging just to the sailor that the world would bear no further trace of. She knew, because she had held him, that he suffered DT's. Behind the initials was a metaphor, a delirium tremens, a trembling unfurrowing of the mind's plowshare. The saint whose water can light lamps, the clairvoyant whose lapse in recall is the breath of God's, the true paranoid for whom all is organized in spheres joyful or threatening around the central pulse of himself, . . . "dt," God help this old tattooed man, meant also a time differential, a vanishingly small instant in which change had to be confronted at last for what it was, where it could no longer disguise itself as something like the average rate; where velocity dwelled in the projectile though the projectile be frozen in mid-flight, where death dwelled in the cell though the cell be looked in on at its most quick. (128–29)

In this dense, compressed passage, while Oedipa cradles the afflicted sailor as a mother would a child, through "that high magic to low puns" and the "act of metaphor" that is "both a thrust at truth and a lie depending where you were: inside, safe, or outside, lost" (129), the verbal and material relation between mattress, matrix, and mother is forged.[14] Jean-Joseph Goux suggests a way in which the "symbolic economy" of paranoia that *The Crying of Lot 49* orchestrates might be read in terms of the linkages between the sailor's mattress (the forcing bed of sexuality and receptacle of bodily waste and desire), the computer matrix (which carries the double meaning of the mapped coordinates on which systems of information and control are erected, and in French, the womb), and the maternal function that Oedipa temporarily assumes at the instantiation of the sailor's temporality—his placement within the "dt" or "time differential" of "vanishingly small" instants that accumulate in the movement toward death.[15]

Goux writes that in the social symbolic derived from anthropological and philosophical narratives, the "phallic dialectic" assigns the functions of "witness and *control*" (219), of "*form, type, notion, idea, or pattern*" (220), to the male (paternal), and the status of negativity, concavity, and "amorphous, transitory, inessential material" (222) to the female (maternal). This dialectic, he argues, has "in social production and reproduction a dimension that far and away exceeds any parental, figurative reduction. These places constitute the minimal landmarks . . . without which subjects are unable to think (and to unthink) themselves as historical subjects" (216). The enactment of the phallic dialectic, for Goux, establishes a privileging of the symbolic over the material order (though the former is founded on and energized by the latter), of "permanence, order . . . and law" over "the sensory, the concrete, the nondeductible" (223), our apprehension of which is lost as the maternal body is repressed or abjected in the constitution of the historical subject under this dialectic. The pietà of Oedipa and the sailor emblematizes the phallic dialectic that governs the whole of *The Crying of Lot 49* and that Oedipa mediates. At the still point of a hermeneutic frenzy, Oedipa is located between control and cry; between the spheres of organization that create the paranoid illusion of mastery over the symbolic order (knowledge) and a recognition of what is lost in the mapping out of our corporeal and linguistic insertion into that order (history). In Goux's terms, she is located within the phallic dialectic. This is to be in between the novel's interconnected discursive systems and the other or outside to them that is figured as an "incorporeal alterity" (219), such as that of the soon-to-be consumed mattress/matrix/mat(t)er that constitutes the disappearing record of the sailor's sensory, corporeal existence across the "dt" of a temporal history.

It is in terms of this phallic dialectic that Pynchon engenders paranoia in *The Crying of Lot 49*. Oedipa occupies a liminal position throughout the novel that culminates in her temporary maternal relation to the sailor. As a woman on an oedipal quest for complete knowledge, and yet as a nomadic figure who traverses the boundaries of a migratory second world, Oedipa is both a trafficker of information and trafficked by the plots in which she is immersed. From this position, she is able to observe the series of connections and disconnections that exist between the articulation of identity mapped onto the "real" organized as "spheres joyful and threatening," and the repressed matrix of that articulation, which is the otherness of the body/corpse and its unrecorded history given over to temporality. This alterity is symbolized in the phallic dialectic as the abject body of the mother or the preterite, disinherited substitutions for it that Oedipa encounters on her journey. Inverarity's vast empire and the systems of discursive and economic exchange that flow from it, as well as Oedipa's own insertion into paranoid systems in the form of control, message sorter, or witness, can be seen as attempts to render into information and silence what is already paradoxically mute in the novel, and always forestalled: the cry, the "direct, epileptic word," which stands for the semiotic/material/maternal origin of "name," "land," "self," "San Narciso," and "the American continuity of crust and mantle" (Pynchon, 177) once it is multiplied and dispersed into all the novel's scripts.

In *The Crying of Lot 49*, Pynchon charts this dialectic rather than resolving or attempting to replace it, or even to ostensibly frame it as a version of the order of things bounded by historical origins and ends. At the novel's conclusion, Oedipa remains suspended between the ones and zeros, between the single unheard cry and its multiple acoustic manifestations, awaiting the gushing of the cry not from "the mouth of a woman," but the auctioneer, Loren Passerine, about to "cry" the sale of Inverarity's postage stamp collection. Oedipa's waiting might be seen as exemplary of both the postmodern condition and the condition of language as we remain suspended in the increasing gap between all the "betweens" of signifier and signified, semiotic and symbolic, maternal materiality and paternal ideality. As I suggested earlier, residing (waiting) within this state of suspended animation complies with the conflation of identificatory and capital fluidity that constitutes a major aspect of the ideology of postmodernity.

Goux encourages us, however, to historically frame these conditions by viewing them as the "legacy of a patrimony of signifiers," which indulges "in the belief that it is the father (enlisting at times the action of a river or the ancestors' breath or a Holy Ghost) who confers both visible and invisible form upon . . . offspring, while the maternal contribution, both physiologically and socially, has the neutrality of an excipient, the inert negativity of the earth" (225). For Goux, because such patrimony is a legacy, something that passes down through time, it marks out a specific and temporal condition of the symbolic order in which capitalist systems of exchange, founded on the trafficking in women, intersect with the emergence of identity into language and particular discursive networks to produce subjects in history who are heirs to this condition. As heirs, they assume certain reproductive "duties" in relation to gender: the reproduction and dissemination of knowledge as opposed to the reproduction of bodies; the production of ideas as opposed to the provision of material. This is, for Goux, the condition of modern subjectivity in history.

The Crying of Lot 49 extends this condition to postmodernity, under which cybernetic technology, multinational capitalism, the multiplicity of identity, and the conception of history as a system of interpretation "conspire" in the production of the subject. The ingenuity of this compact novel lies precisely in this conflation of science, epistemology, and historiography as they effect the formation of paranoid identity. Loren Passerine's appearance implies a pentecostal manifestation to take place entirely within the paranoid rubric of the phallic dialectic thus deployed. Oedipa, carrying conspiracy ("your gynecologist has no test for what she was pregnant with" [Pynchon, 175]), awaits the birth of meaning in this moment, the cry of revelation that will convert all inexpressibility into enunciation and complete her parturition as the knowing subject of the phallic dialectic. At the end of the novel, she remains imprisoned within the confines of Inverarity's paranoid legacy— "the legacy [that] was America"—which legislates between "transcendent meaning, or only the earth" (178), the elect and the outcast, the inheritors of a nation and those disinherited or alienated from it. She therefore continues to be caught up in a dialectic that shuttles endlessly between the paternal extraction and reproduction of value. In this paternal regime, "value" (significance) is derived from an irreducible, inert materiality that accrues a bevy of representations in the novel from that of "bad shit," to abjected bodies, to "that magical Other who would reveal herself out of the roar of relays, monotone litanies of insult, filth, fantasy, love whose brute repetition must someday call into being the trigger for the unnamable act, the recognition, the Word" (180). For Oedipa, there is no other to this dialectic, which appears to be transhistorical in relation to the ever deferred cry of origins and ends. The forestalled cry in *The Crying of Lot 49* thus legitimates the phallic dialectic of cultural paranoia, which regenerates itself by mystifying the multifarious other as the material and maternal while circumscribing the known on this side of the border. In so doing, it authorizes its own work as witness to and legislator of imaginary differences marked as the relation between the subject of knowledge and everything that lies outside knowing in terms of the phallic dialectic— a marking that is ultimately a regressive mirroring of "the legacy that was America."

■ The Umbra of Difference: *The Shadow Knows*

One of the paradoxes that Oedipa must negotiate in her quest is the putative difference between inside and outside, between intelligence that is the result of chance, intuition, or sensitivity to the hum of conspiracy around her, and the factuality of information derived empirically and officially sanctioned by the disciplinary institutions that rule what constitutes knowledge in relation to truth. The relation between inside and outside in *The Crying of Lot 49* is complicated by the manner in which Pynchon, in charting the coordinates of cultural paranoia, maps onto the set of differentiations perennially made between subjectivity and objectivity the postmodernist comprehension of knowledge as partial, transmitted by means of conflicting discursive systems that themselves are always in a process of formation and deformation. As I have suggested, this complexity is essential to the paranoid machinery of a novel that produces an unheard cry articulating Oedipa's entrapment within a dialectic that manages the relation between inside and outside as part of the work of ordaining the known communicated through the patrimony of signifiers.

Diane Johnson's largely ignored *The Shadow Knows*, written in a realist mode that would seem to dictate against its being considered among the reflexive and experimental fictions of Pynchon and Acker, offers a significant alternative to the view of the relation between interiority and exteriority that the phallic dialectic underwrites in terms of sexual difference. In this novel, Johnson—a Victorian scholar and author of several novels, a series of biographical sketches depicting the "lesser lives" of nineteenth-century women, and a biography of Dashiell Hammett—portrays a woman continually beset by fears that she is about to be murdered. "N.," as the narrator refers to herself, is a recently divorced mother of four young children living in a low-rent housing district of North Sacramento and pursuing a graduate degree in linguistics. In the midst of an affair with a married man, Andrew, N. is suddenly beleaguered with threats from an unknown assailant: the door to her house is battered with an ax, the windshield of her car is covered with vomit, her companion and housekeeper, Ev, is physically attacked in a laundry room. *The Shadow Knows*—a preemptory rejoinder to more recent misogynist affirmations of the nuclear family in such films as *Fatal Attraction* and *Someone to Watch over Me*—recounts a week in N.'s life during which she is compelled to come to terms with the embodiment of her anxieties about her identity as one who knows and sees the magnitude of her victimization.[16]

N., who reveals her married name to be Hexam, suggestive of her paranoia (she is hexed) and her role as victimized woman (reminiscent of Lizzie Hexam of Charles Dickens's *Our Mutual Friend*), is convinced that there is a plot to murder her. As the novel unfolds, she runs through a list of suspects—her ex-husband; her ex-maid, Osella, who has been making obscene phone calls to her; her best friend, Bess; Andrew's wife—and so exposes a troubled personal life to the scrutiny of the reader, who is implicitly asked to take on the role of confessor while verifying that there is, in fact, something going on here. The novel proceeds through a series of personal disasters that neither confirm nor deny N.'s status as paranoid victim: Ev dies unexpectedly of pancreatitis (though N. believes she has been murdered); N. miscarries the child she has conceived with Andrew; after a number of indecisive moves, Andrew returns to his wife; Bess confesses to N. that for years, she has hated her and resented her supposedly promiscuous activities. Johnson's novel bears all the characteristics of a dystopic version of a Harlequin romance, a genre whose conventions often inscribe the putative feminine desire to be violated; hence, in the end, N.'s fears are confirmed not by murder but by rape.[17] *The Shadow Knows* thus considers the engendering of cultural paranoia from a significantly different perspective than *The Crying of Lot 49*. In Johnson's novel, the relation of "women's time" and experience to paranoid knowledge is foregrounded in a realm where the representation and enforcement of reality, governed by patriarchal institutions, foregoes the luxury of interpretation.

Focusing, then, on the quanta of experience differentiated from information, *The Shadow Knows* personalizes paranoia by taking it out of the province of stock postmodernity, which elides the relation between subjects and objects in the ubiquity of simulacra;[18] instead, Johnson places the issue of cultural paranoia within what may appear, on the surface, to be an anachronistic existential dialectic that moves between subjective experience and objective knowledge. But, as Johnson represents the affects of experience, the projections of passion, longing, revenge, jealousy, and hatred to be found in this disturbing portrayal of female paranoia both disguise and abet the cultural forces that lie behind the victimization of women. N. is variously stereotyped by her friends, relatives, and neighbors as the other woman, the promiscuous divorcée, the careless mother, the hysteric. She is enclosed in a threatening environment that takes its revenge on any woman who resists its normalizing processes by pressuring its victim into a state of paranoia where a hegemonic reality and marginalized interiority are so divorced that the "paranoid" can only engage in the "narcissistic" activity of reuniting and homogenizing them in acts registered by the state as the symptoms of hysteria.

Faced with circumstances in which she feels that verbal and physical abuse can be inflicted on her at any time from multiple directions, N. resorts to what Julia Kristeva calls a "paranoid-type mechanism" that is "the inevitable product of . . . a denial of the sociosymbolic order and its counterinvestment as the only means of self-defense in the struggle to safeguard an identity."[19] N. is continually marked for exhibitions of abjection and hysteria that signify her separation from the "sociosymbolic order" and designate her as victim and paranoid. She screams at the "Famous Inspector" (the police detective assigned to investigate her housekeeper's death) that Ev has been murdered when all the evidence points to the contrary; she hemorrhages from a miscarriage in a public parking lot. The counterinvestments of N.'s paranoia involve recurrent incidents marking the convergence of inwardness (what is "only" intuited or experienced privately) and exteriority (what falls within the confines of an officially proscribed reality that drives a wedge between a woman's experience and so-called historical truth). The condition of separation is forced on her from without and within when a neighbor proposes that N. spend her money fixing up the outside of her house, versus the inside, for the sake of property values; or when N. declares that "outside I am a round-faced little woman with round breasts and toes, surrounded by round babies; I look like a happy moon—now who would have thought that I am riddled and shot through invisibly with desperate and sordid passions, raging passions and egotism, insecurity and lust?[20] But these investments only result in producing an N. whose paranoia, in response to the paranoia foisted on her, collapses the distinction between inside and outside.

Accordingly, N. cites as proof of "the interrelation between passions and things unceasing" her apparently ludicrously exaggerated violent passion with Andrew: "When we were first in love [we] wrecked each other's houses. It was peculiar. I mean physically wrecked them with crowbars and such, and it seemed quite natural and called-for" (Johnson, 28). She looks for and naturalizes the "interrelation between passions and things unceasing" with escalating anticipation as the evidence that someone is planning an act of violence directed at her mounts, to the extent that by the time of the rape, she seems relieved that "it" has finally happened, that paranoid projection has merged with the real and been converted into knowledge, and that her confrontation with the beast in the jungle is not as apocalyptic as she had imagined: "I don't know. I felt happy. Anything bad can happen to the unwary, and when life sends you the *coup de grâce* you have a way of knowing. So I felt better then, thinking well, that was the *coup de grâce* and here I still am" (276). This is the rhetoric of a survivor in a paranoid system to which N. has been so thoroughly assimilated that she will remain content (now that the "worst" has happened) with her liminal status as one who negotiates between the interiorities of passion and the actuality of violence. As for Oedipa, so too for N., the reward for surviving in such a domain comes in the form of knowledge, though in N.'s case it is a postrevelatory corporeal knowing and disengagement quite different from Oedipa's hermeneutic apprehensions. N. becomes herself in the end, but her identity is that of a shadow, otherness beat into airy thinness, inside and joined in the counterinvestment of the shadow's single dimension, outrage become the street smarts of the "spiritually sly":

I feel better. You can change; a person can change. I feel myself different already and to have taken on the thinness and lightness, like a ghost slipping out from his corporeal self and stealing invisibly across the lawn while the body he has left behind meantime smiles stolidly as usual and nobody notices anything different. You can join the spiritually sly, I mean. Well, maybe I'm making too much of this. I mean your eyes get used to the dark, that's all, and also if nothing else you learn to look around you when you get out of your car in a dark garage. (277)

In Johnson's novel, the price that the woman must pay for knowledge is the maternal body, that of the "round-faced little woman with round breasts and toes, surrounded by round babies," abjected in the aftermath of revelation (as inside and outside merge) so that she may continue to survive as a canny revenant.[21]

In *The Shadow Knows,* Johnson represents the engendering of paranoia in terms of the spectralization of the mother's body, rather than its framing and recuperation within a symbolic order where, as in Pynchon, reflexivity serves as a form of complicit resistance to operations of the phallic dialectic. For Johnson, there is a residue (a shadow) that remains after N.'s paranoid counterinvestments and her encounter with the real, and this remainder evokes the foundations of cultural paranoia in the abjection of the body. In a telling moment, responding mentally to the Famous Inspector's characterization of her as a disreputable and hysterical female, N. ponders "that inchoate masculine fear" that leads to the resentment of bad mothers and other "abnormal" versions of womanhood:

A smirk of comprehension and disgust overspreads the features of the Famous Inspector: this is a negloctful, resentful mother he is dealing with, the sort that gets murdered all the time and the children put in foster homes, usually a good thing, too. Ah, it is not reason which congeals the wellsprings of the Famous Inspector's sympathy, but that he is a man. It is that inchoate masculine fear they all have. Where does it come from? It must be that sometime in his life every little baby boy, rosy in his bath, looking up past the warm, strong arms of his mother into her eyes, one time sees there a strangeness which suddenly reveals to him that she is not him, she is not even like him but is another creation of another race, and however much this terrible recognition may be obscured by subsequent pats, hugs, kisses, coos, years and years of love and encouragement—the terror and isolation of that moment, and the fear of it returning, remain forever. (Johnson, 37)

In this enscenement of the Freudian *fort-da*—when the child realizes that the mother is an "other," a "creature" not within umbilical control to be known as much by her absence as her presence—Johnson's narrator engenders paranoia as the male response to the alien that the mother represents. Fear of the utter isolation contained in this moment or rupture between preoedipal mother and oedipal son, and terror at the thought of its return, leads to a system of suppression that attempts to border off all those "neglectful, resentful" mothers to be recollected in the historical aftermath of this differential instant as aliens, hysterics, paranoids. Kristeva suggests that this moment of separation "preconditions the binding of language which is already syntactical"; therefore, "the common destiny of the two sexes, men and women," is that "certain biofamilial conditions and relationships cause women (and notably hysterics) to deny this separation and the language which ensues from it, whereas men (notably obsessionals) magnify both, and attempt to master them" ("Women's Time," 41). This is precisely the situation in *The Shadow Knows,* where N., in a conflation of hysteria and obsession under these terms, tries to erase the separation between inside and outside through paranoid confirmations. These confirmations, in turn, reverberate in the male system of discipline and control represented by the Famous Inspector, who society has put in charge of sorting hysterics from supposedly normal women, thus reinstating and mastering the distance between experience and event that N. attempts to overcome. Ultimately, N. *is* paranoid, a condition that both marginalizes her and enables her survival in "preparing" for the male violence toward women (that revenge on neglectful and resentful mothers) that this system induces.

In Kristeva's view, to exist within this regime is to exist with the abjection of the "archaic mother," the maternal figure who precedes the splitting of the ego and lives on, deformed, in the alienated, commodified versions of femininity through which women are visualized and anchored within cultural paranoia. Hence, in the climactic scene of *The Shadow Knows,* Johnson portrays N.'s ex-maid Osella performing a striptease at a night club while several of the novel's principals, gathered together for the moment of revelation, look on. This baring of the maternal body might be seen as one realization of the ambiguous moment that Oedipa awaits at the end of her epistemic quest: it is notable that she sees the conspiratorial history unfolding around her as a striptease in "the breakaway gowns, net bras, jeweled garters and G-strings of historical figuration" (Pynchon, 54). But, as Osella strips, the nature of her corporeal disclosure stands in stark contrast to the ever deferred crying of lot 49. Johnson depicts what lies behind the paranoia that afflicts her protagonist in the spectacle of Osella's body. Black, grossly overweight, violent (for it appears to N. that it is she who is responsible for Ev's death), Osella is the embodiment of racialized and gendered otherness theatricalized and commodified within the paranoid system that channels the "creature" of the maternal figure supervising the child's bath into a loose, violent woman or bad mother. In Osella, a figure of alterity and multiplicity, these designations are conflated when she performs as a degraded, promiscuous "mammy." As N. remarks, "the naked Osella makes everything clear" (262) in a scene that constitutes the unveiling of the real where the primal moment of separation and abjection is reenacted and contained. Here, Osella receives the mythic investments of the archaic mother, but now she is objectified, her uncanny and bizarre attributes (in the Club Zanzibar) zoned off and normalized, for she is soon to be a star in Las Vegas:

the naked Osella, a sight at first so horrifying and then so immensely fascinating that the people watching it all drew in their breath. . . . But Osella did nothing at all, merely radiantly stood which was enough, with the light gleaming down on the folds of her body, on her tremendous breasts. She seemed to have been oiled for she shone so; one saw nothing but the gleaming immense breasts lying across her huge belly, breasts astoundingly full and firm like zeppelins overhead. (267)

In this racist image of the archaic mother commodified, multiplied, and circulated, Johnson fabricates a gendered source of cultural paranoia that in effect is a symptom of its bifurcative functionality. The survival politics of *The Shadow Knows* dictates that women have the choice of either internalizing paranoia and becoming ever watchful or, obversely, becoming a spectacle, their corporeal visibility the sign of their objectification and containment of otherness.

For Oedipa Maas, the work of paranoia is founded on a mimetic logic: the desire to know the meaning of all the puns, riddles, and clues. To reconnect all the loose ends in order to resist conspiracy is, in fact, to replicate its discourse of mastery. In the paranoid epistemology of *The Crying of Lot 49,* Pynchon shows the reach of the complicitous relation between semiotic play and the obsessive quest for discursive mastery disguised as the need to know. Johnson, too, sees the desire to know as a primary condition of contemporary cultural paranoia, but in *The Shadow Knows,* she reveals the extent to which this desire is caught up within a network of sexual and racial differences that the paranoid system always works to contain or eliminate. In both novels, through a series of figural enforcements, the woman is falsely determined in the connection established between maternity and violence: Oedipa, pregnant with knowledge at the novel's end, awaits the violent epiphany of the auctioneer's cry; N., awaiting the manifestation of her attacker, is stereotyped as the woman who wants violence.[22] More pointedly for Johnson, paranoia is a political matter, where enforced cultural relations stemming from anxieties about otherness result in specific consequences for women. In *The Shadow Knows,* a novel filled with scenes of violence toward women, a black woman is possibly murdered and her murder is ignored because N., a paranoid, is the only one who wishes to pursue the issue. Ev's corpse represents a stark contrast to Osella's living body, but they are both transformed into objects in the system of terror and domination that passes for middle-class culture in Johnson's novel.

For Johnson's protagonist, a nominal cipher, paranoia is not so much a matter of seeing through the fog of conspiracy—for she sees clearly enough—as it is surviving warily and invisibly in an unrelentingly threatening environment. That she does so "existentially" within the framework of postmodernity (the commodification of bodies, the multiplication of identity, the fragmentation of the real in the splitting of interiority and actuality) speaks to the incongruity that Johnson sees between a paranoid regime and the agency of women within it as she reflects the violence that must be deployed in order to ensure their containment. Because of that incongruity, the identification of women with the dominant order in *The Shadow Knows* is registered on and in their bodies. N.'s shadowy transformation in the novel's concluding pages is only the obverse of Osella's presence on the stage: theatricalized or underground, star or paranoid, these estranged women are precisely placed. The belittling and shameful consequences of their siting are not, as the Famous Inspector insists of Ev's murder, in another Dickensian echo reminiscent of another story about a "little" woman (*Little Dorrit*), "nobody's fault." These consequences, Johnson's novel powerfully argues, are no accident.

■ Exposing Paranoia: *Empire of the Senseless*

To move from the 1960s and 1970s' California of Pynchon and Johnson's novels to the apocalyptic, postrevolutionary Paris of Kathy Acker's *Empire of the Senseless* is to traverse a terrain that extends from the activation of contemporary cultural paranoia to the return of its repressed content. In contrast to the drawing of the relation between inside and outside to be found in *The Crying of Lot 49* and *The Shadow Knows, Empire of the Senseless,* like all of Acker's novels, is ostensibly a comedy of exteriority in which everything is outed, "transparent," the tabooed hyperbolically externalized and acted out under millennial conditions in which the unthinkable, strangely normalized, operates beneath and contests against the "concrete of repression."[23] In Acker's Paris, the Algerians have taken over the government, but the mechanisms of control instituted by the revolutionary, postcolonial regime are identical to those that have been replaced, the crucial difference being that the location of the conflict between cultural dominance and the enactment of desire has materialized on human bodies: "My body is open to all people: this is democratic capitalism," proclaims Abhor, the novel's female protagonist (Acker, *Empire,* 55). This city of Paris is one without "bosses," "a bloody city" that "looked as if it was made of glass" that "cuts through the flesh" (110), a realm of mirrors seemingly inhabited by only two classes, the agents of control such as the Algerian secret police, and the nomadic sailors, pirates, and tattooers who wander the streets on fragmentary quests that simultaneously entail the liberation and marking or cutting up of the body. On the one hand, the novel may appear to enact a deconstruction of the West and the "end of this white world" (119); on the other, the Manichaean contest between "Discipline and Anarchy" (221) that continues to ensue in the wake of cultural revolution, mapped onto the novel's scarred and tattooed bodies, foregrounds and clarifies the paranoia of oedipal identity that, for Acker, retains its power as the primary construct of the new order. *Empire of the Senseless* is, above all, a critique of and satire on identity as the fundamental unit of social organization—one whose consistency *as* construct relies on the maintenance of a binary relation between the multiplicity of identity's performativity and its location within gendered positions and relations of power.

Empire of the Senseless is made up of a series of monologues, ventriloquizations, and dialogues between Abhor and Thivai, two terrorists who roam aimlessly through a postapocalyptic, recolonialized Paris while recalling disastrous childhoods filled with mutilations and violence. They are deployed in the novel as allegorical figures through whom the crises of postmodern identity are negotiated in a "senseless" world: "Since the world has disappeared: rather than objects, there exists that smouldering within time where and when subject meets object" (38). In this hypervisible realm where the distance between all the Western binaries of subject/object, self/other, and inside/outside ostensibly has been foreclosed, identity is a nomadic and deterritorialized conglomeration of forces and vectors rather than a constituted entity, and unleashed desire is the motor of agency. In their meanderings, Thivai and Abhor encounter a host of fellow travelers in abjection who are perennially pitted against the forces of control represented by the secret police, the CIA (which has taken over the government in the United States), and the revenants of parental authority.

The paranoid domain of *Empire of the Senseless* is one where a dystopic version of total dissimulation along the Lyotardian "great libidinal skin" is coterminous with the global extension of control over nations and bodies to the extent that mastery and libidinality have become mirroring processes. Here, the nuclear family has self-imploded: all of the novel's dead fathers and suicided mothers indicate the degree to which the oedipal structuration of the family lies in ruins, its repressed contents now fully exposed in acts of incest and parricide. As Kathleen Hulley has argued, Acker's fiction suggests that

the objective correlative for the new forms of subjectivity is territorialized demands. . . . All her treatment is obsessional: father/daughter incest, unmitigated female masochism, the colonized body. Every narrative circles around a mother who commits suicide, an incestuous and promiscuous father, a sexually victimized daughter desperately seeking love along limited channels of possibility. In her work, we are in the presence of that abject and terrifying realm of desire so insatiable that its invasions and betrayals reveal themselves as a frantic reconstruction of a fictional self that returns us only to the scene of our own obliteration.[24]

In *Empire of the Senseless,* this obliteration of the oedipal subject that is at once the articulation of the desiring subject without boundaries is always expressed under the aegis of control, as if desire cannot be known unless it is refracted in the mirror of the other.

The nomads of *Empire of the Senseless* are supposedly politically and libidinally liberated as they wander where they will, yet they always exist under the umbrella of revolutionary governmental control. Unlike Pynchon's preterit, the identity assemblages in Acker's Paris are totally disconnected from each other, colliding only by chance as they move along random libidinal paths. Speaking "the language of the 'unconscious,' " a language of "nonsense" that "must be taboo" (Acker, *Empire,* 134), they are allowed to give voice to the furthest extremities of desire and experience in the continuous reliving of the spectacles of incest, rape, paternal and maternal violence, and introjection and abjection that constitute the novel's literalized, "unrepressed" primal scenes. As Abhor, her name connoting her status as both abject and commodified subject, says:

I am a witch, an evil almost inhuman because I am in the act of brewing my own blood. . . . I'm playing with *only* my blood and shit and death because mommy ordered me to be only whatever she desired, that is, to be not possible, but it isn't possible to be and be not possible. By playing with my blood and shit and death, I'm controlling my life.

Paradoxically, within the libidinal economy of *Empire of the Senseless,* for Abhor "to be," even as she revels in the conflated maternal abjections of death and eroticism, she must exert control over desire through a reflexive "play" that parallels the visibly borrowed and highly foregrounded strategies of Acker's writing—strategies that include plagiarism, the citation of Arabic scripts, and the grafting and interbreeding of multiple genres. At bottom, Acker assets, postoedipal identity, freed of discursive constraints, encounters the impasse and circularity of a desire that inevitably reflects the narcissistic, self-mirroring order and language of identity seeking to trangress itself. Thus, a sailor, Don, exclaims, "We're the real children of the revolution. I go where I want in this city. Now. I might be a physical mess, filthy, crazy cause I'm wrapped up in my own thoughts which still are mirrors of their desires to enslave me: but now I see this. Me" (108). Another nomad, Agone, about to be tattooed, reflects in more Emersonian rhetoric on

how there were goals of desire, objects of desire, resting places, beds, and he never sailed to these places directly. There were no straight routes, except by chance. Rather, the soul travelled such turns and windings, snails, that a world was found, defined. The soul created out of its own desires. But suddenly, in his swerves and curves, he found himself stopped. Unable to go further. (136)

It is exactly this roadblock, what Hulley calls "the scene of our own obliteration," reached only through the "de-repression" of identity that constitutes one of the desiderata of postmodernity, which necessitates a concomitant reinscription of a dominating political and psychological order in *Empire of the Senseless*. This, I will argue, is the engendering order of reproduction that Acker's novel both demythologizes and recasts as the paranoid regime of postmodern identity's memorium.[25]

In *Empire of the Senseless,* it is as if libidinal liberation—in more anachronistic terms, the demolition of the superego or, more precisely, the collapse of the superego into the id, which results in the annihilation of the ego—necessitates the erection of new empirical orders and assemblages of control. The old power structures made up of the unitary identities called the bosses may be gone, but control is everywhere in the novel. It is in the information systems: "The AI [American Intelligence] control information. The AI control the medical mafia. Democracy controls its own death, its medical knowledge and praxis" (Acker, *Empire,* 41). It is amongst the terrorists:

The modern Terrorists are a new version . . . of the hoboes of the 1930s USA. Just as those haters of work (work being that situation in which they were being totally controlled; the controllers didn't work), as far as they were able took over lines of communication, so these Terrorists, being aware of the huge extent to which the media now divorce the act of terrorism from the original sociopolitical intent, were not so much nihilists as fetishists. (35)

And it exists between incestuous bodies:

My brother Don . . . coldly informed me that if I didn't do exactly as he said I'd be shot. I took my clothes off. But I wasn't able to entice this real commander away from his commands with just my body because he didn't care about sensuality. Both of us were unable to touch a person physically. In order to touch he had to command. He commanded me; he commanded positions; he invented a world. (95)

Paris is filled with identity constructs such as Abhor, who is part cyborg, and even though the incestuous father-rapists have been slain and the cannibalistic oedipal mothers have committed suicide or died in childbirth, even though a cultural and political revolution has occurred, the world remains one in which language and relationality operate through systems of domination and control. Indeed, Acker's point seems to be that in this fictional experiment, the attempted wrecking of the symbolic order and the deconstruction of identity only serve to magnify the permanence and reproducibility of their fundamental elements.

The primary order of the new world of the future Paris, which increasingly resembles the world it has replaced as its obverse, is that of reproduction; and it is the paranoia of reproduction on multiple levels —biological, scriptural, political—that Acker both critiques and replicates in *Empire of the Senseless*. In Acker's satire on the nuclear family, the oedipal identities it engenders, and the politics it entails, biological reproduction is assailed as the mechanism through which new bodies are produced to be seduced, marked, and controlled by fathers, thereby serving their functional purpose as instruments of paternal reflection. Abhor's daughter's body, for example, becomes a site of self-mutilation as she practices a "final trick" taught to her by her father:

He showed me how to insert a razor blade into my wrist just for fun. Not for any other reason. Thus, I learned how to approach and understand nature, how to make gargantuan red flowers, like roses blooming, drops of blood, so full and dripping the earth under them, my body shook for hours afterward. . . . This was relief that there were no decisions left. (9–10)

To her father, Abhor "was his mirror. I was his knight" (10). Abhor's biological mother has committed suicide, typifying the role of the mother in *Empire of the Senseless* as the abject bearer of death who confers on her progeny a life of mortality; accordingly, Thivai views his own birth in this manner:

I was a placenta which had been cut open. Yours. Then you, mommy, cut the red cord which united you to me. After you alienated or murdered me, you kissed my mouth and told me you loved me. I awoke: anger made my heart awake. I murdered you: I cut through the red blood that united your mouth and mine: I cut out all emotion which is hatred. I woke up in the only democracy of freedom. (106)

From the father's side, biological reproduction in the novel is a means of control; from the mother's side, it is a mechanism by which the death of identity is executed.[26]

Yet, if Acker undertakes an antioedipal critique of modes of biological reproduction that generate embodiments of paternal narcissism and abject maternity in the form of democratic subjects ("I woke up in the only democracy of freedom"), she manifests the extent to which the ideology of reproduction maintains its footing even when identity is conceived in the cases of Abhor, Thivai, and the nomads they encounter as molecular "desiring-assemblages" of "passional mutation."[27] *Empire of the Senseless* is replete with substitute fathers and fake mothers cast in the form of cyborgs, mutations, and reduplications, suggesting that the metonymical work of reproduction thrives in this revolutionary regime where the displacements of the symbolic order, in their deterritorialized multiplicity, serve to reconstitute it. Chief among these are such figures as the sadistic "Madame" and "Mommy Death" representing the conjunction between sexuality, death, and abjection that Acker locates in the maternal figure. Among the patriarchs, there is none other than "Schreber," Abhor's former boss, who offers Thivai an "enzyme which could change all [his] blood," converting him into a "construct" (Acker, *Empire,* 45). Schreber is a proxy for all of the novel's rapacious paternal authorities. Mutilated by his parents, who have used various mechanical devices to deform his body, transformed into a surveillance cyborg as a result of wounds suffered in the Korean War ("his arms legs and eyes had been lopped off. . . . The Americans saved him . . . by sticking in some new plumbing. . . . Practically, he was dead. Dead, the only possible work for him was to be a spy. He spied on spies who spied on spies" [46]), Schreber invents torture devices and assembles identity constructs to be controlled. He is described as "paranoid, schizophrenic, hallucinated, deluded, disassociated, autistic, and ambivalent" (45), and in his multiplicity, he appears omniscient and immortal.

As the last of the bosses removed from Paris, Schreber is murdered by Abhor, an act that parallels the scene of his mother's death in giving birth that Thivai imagines, and one that would seem to portend the death of the primal father and end of the despotic reproductive regime under which Thivai and Abhor have suffered. Yet Schreber survives in the succession of ghouls and specters that replace him as the living dead in the eternal regress of a symbolic order that most reveals its fragile consistency in the slain patriarchs and monumental figures that constitute its memory in the form of eternal return.[28] The Schreber of *Empire of the Senseless* has achieved the godhead he sought in his memoirs, but as a perverse mutation who represents the nightmare version of the cyborgs populating what Donna Haraway calls the "cyborg myth" that is "about transgressed boundaries, potent fusions, and dangerous possibilities," exemplers of a "powerful infidel heteroglossia" in works that offer a utopian alternative to the politics of global capitalism and its proliferate paranoias.[29] In *Empire of the Senseless,* Acker is interested neither in myth nor utopia but in showing the capacity of the reigning sociopolitical construct satirized in all her fictions—the nuclear family, with its violent patriarchs, abjected mothers, paranoid sons, and victimized daughters—to reproduce itself in the aftermath of its destroyed paternity.

To employ different terms, Acker, employing the stratagem of transparency that allows her to foreground "that which the codes forbid" (*Empire,* 134), lays bare the violent, thanotopic logic of reproduction through which identity is sutured to the social order—even if that order is allegedly revolutionary, even if identity is multiple, machinal, deconstructed. In this manner, she implicitly critiques the notion of desire as an alterity to the social. It is, for her, the binding of desire to the logic of reproduction with its positioned controlling paternal and voided maternal figures that engenders identity. Such desire is always narcissistic (its centripetal line of flight directed toward the monstrous, indeterminate self) and paranoiac (its centrifugal line aggressively directed at the other on whom this monstrosity and indeterminacy is displaced). In *Empire of the Senseless,* Acker identifies reproduction, which in Judith Roof's terms "provides the model for social order," and which "in its various mechanical, artistic, and biological guises becomes the terrain for the Symbolic's renegotiation," as "a governing representational fiction in western culture."[30] Her project is not to mystify or mythicize these renegotiations as they take place in an imagined future of dead paternity and libidinal extension but to measure their sheer reproducibility in a narrative of apocalyptic anxiety about identity's continuance as a social construct or object of representation. If Pynchon, in *The Crying of Lot 49,* projects a future where paranoia is matched by indeterminacy in the atemporal instant of revelation, Acker projects a present that can only replicate itself as the null set of potentiality. As Abhor says, "Time which will come, the future, is never present. Since everything will happen in the future: the present, me, was null. . . . I was the only end which could be present. . . . I was an end to the present" (Acker, *Empire*, 113). *Empire of the Senseless* thus satirizes familiar versions of postmodern identity—nomadic, cybernetic, phantasmic—in an effort to represent them as examples of, not departures from, "the Symbolic's renegotiation" within the history of the present.

Ultimately, for Acker, representation—that conceptual twin to reproduction—is the central issue. In reinscribing "the ego's era" laid bare with its defenses down, as it were, Acker enscenes her own writing as a reproductive act. She does so even as she exposes the prosthetic logic of reproduction that continues on by virtue of a metonymic process that replaces mom and dad with such mutations—such multiplicities—as Mommy Death, Schreber, and their substitutes. Of representation, the terrorist Thivai says:

We should use force to fight representations which are idols, idolized images; we must use force to annihilate erase eradicate terminate destroy slaughter slay nullify neutralize break down get rid of obliterate move out destruct end all representations which exist for purposes other than enjoyment. In such a war, a war against idolatry, ridicule'll be our best tool. (95)

Arguably, Acker follows this dictum in her own work as she makes war on "logocentrism and idealism, theology, all supports of the repressive society. Property's pillars. Reason which always homogenizes and reduces, represses and unifies phenomena and actuality into what can be perceived and so controlled" (12).

Like all her novels, *Empire of the Senseless* is replete with acts of plagiarism, ridiculing imitations of familiar canonical works, and what Meaghan Morris lists as instances of "piracy": "appropriation, strategies of quotation, revision, mimicry, and for that matter . . . image and discourse *piracy* (or, more recently, 'poaching')."[31] As movements in the war on idolatry and representation, one can find in *Empire of the Senseless* eradications of punctuation, destructions of syntax, disruptive shifts between levels of discourse and point of view, scandalous language, "unreadable" (i.e., Arabic) inscriptions, pornographic descriptions of sexual acts between relatives, friends, and strangers, and stylistic and generic parodies of works ranging from Saint Augustine's *Confessions* to Mark Twain's *Huckleberry Finn,* along with all the pirates, criminals, terrorists, fake mothers, and substitute fathers who are the actants in Acker's discursive fakery/terrorism. Moreover, in the frequent acts of tattooing that occur in a novel that Acker dedicates to her tattooist, "writing on the body" is viewed as a criminal act, a form of inscription in which "the power of the tattoo becomes intertwined with the power of those who chose to live beyond the norms of society" (Acker, *Empire,* 140). An art of images, tattooing is potentially a force in the war on representation because it is a "direct" writing, "flesh on flesh" (ibid.), that cuts out the representational middleman; rather than being a reproduction, it is potentially a unique production, or enactment, of desire on the flesh, and it is criminal because it exhibits a resistance to the imposition of control of images from outside the body as it merges desire and (self)discipline.

Yet in the syntactical and corporeal war on idolatry conducted by her writing, Acker's own version of the phallic dialectic manifests itself when forms of resistance—even the resistances of mimicry, plagiarism, and tattooing—are unveiled as reinscriptions of the reproductive order where desire is equated with the reduplication of gendered positions. The most extravagant instance of reinscription in the novel occurs during a long sequence in which Thivai and Abhor reenact the concluding scenes of *The Adventures of Huckleberry Finn.* Like Huck and Jim, the terrorist runaways Thivai and Abhor have been floating down a river and encountering an assortment of other deterritorialized entities when Abhor suddenly disappears. Discovering that she has been picked up by the Revolutionary Algerian Police, Thivai formulates an elaborate plan for her escape and initiation into piracy with a newfound friend, Mark. As is the case with Huck and Tom's plan to free Jim in *Huckleberry Finn,* Thivai and Mark's plan is designed to extend Abhor's term of imprisonment and her victimization for as long as possible while they play at being liberators in a performance that reproduces the master/slave, male/female dialectic that the revolution is supposed to have sublated. The goal of the two men is to transform Abhor, "though she was uneducated, into a great writer so that she'd have a reason for being in jail for the rest of her life. And at that time, society needed a great woman writer" (203). In order to mark Abhor as this embodiment of the writer "who need[s] disability or madness [she] can overcome in order to write" (203), Thivai and Mark "tattoo" her with three hearts written in her own blood; as Thivai explains, "These hearts were applicable because they were senseless. To write is to reveal a heart's identity. Abhor heard me, squeezed some more blood out, and traced, rather than drew, her own lonely heart" (204).

In this symbolic enactment of the heart's desire—or the desire of desire—the drawing and tracing on Abhor's skin via the revolutionary art of tattooing merely reduplicates the conditions of her subjectivity and victimization, for it is the desire of these men that is being made visible through her inscribed body, which is yet another representation of "the sensory, the concrete, the nondeductible" always associated with "woman" in the phallic dialectic. Abhor's desire, her writing, does not exist as such because it would fall entirely outside the confines of representation: when Abhor prints the words "*FUCKFACES ALL MEN*" then "*THE SHIP IS SINKING* right over the bloody heart," Thivai remarks that "these words weren't good writing because they had nothing to do with nothing. With Abhor. . . . To write or describe a heart, I explained, demands accurate observation of the self and the self's world" (204). In the process interpellating Abhor as pirate and great woman writer, Thivai effectively replicates a paranoid system of surveillance that enables "the accurate observation of the self," paralleling his and Mark's elaborate spying operations on Abhor. Protesting the dominion of observation and reason, Abhor's blood writing is both material and nonreferential, having "nothing to do with nothing." In Acker's dystopia, the mechanisms of writing and reproduction that entail the positioning of the woman as victim, criminal, and site of male desire's inscription (the only place where it is known), thrive within a revolutionary, postsubjectival regime through the ciphering of women. The paranoia of Acker's revamped Huck-Tom scenario is evident in the relation between Thivai and Mark enacted across the transparency of Abhor's body—a relation that depends on the surveillance and control of women in order to effect their authoring.

As Abhor writes in a letter to Thivai and Mark,

The whole world is men's bloody fantasies. . . . You two collaborated in keeping me in jail by planning escapes so elaborate they had nothing to do with escape. That's western thought for you. . . . This is what I'm saying: you're always fucking deciding what reality is and collaborating about those decisions. (210)

Abhor's formulation suggests the extent to which she remains trapped in a patriarchal system of discursive control that confines her to the realm of her own conspiratorial knowledge of reality collaborating against her. *Empire of the Senseless* can only indicate what lies beyond the phallic dialectic and the collaborative construction of reality by men, contradictorily, by means of a pastiche of reproduced and variegated Western thoughts, inscriptions, genres, and stories. The problem, for Acker, lies in the nature of desire as such, or more accurately, the available means for representing desire, which as Roof contends, inevitably involve a renegotiation, or reproduction, of the overthrown symbolic order that positions men as the scribes of desire and the abject bodies of women as the surveyed scene of that inscription.[32] Equally, in *Empire of the Senseless,* Acker posits the nuclear family and its substitutes—the revolutionary triad of Abhor, Thivai, and Mark that survives in the wake of dead fathers and suicided mothers—as the sociopolitical entity through which this process of twinned biological and discursive reproduction is mediated. As we have seen, Pynchon offers postponed revelation, projected into a future that stretches to infinity, as the other of cultural paranoia that may only confirm its reach. Acker, conversely, resituates paranoia in a near future where the very mechanisms that play a major role in constituting it—Western thought, reproduction, objectivity, the gendered construction of the subject of knowledge through surveillance—are on the verge of breaking down, yet are ever renewed in the face of a postmodern crisis of representation that unfailingly reproduces itself *as* crisis.

Acker, therefore, depicts paranoia as part of a series of cultural processes that produce identity, and when put under the pressure of extinction, reveal the capacity to assimilate multiplicities, nomadisms, and deterritorializations of writing and identity in the work of reproduction that underwrites "the Symbolic's renegotiation." Acker's mapping of this renegotiation in *Empire of the Senseless* discloses the engendering of cultural paranoia occurring in the relation between the collaborative construction of reality—that pragmatist fantasy— and the bloody marking/domination/mutilation of bodies that reproduces the effects of this construction as history that "runs human blood through the river of time" (Acker, *Empire,* 66). From this, she offers no escape, however temporary, into the chimera of Pynchonian revelation, or even into the canniness of Johnson's survivalism. Nevertheless, she does offer through Abhor, who is "nothing" but a bloody medium ("I'm taking layers of my own epidermis . . . and tearing one of them off so more and more of my blood shoots into your face. That is what writing is to me a woman" [210]), a "symptom" or "externalization" of all that humankind's "ontological consistency hangs on, is suspended from." [33] In effect, Acker is a postmodern realist who shows the degree to which the "whole world" of men's "bloody fantasies," reproduced on the body and as history, depends on the stripped, abjected subjectivity that gives lie to the consistency and permanency of the symbolic order, forcing its continuous renegotiation, exposing its fragility. Taken as a whole, Acker's fiction suggests that in this repeated exposure—literally in your face—resides the possibility of a renegotiation that might at some point produce "a society which wasn't just disgust" (*Empire*, 226). But for Abhor, this lies beyond the current order in which the relation between desire and knowledge is a matter of reproduction: "I stood there in the sunlight, and thought I didn't as yet know what I wanted. I now fully knew what I didn't want. . . . That was something" (227).

Criminality and Paranoia

The criminal act calls into question the general sphere
of the law itself, the law as such.
—Slavoj Žižek, *For They Know Not What They Do*

But to live outside the law you must be honest.
—Bob Dylan, "Absolutely Sweet Marie"

■ In *Empire of the Senseless,* one of Abhor's monologues is titled "The
Beginning of Criminality/The Beginning of Morning," suggesting for
Acker's protagonist that the illegality of piratical status and the marginality it confers comes as an awakening that illuminates the borderland
between official or national identities and their alien, illicit counterparts. As Žižek writes, criminality questions the nature of "law as such,"
and does so in ways that reveal the enforced connection between legality and such symbolic entities as the state, nation, and identity of the
citizen. In this conception, the law comes before identity; thus identity, when criminalized, both reflects the paranoid formations that are
symptomatic of the suturing of the self to the symbolic order and, by
virtue of being alien or criminal, reconstitutes the conditions that produce the law and those outside it, whose "honesty" is the contradictory negation and affirmation of the law's reach.[1] With Abhor's awakening into criminality, there comes the ignition of the narrative engine by

means of which she is transformed into the imprisoned woman writer, just as, for Michel Foucault, the "category problem" presented by the nineteenth-century parricide Pierre Rivière results in the designation of both his monstrosity and new juridical and medical categories to contain and explain it.[2] The criminal subject is, as films as various as *The Godfather* and *Heat* suggest, a mirror that reflects the lineaments of the legal subject in a system of surveillance that depends on the advent of the outlaw as well as the disciplining of criminality in order to sustain itself.

The relation between criminality and paranoia is, counterintuitively, multiplied and deepened when one considers the subjectival fluidities and soft, permeable borders that inhere in the postmodernist conceptions of identity that I have introduced. In tracing transformations in criminalized subjectivity across a history of punishment and execution that runs from the premodern to the modern, panoptic epoch, Foucault argues that the more mobile and irregular identity is conceived to be, the more accountable it must become to disciplinary systems of enumeration and control:

The body of the king, with its strange material and physical presence, with the force that he himself deploys or transmits to some few others, is at the opposite extreme of th[e] new physics of power represented by panopticism; the domain of panopticism is, on the contrary, that whole lower region, that region of irregular bodies, with their details, their multiple movements, their heterogeneous forces, their spatial relations; what are required are mechanisms that analyse distributions, gaps, series, combinations, and which use instruments that render visible, record, differentiate and compare: a physics of relational and multiple power, which has its maximum intensity not in the person of the king, but in the bodies that can be individualized by these relations.[3]

Under Foucault's logic, the hypervisible, heterogeneous identities of postmodernity, mobilized by the flows of capital through which the intensities of libidinal desire are channeled, become more—not less—subject to an exfoliation of legal boundaries and restrictions that operate under a panoptic authority whose center is nowhere, but whose effects are felt everywhere. Enhanced technologies of surveillance, the arrival of prisons as a growth industry in such states as California where the public funding for the incarceration of its citizens exceeds that for their education, the fetishizing of lawyers and the legal process discernible in *Law and Order* and Court TV, and the national obsession with trials: all are scattered manifestations of the degree to which we feel that we are increasingly under the eye of the law, even as the celebrated hybridization of identity is played out across the fluid economy of a mobile society. Within this economy, the criminal, as public spectacle, becomes the visible representation of the point at which the contradiction between subject mobility and panopticism—between the deterritorialization and commodification of identity—breaks down. Both outside the law and subject to it, the criminal reveals how normalized identity, as a form of negotiation that represses this contradiction, instantiates the cultural paranoia that squares the production of postmodern subjects with official or legal histories.

The narratives I consider in this chapter contain representations of criminality that place the "criminal" as a component of postmodern identity at the liminal point on the border of the law. This positioning, in turn, produces the law and legal subject within various national, subjectival, and corporate frameworks. In Mailer's *The Executioner's Song,* Gary Gilmore is articulated by a seemingly absconded narrative authority as the public citizen/criminal who incorporates the desire for a punishment—an execution of the law—that responds to the perceived historical individuality of the transgressor, yet who serves at the moment of execution as a testament to the universality of the law and the cosmic fatefulness of historical process. Fabricated as a postmodern spectacle whose process of assembly is foregrounded and overseen in the novel, Gilmore is the embodiment of the federal subject whose meeting with fate, like that of *Libra*'s Oswald, apparently occurs by chance and through the eccentric will of the individual, yet coheres with the unfolding of a national destiny. In Jim Thompson's *The Killer Inside Me,* the interiority of the criminal is instantiated in a narrative secretion of felonious identity; Thompson's examination of the criminal's "insides" is analogous, in many ways, to that of the paranoid woman in *The Shadow Knows.* By conflating the narrator, perpetrator, and adjudicator of criminal activity into a single paranoid entity, Thompson achieves an identificatory collapse of the homologous, panoptic relation between the law and those subject to it—a relation that arises at the birth of the individual and the discovery of his "insides." The schizoid deputy sheriff and multiple murderer of Thompson's novel is a study in heterogeneity, yet it is his very ability to move across subject positions and the observatory capacities enabled by his mobility that allow him to legally authenticate and categorize the criminality of identity. Quentin Tarantino's *Reservoir Dogs* provides a corporate model for the national, (il)legal subjects represented in *The Executioner's Song* and *The Killer Inside Me.* The uniformity of the gangsters in Tarantino's film is superficially matched by arbitrarily imposed differences used to distinguish individual criminals, but this spurious play of homogeneity and multiplicity only produces the commodified, corporate felon whose unlawful acts mirror the hetero-normativity of subjects operating under the eye of the law. Significantly, each of these three narratives negotiates the connection between felony and paranoia in terms of mediated homoerotic and homophobic exchanges between men that occur within the capital, phallocentric order that adjudicates their criminality. Each thus offers a strong critical reflection on the relation between sexuality, criminality, and the cultural paranoia that informs the mirroring relation between legal and illegal mobilities.

■ The Voice of Paranoia: *The Executioner's Song*

Sometime in the early morning of July 20, 1976, barely three months after his release from a twelve-year sentence for armed robbery served in the federal penitentiary at Marion, Illinois, Gary Gilmore drove into a gas station in Provo, Utah, robbed station attendant Max Jensen, and demanded that he lie facedown on the ground. Gilmore then fired twice into Jensen's head at point-blank range with an automatic pistol; Jensen died immediately. In the evening, fifteen hours after the first murder, Gilmore drove up to a motel situated next door to the house of his relatives, Vern and Ida Damico, who had given Gilmore refuge and found him a job on his release from prison. Gilmore demanded money from Benny Bushnell, the owner of the motel, asked him to lie facedown on the floor, and then pumped one bullet into his head; Gilmore had intended to shoot him twice, but his gun jammed, and it was several hours before Bushnell would die of his wounds. One day later, Gilmore was arrested for the murder of Bushnell. He was tried, found guilty of murder in the first degree, and sentenced to death: his choice of punishment was execution by firing squad. Though his mother and the American Civil Liberties Union attempted to block the execution, Gilmore insisted that the state of Utah carry out the sentence. On January 17, 1977, he was shot to death by a team of four handpicked riflemen. His was the first public execution to have taken place in the United States in over a decade.

Such are the bare facts of the Gilmore story as told by Mailer in *The Executioner's Song,* which follows Gilmore from his prison release to his death. The novel, proclaimed to be a "true-life story," is, as Mailer notes in the afterword, based on hundreds of hours of tape-recorded conversations with Gilmore himself, as well as his friends, family, and associates; on letters written between Gilmore and his lover,

Nicole Baker; and on scores of public documents that relate this story of crime and punishment in contemporary times. *The Executioner's Song,* seemingly a novel of a thousand voices, is divided into two symmetrical halves. The first, titled "Western Voices," details Gilmore's life after his release, his relationship with Nicole, and the murders; the second, "Eastern Voices," describes the publicizing of the story and Gilmore's execution. The books mirror each other, the complex aspects of Gilmore's private agony and psychosis in book one echoed and disseminated in the spectacle of book two. Thus, "Gilmore" in the novel becomes the sign for the relation between private and public life in the United States or rather, for the collapsing of this relation in Mailer's paranoid view of history as a system and personal agency as the extension of Foucauldian discipline.

In some respects, *The Executioner's Song* is a perverse bildungsroman, the young man from the provinces making it into the incarceratory big leagues and becoming the public spectacle of the victimizer with principles, himself, a victim of the system.[4] Mailer's presentation of the story reveals his own assumptions about heroism, manhood, and the publicizing of identity in the United States. As we shall see, the homoeroticism that Mailer attributes to Oswald as an aspect of a potential or alternative identity becomes associated through inversion with paranoid criminality in his portrait of Gilmore. More broadly, *The Executioner's Song* reflects elements of a cold war habitus, or in Pierre Bourdieu's sense, a configuration of "transposible dispositions," "structuring structures" that "generate and organize [cultural] practices and representations."[5] According to Bourdieu, "The practical world that is constituted in the relationship with the *habitus,* acting as a system of cognitive and motivating structures, is a world of already realized ends—procedures to follow, paths to take—and of objects endowed with a 'permanent teleological character,' in Husserl's phrase" (53).

As I have suggested previously, in cultural paranoia the "already realized ends" of historical destiny contend with the fluidity and mobility of the postmodern subject. In *The Executioner's Song,* Mailer projects Gilmore as a protean, criminal identity within a "habitus" of consensus—the voice of the people—that contains him as a contradiction within the political condition of late–cold war culture. Its "dispositions" include the polarization of reality in opposed, binary systems; the conflating of mass hysteria with popular consensus, and the investment of social and political institutions with the power to legitimate such formations; the comprehension of history backward as a retrospective unfolding of conspiratorial designs; and the projection of criminal identity either as a marginal, illegal subject who revolts against systems and is ultimately crushed by them, or as a demonic genius who has the capacity to manipulate them. In between these extremes lies the zone of normality whose ruled subjects and governing agents replicate the roles of the alien and panderer. In *The Executioner's Song,* the discrepancies of these circumstances within which the criminal is identified as both abject and, yet, the product of agreements about what constitutes criminality are registered in terms of Gilmore's mobility, spectacularity, and randomness. It is because he is the radically unstable sign of consensual certainty about what comprises legality within the cold war habitus that Gilmore, in his "own" voice, which is at once the recorded vox populi, can conspire with the public in calling down punishment upon himself as witness to and embodiment of criminality.

In the novel, Gilmore, compared by various informants to John F. Kennedy, Mohammed Ali, Joe Hill, Christ, Satan, and Harry Houdini, appears as the antihermeneutic opposite of Pynchon's Oedipa, engaged in hermeneutic frenzy. Though others may make of him what they will, Gilmore kills with little comment and no explanation, and his monotone responses to all questions regarding motivation suggest that he firmly believes in a fatality that in the short view may appear to be a collation of accidents, but in the long run is the linear narrative of what was "meant to be." Whereas Oedipa seeks the hidden connection between objects and events as the sign that she is traveling briskly down the road leading to the site of final revelation in the auction room, Gilmore, a kind of outlaw pragmatist, just acts, and expects the state to do the same when it sentences him to die in the chamber of execution, without legal prevarication or moral agonizing in the attempt to make sense of the deed or reform the doer. In contrast to the overdetermined realm Oedipa negotiates, replete with symbolic riches and paranoid possibilities, Gilmore's world is as flat and disjunctive as the recorded voices on the novel's tape machine, and Gilmore himself becomes the passive site of diverse, yet phonetically, remarkably similar responses to multiple roles as criminal, prophet, and revolutionary. The novel is indeed a mechanism in which the author/interviewer assumes the illusory role of magnetic sensor registering slight variations in the tight-lipped voices of his interlocutors.

The Provo that Gilmore inhabits during his short hiatus between incarceration and execution is "laid out in a checkerboard" with

very wide streets and a few buildings that were four stories high. It had three movie theaters. Two were on Center Street, the main shopping street, and the other was on University Avenue, the other shopping street. In Provo, the equivalent of Times Square was where the two streets crossed. There was a park next to a church on one corner and diagonally across was an extra-large drugstore.[6]

Unlike Pynchon's use of indirect free discourse to describe Oedipa's perception of San Narciso as paranoid system and structure, Mailer's anonymous narrator refuses to comment beyond just the facts, though it is clear that the description is a composite of positions and perceptions. Who would be making the urbane comparison of Provo to Times Square? Certainly not the same voice who would depict the drugstore as "extra-large." Tone and point of view in this passage are mobile, almost random as the subject-position of the narrator slides from that of a Manhattan executive on the Kennedy-LAX route looking down at the checkerboard of Provo amid the vast wastes of the western desert, to that of a local citizen siting along the diagonal the drugstore that seems real big by Utah standards. The composing of angles and voices—high and low, citified and redneck, lyrical and profane—that occurs here and throughout the novel lends a form of consensual objectivity to such descriptions, as well as to the thousands of opinions and responses to Gary and his deeds in the novel. Contradictorily, this narrative authority appears to be without intention or direction. Gilmore may be perceived as a satanic manipulator, or one of Mailer's perverse, existential anti-heroes willing to cross the boundary between life and death, but it is equally likely that he is just another psychopath who stumbled into murder and notoriety. If readers want to make something of Provo, beyond its dullness and mediocrity, then as far as the composite narrator of *The Executioner's Song* is concerned, they will have to do so on their own, for Provo is just a place you see from an airplane on a cross-country flight if that is where you happen to be one day while, down below, Gary Gilmore wreaks havoc.

At least this is what appears on the surface of *The Executioner's Song,* which may seem merely a distended transcript, the voices, impressions, and documents reeling off one after another, chronology the only order. Mailer, the titular organizer of this massive amount of information, is already at one remove from the material since most of it was recorded during interviews conducted by a former *Life* journalist, Larry Schiller, who later sold the story to Mailer; throughout, the passive recording voice he generates seems unconcerned with the hash everyone is making of the Gilmore story. Whereas Pynchon engages epistemology, Mailer appears to inscribe the poetics of the knee jerk in the novel's transcript: things happen; people respond; someone, anyone, is there to videotape, record, or write it down. *The Executioner's Song* would then seem to be remarkably antiparanoid since it implicitly promotes a peculiar form of chaos theory.[7] Things may be ordered according to some design or plan: Gilmore may be the institutionally fated murderer of two men in cold blood, or he may be the demonic tester of the system that articulates him as its subject on trial, just as Oedipa is a quester amid disciplinary matrices. But this is never *necessarily* the case since one strategy of the novel is to suggest that any detected patterns of fate or contingency come after the fact of recording and registration, after history and before interpretation, thus driving a temporal wedge between inscription and reading. Arguably, we witness in *The Executioner's Song* a powerful example of Mailerian undecidability, where historical parallels, accidents, and coincidences can lead willynilly to consensual views about what happened, and equally serve to refute the notion that the examination of events and their afterlife will yield patterns of significance. Hence, like Mailer's *Why Are We in Vietnam?*, *The Executioner's Song* may be viewed as a parody of "historiographic metafiction"—that is, work that merges fiction and history in order to offer pluralistic interpretations of real events or advance the idea that history is a fictive construct.[8] Amid the plethora of competing explanations that may provide a narrative rationale for Gilmore's actions, Mailer offers the possibility that no explanation is available or necessary in the historical compressions of postmodernity. Events occur and are recorded at such a rapid pace that they cannot be assimilated into any hermeneutic system, paranoid or otherwise, for the next catastrophe is on the way before the last one has ceased. Gilmore, it seems, is a walking disaster, and his transcribed life is a form of institutionalized or disciplined chaos that reveals the fragile purchase of any consensus formed around him.

But this is to accept the narrative authority of *The Executioner's Song* on its own terms, and leave unquestioned Mailer's implied polemic: if we can make nothing of Gilmore, we can make everything of him. As almost anyone who draws close to Gilmore in his final days can agree, while they are appalled by his inexplicable crimes, they admire his intelligence, courage, and vision. Such gifts, they conclude in a vast assemblage of sound bites, must not have been conferred without a reason, even on this wasted life; hence, they consensually engage in the insipid mythologizing of the mass murderer who grew up next door and always seemed a perfectly nice boy, a process that both links criminality to normalized origins and abjects it as the betrayal or monstration of those beginnings. Gilmore passes easily from cipher to symbol as the novel progresses, and in the end, it makes no difference who or what Gilmore is or has been: when he becomes a public spectacle, he also becomes public property, his words, letters, poems, thoughts, and memories capitalized on and commodified.[9] As David Guest has written, within weeks of his imprisonment,

Gilmore would sell exclusive rights to his story for one hundred thousand dollars plus a stake in a future book and movie deal. . . . By the date of the execution, Gilmore had received more than forty thousand personal letters at the Utah State Prison. Within a few months, he was featured, posthumously, in a lengthy interview in the April 1997 edition of *Playboy* magazine. The deal eventually led to Mailer's "true life novel" and to a made-for-television movie bearing the same title.[10]

Gilmore, like Mailer's versions of Oswald, Marilyn Monroe, and Jack Henry Abbot, becomes what can be made of him. Passing into a spectacular history, these characters are transformed into fluid identities subject to rates of exchange as they become the symbolic reservoirs of public consensus about what constitutes the criminal and the normal.

All the more curious, then, that in *The Executioner's Song* what appears on the surface to be a manifestation of the narrator as passive recording device registering disparate voices that coalesce into the public view of Gilmore turns out to be something quite different as Mailer engages in a form of dubbing through which coincidences are noted and bound over to evolving patterns of fatality, and the composite heteronomy of voices is reduced to the monotone of a singular, coded message. It happens, for instance, that Gilmore and girlfriend Nicole own exactly the same model and year; Gary has his car painted blue to match Nicole's after they meet. Jim Barrett, one of Nicole's former husbands, leaves Provo for "Cody, Wyoming, with a friend of his also named Barrett" at the same time that Nicole finds a house in Spanish Fork where she will briefly share her life with Gilmore, "like something out of a fairy tale" (Mailer, *Executioner's Song,* 117). Kathryne, Nicole's mother, is the spitting image of Nicole's half sister, also named Kathy. Ida Damico has a twin sister, Ada, who is deceased. (The Ida/Ada connection, in particular, is a signal example of Mailer's uncanny ability to turn a fact into a cultural marker that will surely ring differently in the ears of locals and urban intellectuals, the former hearing country cute in the tendency to give siblings rhyming names, the latter registering the title of Nabokov's parodic family romance and his Poesque fascination with the dead, doubled other.) Max Jensen, the gas station attendant who

Gilmore slays, has a sister and wife who share the same name: Colleen. Gibbs, Gilmore's cellmate in the Logan County Jail, has "a kid sister living in Provo who was married to a fellow named Gilmore" (367). The maiden name of Grace McGinnis, a dedicated teacher who attempts to help Gary's brother avoid the family curse of violence and early death, is Gilmore. And so on. The doublings and repetitions of the novel that, when listed, sound like the litanies of coincidence that the Oswald of *Libra* recites to himself as he articulates his presence as a historical subject, begin to add up to something: a "synchronicity," as one of the novel's chapters is titled, a sense that unrelated events—even facticity itself—are harmonized into some pattern of correspondence that, formulated in retrospect, anchors Gilmore's catalytic acts of random violence in a spatialized temporality.

The word *paranoid* is used not only in reference to Gilmore, who may be so because of the massive doses of Prolixin given to him in prison, but also in reference to Gary's cousin Brenda Nicol (her name echoing that of Gilmore's paramour), to Nicole Baker, to her former husband Kip, to her sister April, to Gilmore's mother, to Debbie Bushnell on the day of her husband's death, to Gibbs, and to John Woods, one of Gilmore's psychologists. Paranoia is contagious in *The Executioner's Song,* and almost every one of its dozens of characters is afflicted with it at some point. Moreover, it seems that almost everyone—from the soft-brained freelance journalist, Dennis Boaz, who first attempts to break the Gilmore story and who believes in obscure theories of numerology, to the most hard-nosed reporter in the field—has some sense that events are taking place within patterns of significance. Theories about reincarnation, the cabals of Mormonism, and prison surveillance systems circulate among the novel's interlocutors as systems of belief, explanatory assemblages, and disciplinary mechanisms seem to conspire to articulate Gilmore as criminal historical subject. Remarkable public and private historical coincidences abound, ranging from the fact that George Latimar, chair of the Utah Board of Pardons that will decide Gilmore's execution, turns out to have been the chief civilian attorney in the Lt. William Calley trial, to Gilmore's implicit claim that the randomness of the murders exemplifies the transformation of contingency into historical "fate":

"Gary," said Nielsen [the detective who interviews Gilmore after his capture], "I have to think like a good policeman doing a good job. You know, if I can prevent these kinds of things from happening, that makes me successful in my work. And I would like to understand—why would you hit those places? Why did you hit the motel in Provo or the service station? Why those particular places?"

"Well," said Gilmore, "the motel just happened to be next to my uncle Vern's place. I just happened on it."

"But the service station?" said Nielsen. "Why that service station in the middle of nowhere?"

"I don't know," said Gilmore. "It was there." He looked for a moment like he wished to help Nielsen. "Now you take the place where I hid that thing," he said, "after the motel." Nielsen realized he was speaking of the money tray he lifted from Benny Bushnell's counter. "Well, I put that thing in a particular bush," he said, "because when I was a kid I used to mow the lawn right there for an old lady." (288–89)

Historical parallels, accidents, and unplanned or manufactured coincidences like these (who would not perceive artifice in the correspondence of "bush" and "Bushnell" as Gilmore struggles to covert contingency into fate?) are conflated to such an extent in the novel that it is impossible *not* to think that Gilmore is more than he appears to be, that he stands at the crossroads of events converging on the media-made, postmodern antihero. Thus, we are jawboned into accepting as consensual truth the demonization of Gilmore, where, as in this anecdotal aside, what is clearly a thought proceeding from Gilmore's self-aggrandizement becomes yet another example of his charismatic power: "In the morning, it was the Mustang. His car would not start. It was as if something in Gary's makeup killed off the electrical system every morning" (148). An authorial joke at Gilmore's expense? If so, it is part of an elaborate routine through which Gilmore becomes the focal point for public fears and expectations that the worst will inevitably happen and it will inevitably make sense. Gilmore becomes in *The Executioner's Song* the subject of history conceived, like a Freudian dream text, as a palimpsest of riddles, displaced and condensed signs, enigmas, false leads, puns, and coincidentally bad jokes. Perhaps one of the most painfully obvious of the latter in the novel occurs when Gibbs, released from jail after ratting on Gilmore, finds himself the victim of an auto accident and at the hospital asks "for the best doctor in town. There it was. The fellow's name was Best. Dr. Robert Best. One of Evel Knievel's own personal doctors" (767). If such flukes offer compelling evidence of the black humor of fatality, then so much the better for the disposition that confers a perceptible intentionality on destiny, even if, for Gilmore, it is comic in comparison to the tragedy that must cohere around Mailer's Oswald.

But who makes note of this curious array of coincidences and parallels—pure chance (Gilmore is characterized by Gibbs as "a roulette wheel . . . [that] just depended on which number came up" [359]) made over into the significant patterning of self-determining circumstance? Mailer, noncommittally, might have us believe that history works in this way, the novelist-cum-all-seeing-eye-cum-tape-recorder sifting through the voice transcripts and discovering synchronicity where one expected only a chaos of details. But it is his voice, or more precisely his overvoice, that gives Mailer away. To return to the description of Provo and the "extra-large" drugstore on the corner: it is a word, as I have suggested, that comes from someone walking the streets of Provo—a citizen, or perhaps Gilmore himself, or Nicole—but not one generated, apparently, by the recording angel of a narrator who merely registers what others say. Yet, if we listen more carefully, we "hear" this: Mont Court, Gilmore's probation officer, portrays Gilmore as "supernice" and himself as "neither a hardnose, nor superheat" (53); Spencer McGrath, Gilmore's boss, remarks that Gary and Nicole seem to be in "supergood shape" (63–64); Mormon missionary Pete Galovan suffers from "super-excitement" (130); Gary tells Nicole a "supergross" prison story (141); April, Nicole's sister, is "superfreaky" (166); Nicole feels "double-loyal" to Gary, and regards Roger Eaton, another lover, as "superclean" and "supersweet" (177); Dean Christiansen, Ben Bushnell's bishop, bears a "super-Mormon" name (258); Gilmore describes events in a letter as "supershitty" (360); prison guard Jerry Scott resents the fact that everyone is "extra nice" to Gilmore (448); Nicole's former husband, Kip, considers her a "super chick" who is "superdaring" (514); Dennis Boaz calls Barry Farrell, soon to be Schiller's cowriter on the Gilmore story, a "superpipeline" (629); and Gilmore, in an interview, maintains that "you don't have to be superintelligent to get away with shit" (798). The proliferating examples acquire a cumulative force that leaves the reader with the impression that the novel's many voices—mediated through recordings, transcripts, and newspaper accounts, and remembered, overheard above constant background noise, distorted over the telephone—either all speak the same language or are the same voice. In the novel, a consensual identity gradually forms around the figure of the criminal, Gilmore, a linguistic community with its own vocal tics manifesting the paranoid sense that events are unfolding according to a singular, external design marked by a common language, no matter how dispersed individual speakers and speech acts may be. Through this processing of linguistic consensus in Mailer's "overvoice," Gilmore becomes the disciplined subject whose alterity enables the formation of a body politic, a community or nation of speakers with shared assumptions about what constitutes the criminal as subject to (a) history, and at the focal point of its revelatory narrative.

The overvoice of *The Executioner's Song* provides evidence of Mailer's intention mapped onto events that otherwise would appear to be random, as in terms of its victims, Gilmore's violence is random. Merely by just taking note of the communal speech patterns and amazing coincidences that seem to circulate through the Gilmore story, and by generating a "random" assemblage in which Gilmore is recollected as a protean aggregate constructed from multiple, overlapping perspectives, the narrative authority of *The Executioner's Song* establishes synchronicity as the novel's temporal register in which repetition and contiguity (read proleptically) signify the inevitability of occurrences in the aftermath. In this fatal narrative, Gilmore is heroicized because, as a postmodern disciplinary subject, he fits into the wholly paranoid schema of history that fascinates Mailer and fulfills the expectations produced by a social order in which the exercise of punishment ("the executioner's song") precedes the law as the guarantor of its efficacy and universality in separating the normal from the criminal. The local version of this schema in *The Executioner's Song* is comparable to that of *JFK* in a variation of the familiar oedipal pattern where a revolutionary, amoral son takes on not the father in the usual sense but the paternal disciplinary system. Mailer's "son" first attempts to transgress this system, and then, in a contradictory act of submission and revolt, demands that the system keep its word and acquit its mission by exacting just punishment from the former victimizer and current victim of the same process that calls him into order.

The tactic that Mailer pursues in instantiating this pattern as the narrative backbone of the consensus that forms around Gilmore is remarkably like that of Mailer's infamous political essay, "The White Negro," where as Thomas Schaub claims, the "invention of the 'white Negro' . . . is a romantic strategy of converting a struggle between racial colors into the opposition between self and society, imagination and ego repression."[11] With *The Executioner's Song,* Mailer engages in a similar conversion process where public opinion, metabolized by the novel's quiescent, panoptic authority, everywhere reflects Gilmore's private struggle; and where class difference, systematic institutional violence, and Mormon banality are transformed into opportunities for the exercise of a form of liberal individualism operating under the postmodern ethos of multiple, rhizomic agency constructed within and resisting the symbolic order. By virtue of this process, Gilmore becomes the central spectacle in the novel's manifold and intersecting plots. This centrality is what gives his life and death meaning, and the author a job to do in exacting meaning in the form of public consensus about the spectacle. Only in the egotism of the oedipal nightmare of Gilmore's life—a life spread over the entire community of speakers in *The Executioner's Song*—can Mailer elicit the sense that this "true-life story" adds up to something in a devastating self-performance.

Devastating, that is, because Gilmore's story is a communal one, authorized by Mailer—a fable of contained violence that performatively contributes to what Donald Pease terms the "Cold War consensus." [12] Everyone in this post-Vietnam novel, from Gilmore himself to the priest who hears his last words, thinks that Gilmore must add up to something, that he must play a leading role in the story of the opposition between the marginal, criminal individual and the repressive social order that forms the metanarrative of contemporary existence for Mailer and the interlocutors of *The Executioner's Song*. In Provo, it seems, there is no random violence, only contingent acts, however brutal, that can be woven into the ongoing story of the fated, paranoid conflict between social authority and radical individualism. Mailer's camouflaging of his own narrative authority in telling the story under the guise of recording angel is evidence of the enabling force behind such consensual fictions. The fabrication of communal authority through the deployment of the celebrated "heteroglossia" that attends conceptions of decentered and fluid postmodern identities works here, as elsewhere, to demarcate polarized zones of normality and otherness. *The Executioner's Song* reflects these circumstances by placing criminality at the service of normalization as part of the process of achieving consensus about what, or who, constitutes "Gilmore." The novel's consensual fiction has many filiations, but to pursue one of these threads that symptomatically reveals the cultural paranoia of Mailerian pragmatic consensus, I turn to its inherent, and seemingly contradictory, inscriptions of homophobia and homoeroticism.

For *The Executioner's Song* is, above all, a tale of exchanges between men: the Gilmore story passes from Dennis Boaz to Larry Schiller to Norman Mailer. The story itself is one of men conferring death on each other: in exchange for the four bullets Gilmore intends to fire into his two male victims, four male riflemen shoot four bullets straight into his heart; he is punished, in the end, by the judges of the Mormon patriarchy and the United States Supreme Court; his tales of incarceration are replete, as one would expect, with instances of male rape. Amid this bevy of male exchanges of scripts, bullets, sentences, and semen, there is the figure of Nicole Baker. Gilmore refers to her as his "elf," and offends by calling her "Pardner" (which Nicole takes as an accusation of lesbianism), "but as he tried to explain later, he often called men and women alike by Buddy or Pal, Pardner, things like that" (Mailer, *Executioner's Song,* 147). Nicole's promiscuity (read, in the eyes of Provo morality, as nymphomania) is, for some, what leads Gilmore to murder in the first place. Gilmore is obsessed with the idea of possessing Nicole in life and death, so much so that he talks her into a failed suicide pact, and Boaz/Schiller/Mailer are obsessed with the notion of getting hold of Baker's hot letters to Gilmore—clearly, not only because they are interested in their historical value. As the Gilmore story evolves in *The Executioner's Song,* Nicole emerges as the object of scriptive and bodily exchanges in a world of violent, ambitious men. She is the medium and catalyst for male rivalries that are acted over her female, yet "elfin," homoeroticized body as well as the texts of her letters and interviews.

At one point, Gilmore reminds Nicole—whose voice, in the mind of the novel's narrative authority, "never stumbled when it told the truth"—that in an early letter "you talk of climbing in my mouth and sliding down my throat with a strand of your hair to mend the worn spot in my stomach (486–87; italics deleted). In this grotesque image, supposedly generated by Nicole herself, the female body becomes the consumable item in the formation of criminalized identity. Through this figure, Nicole is incorporated into Gilmore's soon-to-be-executed body in the final spectacle of Deleuze and Guattari's "paranoid regime" of signs, where embodied forms of signification refer in endless, metonymic chains to other forms of signification; or in Deleuze and Guattari's domestic example:

Your wife looked at you with a funny expression. And this morning the mailman handed you a letter from the IRS and crossed his fingers. Then you stepped into a pile of dog shit. You saw two sticks on the sidewalk positioned like the hands of a clock. They were whispering behind your back when you arrived at the office. It doesn't matter what it means, it's still signifying. The sign that refers to other signs is struck with a strange impotency and uncertainty, but mighty is the signifier that constitutes the chain.[13]

The paranoid regime of *The Executioner's Song* extends this process to the community of Provo, for whom Gilmore is the master signifier who constitutes the chain, and within which Nicole is a cipher who serves as the excuse, as it were, for male exchanges. Figuratively, she is consumed by and heals Gilmore's body, itself soon consumed by the state and body politic in order to heal the necessary and constitutive wound caused by his violence, now (after the execution) contained and explained by the disciplinary procedures—taped story and trial transcript—of Provo and its citizens.[14]

In the novel's afterword, Mailer notes that he has edited some of Gilmore's letters to match the expression with the quality of mind he senses in a man he apparently never met; on the other hand, he does not mention making even minor changes to Nicole's telegraphic and often ungrammatical letters. Baker, then, is one kind of transparency among many in *The Executioner's Song* that men talk over or talk through in an effort to get at Gilmore and maintain the system of male exchanges. Nicole serves, at the heart of the novel's consensual fantasy, as one sign for coincidence writ large, a translucent and illusory difference floating amid an all-encompassing assemblage of concordant representations both centered on and issuing from the inverted paranoid subject, Gilmore. Nowhere is this more evident than in a jailhouse exchange between Gilmore and Gibbs, the latter having just revealed that he has "a kid sister living in Provo who was married to a fellow named Gilmore" (Mailer, *Executioner's Song*, 367). The cellmates then decide to compare curricula nitae:

Gary made a list: they had both spent a lot of time in prison, Gibbs in Utah and Wyoming, himself in Oregon and Illinois. Prior to prison, they had gone to Reform School. Both were considered hard-core convicts. Both had done a lot of time in Maximum Security. Both had been shot in the left hand whilst in the commission of a crime. Neither of them cared for their fathers. Both fathers were heavy drinkers and dead now. Gilmore and Gibbs both loved their mothers, who were religious Mormons and lived in small trailer courts. . . . On top of that, the first two letters of both their last names were "GI" although neither had ever seen the armed services. Their first experience of drugs was in the early '60s and they both used the same drug, Ritalin, a rare type of speed not in common use.

"Had enough?" Gilmore asked.

"Hit me," said Gibbs.

Well, Gary could point out that prior to their arrests, they had both been living with 20-year old divorcées. Each of them met the girl through her cousin. Each of the girls had two children. The first was a 5-year-old daughter, a brunette, whose name started with an *S*. Each girl had a 3-year-old son by another marriage. Both little boys were blondes and their names started with a *J*. Both Nicole and Gibbs's girlfriend had mothers whose first name was Kathryne. (368)

Gibbs is impressed with Gilmore's ability to draw parallels, and begins to seriously consider Gary's theories regarding fate and reincarnation as a result of this astounding, if absurdly protracted, list of similarities borne of prison-cell boredom and bull. Meanwhile, the voice of narrative authority masked as indirect discourse (Gibbs "speaking" after the fact) opines, "of course, Gary hadn't hit the difference. Gibbs's girl was nothing to look at, and Nicole was beautiful. After Gibbs saw the way she put herself out for Gary, he decided she must also be beautiful inside" (368). In this offhand manner, Nicole is transformed into a kind of capital as she becomes the specious embodiment of negated difference that allows these inmates—who otherwise spend much of their time telling each other stories of violence against men—to grow intimate with each other. She is "beautiful inside," Gibbs voyeuristically imagines, because she "puts out" for his roomie, her interiority exteriorized, her body converted to sign as she becomes the object of discourse. This is a difference that makes no difference, for Nicole becomes the symmetrical grammar through which Gibbs and Gilmore mirror themselves as the same. As Lynda Zwinger has argued, "the desire for symmetry . . . turns out to be a particularly effective policing device for heterosexual ideology," one of many ideologemes of symmetry that reinforce each other in the fiction of consensus that relies on the historical centrality of Gilmore's criminality.[15] Heterosexual ideology inheres in the Gilmore story, where the female body functions as the homoerotic medium of exchange between men, the illusory difference (as with N. in *The Shadow Knows,* her inside and outside conflated) that mediates, as a form of representation, the bipolar system of crime and punishment exhibited in Gilmore's killings and execution.

The Executioner's Song portrays a cultural order in which the repression of homoeroticism leads to a version of heterosexuality where women become objects of exchange, but just barely so, within the terms that Gilmore employs in the representation of his elfin "Pardner." The work of this repression is present in the violence against men that Gilmore inflicts on his victims and that, in turn, is inflicted on him; male violence and its consequences signal that the system of crime and punishment that depends on the consensual, paradoxical abjection and assimilation of criminality is operating smoothly. No wonder, then, that Gilmore, who styles himself in the mode of the cowboy outlaw, is more than a little disturbed to find that the name on his birth certificate reads "Fay Robert Coffman," a name his stepfather insists on but that his natural mother, Bessie, later changes because she thinks it will embarrass him. She renames him Gilmore, her married name at the time of her son's birth, and Gary, "because she loved Gary Cooper" (Mailer, *Executioner's Song,* 313). We only have to think of the eerily similar nominal conversion of another celluloid cowboy hero—that of John Wayne (born with the first name of Marion, which to indulge in the harmonization of contingencies typical of *The Executioner's Song,* is also the name of the Illinois town where Gilmore is imprisoned before coming home to murder in Utah)—to see how unwittingly accurate Mailer's novel is in making the connection between male paranoia and gender anxieties. The cultural paranoia of *The Executioner's Song,* doubly disseminated by means of the consensus reached over Gilmore in Provo and the formation of that consensus through the novel's overdubbing of voices, is activated through a system of reciprocity that implicitly affirms Gilmore's decision to make the law keep its word about the retributive chain of male exchanges he has initiated: an eye for an eye, a bullet for a bullet.

Pursuing the thread of male violence and homoeroticism enacted across the bodies of women in *The Executioner's Song* reveals the degree to which the processes of normalization and consensus that operate across the multitudinous stories and voices of the novel are integral to the formation of a narrative community, homologous to the national formations of *Libra* or *JFK,* in which Gilmore becomes the retrospective, fated, paranoided subject of a disciplinary history that preserves the symmetry of violent reciprocity. As an assemblage sutured up or voiced over into a singular history, *The Executioner's Song,* fittingly, enables a reflection on the nature of "true-life stories" as they are represented in a novel where the question of how Mailer got the story is elided in the author's forging of a consensual fiction. The commodification and consumption of stories is at issue here, for the Gilmore story becomes interesting only when it is made consumable, that is, only when the spectacle of his body being consumed by the state in payment for other bodies becomes an imminent possibility. As Nicole is figuratively swallowed by Gilmore, so Gilmore and his story are swallowed whole by the public to "mend the worn spot in [its] stomach" as a kind of medicine or food that will satisfy the hunger for stories that construe imaginary differences within the paranoid regime of repetition, symmetry, and reciprocity (the quanta of consensus), while simultaneously patching over any holes in the logic of that regime: this illuminates Gilmore's commodification as both symptom of and cure for the disorder—as nomad, criminal, or other—that he brings into the habitus of Provo.

As Gilmore comes to know Nicole, he tells her prison stories. In an odd moment of either self-consciousness, or concealed, postmortem Mailerian commentary, Gilmore acknowledges that "when his stories got too boiled down, when it got like listening to some old cowboy cutting a piece of dried meat into small chunks and chewing on them, why then he would take a swallow of beer and speak of his Celestial Guitar" (104). Reinvigorating the metaphor of historical actuality as "cut and dried," Gilmore/Mailer figures "story" in terms somewhat less appetizing than those attributed to the embellished tales of Bessie, Gilmore's mother, who "had a fund of stories and passed them out like confections. It was as if she naturally preferred tasty little stories to the depth of those echoes that came up from the past" (465). Whether conceived as beef jerky or bonbons, whether harmonized or sugarcoated and eaten whole in preference to facing the contingencies and derailments of the past, the stories of *The Executioner's Song* are consumable items that satiate the consensual and clearly phallocentric need to construct a version of history that promotes and naturalizes in the convergences of syntax, characteristic, and event the inevitable alignment of things as they are, played on a "Celestial Guitar."

Larry Schiller, the reporter who put the Gilmore story together and whose previous triumph was the selling of "a nude photograph of Marilyn Monroe to Hugh Hefner" that had "obtained the highest price ever for a single picture up to then, $25,000" (600), claims credentials as a true historian because he has mastered "the secret of people who had class[.] . . . they remained accurate to the facts. Schiller called it history. You recorded history right. If you did the work that way, you could end up a man of substance" (ibid.). As Boaz sold tapes of Gilmore recounting jailhouse stories he has shared with Gibbs to Schiller, so Schiller, alleging he has gotten too close to the story, sells it to Mailer, himself a man of substance who has made a fair amount of money from *his* book on Monroe. Like the gossip passed between soldiers in Stone's antihermeneutic figure of historical knowledge, history in *The Executioner's Song* becomes yet another "substance" passed between men as it is processed through a discursive array of aligned signs and ciphers. The novel entails a disciplinary history of law and order, crime and punishment that explains itself as a repression of difference that depends for its work on Gilmore's multiplicity, and the contradictory fear and fetishizing of sameness that fuels this repression. There is money to be made in the tales of the Gilmore murders and execution, there is the social ordering of class to be attained, precisely because they are stories that patch the tears in the cultural fabric that threaten its wholeness and homogeneity. Such paranoid stories sate, as well, the appetite for contrived otherness that substitutes for a confrontation with the terror of history, the nonassimilability of event into pattern, the utter heterogeneity and incomprehensibility of that which cannot be consumed or exchanged. Capitalism and capital punishment, like love and marriage, go together in the Gilmore story. It is a sad, banal, oedipal story that positions Nicole Baker as the body across (or for which) men murder and punish each other, and Gary Gilmore as the body that must be sacrificed for this to go on. Taking place in the far reaches of the new West, *The Executioner's Song* is ultimately an American, Western story, one that articulates Gilmore as a leading symbol in a paranoid cultural imaginary on which systems of discipline and their punitive victims depend.

■ The Cultural Logic of Paranoia: *The Killer Inside Me*

Now, if there is anything worse than being subject to the law of others, it is surely being subject to one's own law. —Jean Baudrillard, *The Perfect Crime*

The superego is a Law in so far as it is not integrated into the subject's symbolic universe, in so far as it functions as an incomprehensible, nonsensical, traumatic injunction, incommensurable with the psychological wealth of the subject's affective attitudes, bearing witness to a kind of "malevolent neutrality" directed towards the subject, indifferent to his empathies and fears. —Slavoj Žižek, *Metastases of Enjoyment*

Like Mailer's Provo, the West Texas towns depicted in Jim Thompson's pulp noirs, bearing such titles as *After Dark, My Sweet, The Grifters, Texas by the Tail, Pop. 1280,* and *Nothing More Than Murder,* are sites of containment and consensus. The "Central City" of *The Killer Inside Me* is depicted as a locale where the conflict and connection between the rule of desire and the "malevolent neutrality" of a communal superego, both homologous to and opposing "one's own law," are negotiated in terms of a paranoid criminality. As its name implies, Central City— a representation of the "All-American" small town of the cold war era with all its racism, misogyny, and celebration of mediocrity—is the embodiment of a "normality" that the novel's narrator both scorns and relies on as cover for the series of murders he commits:

I've loafed around the streets sometimes, leaned against a store front with my hat pushed back and one boot hooked around the other—hell, you've probably seen me if you've ever been out this way—I've stood like that, looking nice and friendly and stupid, like I wouldn't piss if my pants were on fire. And all the time I'm laughing myself sick inside. Just watching the people.

You know what I mean—the couples, the men and wives you see walking along. The tall fat women, and the short scrawny men. The teensy little women, and the big fat guys. The dames with lantern jaws, and the men with no chins. The bowlegged wonders and the knock-kneed miracles. The . . . I've laughed—inside, that is—until my guts ached. It's almost as good as dropping in on a Chamber of Commerce luncheon where some guy gets up and clears his throat and says, "Gentlemen, we can't expect to get any more out of life than what we put into it."[16]

Voyeuristically scrutinizing the quotidian life of Central City as a freak show, its normalized, heterosexually arrayed citizens, "the politest people in the world" (Thompson, 174), converted into grotesque jokes in the eyes of the criminal, the narrator of *The Killer Inside Me* stands in a schizophrenic relation to the inhabitants of the town and the laws they live by, for he is both a multiple murderer and deputy sheriff. The novel, written in the form of a confession, is Lou Ford's attempt to explain the logic of his crimes as well as the contradictions of his status as both inside and outside the law, a complexity that is enhanced by his naturalistic sense that the internal laws of compulsive instinct are in eternal conflict with civil law. Yet Ford's confession—the disclosures of a self-avowed psychopathic paranoid—reveals the extent to which the opposition between the social organization of Central City and the internal drives of its leading criminal is founded on their interdependence. Ford's violent misogyny (what he refers to as "the sickness") is tolerated by the community as a legitimate means of maintaining the symbolic order as long as it remains concealed, "inside" him, and is "properly" deployed to police those marginal to Central City. It is only when this invisible underside of Central City's cultural logic becomes too apparent—when the sadist in the sheriff becomes too visible—that Ford must be expelled as the alien, monstrous element within the body politic.

The murders begin soon after Ford befriends a prostitute, Joyce Lakeland, who lives on the fringe of town. Their brief, sadomasochistic affair allows Ford the opportunity to arrange for the murder of Elmer Conway, the son of a corrupt local contractor who Ford holds responsible for the death of his foster brother, Mike Dean. Ford persuades Elmer, who believes he is in love with Joyce, to elope with the prostitute; the deputy sheriff then beats Joyce nearly to death moments before Elmer's arrival at her house, and kills Elmer with a handgun when he comes on the scene. The sheriff is convinced that he has committed a perfect double murder: the townspeople and authorities, in his view, will believe that Elmer beat Joyce to death in an argument, then shot himself in despair.

Since the story is told after the fact, from the retrospective of the grave (in the novel's climax, Ford is shot and killed by the police), the narrator purposefully withholds information about his own actions until he is ready. In confessing to the reader another murder, which he states has occurred "on the fifth of April, 1952, a few minutes before nine o'clock" (170), he pleads that "I guess I'm not ready to tell about it yet. It's too soon and it's not necessary yet" (171). The confessional point of view of the narrative corresponds to the narrator's obsession with getting the story right, allowing him to generate the illusion, speaking from a time after his own death, that he is reliving events as they occurred. This "reliving" in a proleptic mode, however, also allows him to secrete his crimes (we don't know how he murdered his victims until he tells us), and at the same time, reveal them within the framework of public knowledge and historical fact (we do know, as if reading a confession in the wake of newspaper accounts of the murders, that they have already occurred). The contradictions of the narrator's position vis-à-vis the reader replicate those of his relation to the community of Central City as both its deputy sheriff and local serial killer—a relation, I will argue, that depends on maintaining Ford as the open secret of the law, simultaneously the known and the repressed element of its criminal underside. The error in Ford's modus operandi is that he assumes omniscience about what happens both inside and outside, and thus partakes of an internal fallacy, where gut instinct is always assumed to correspond with occurrence. What he does not know, for example, is that Joyce Lakeland is not really dead but lies in a coma in a Houston hospital where Elmer's father, Chester Conway, has taken her in the hope that she will awaken to reveal the real perpetrator of the crime. The novel's confessional logic has the narrator revealing this "tragic flaw" in his own time (postmortem), thereby reasserting control over the conversion of secrecy into knowledge, even if the secret has been unknown to him in "real time." Thompson's narrative irony in *The Killer Inside Me* suggests that the whole truth can only be spoken after the fact, through a death mask.

The paranoid dialectic of secretion and revelation played out between the narrator and reader, and across the narrator's life and death, is repeated in the game that Chester Conway and the county attorney, Howard Hendricks, play with Ford as they attempt to trap him in the murders that they know he will commit in order to cover up that of Elmer. Their objective, of course, is to frame Ford as a known criminal—as the man who committed the original crime—but in the process of giving him enough rope to hang himself, they must allow for further violence, and yet repress the knowledge of its inevitability and their complicity so that they can apply the law (as the narrator insists on telling the story) in the right way.

Lest we think that the rubric of knowledge/secrecy/disavowal only applies to the aberrant situation of multiple murder, a conversation between Ford and Hendricks reveals that it is standard operating procedure for "normal" life in Central City:

"I guess we're a pretty stiff-necked lot out here, Howard," I said. "I suppose it comes from the fact that this country was never very thickly settled, and a man had to be doggoned careful of the way he acted or he'd be marked for life. I mean, there wasn't any crowd for him to sink into—he was always out where people could see him."

"So?"

"So if a man or woman does something, nothing bad you understand, but the kind of thing men and women have always been doing, you don't let on that you know anything about it. You don't, because sooner or later you're going to need the same kind of favor yourself. You see how it is? It's the only way we can go on being human and still hold our heads up." (67)

"Being human" in the thinly settled plains of West Texas (recall, by contrast, Mailer's commentary on the imaginative paranoia of a thickly settled America) means being inevitably involved in a process of steadily watching one's neighbor who openly discloses her or his small sins under the pretense of secreting them, and acknowledging those transgressions while suppressing that knowledge.[17] This formula is perfectly mirrored in the pursuit and execution by the legal authorities of those criminals who, like Ford, have crossed the line and, in the violent excess of their crimes, too openly reveal the dirty secret of the law. It is, clearly, a formula that enables the prevailing corruption of Central City, extending from the government to the labor unions, as well as its misogyny and racism:

Out here you say yes ma'am and no ma'am to anything with skirts on; anything white, that is. Out here, if you catch a man with his pants down, you apologize . . . even if you have to arrest him afterwards. Out here you're a man, a man and a gentleman, or you aren't anything. And god help you if you're not. (Thompson, 8)

For one character in the novel, Ford's friend Sheriff Bob Maples, this position is untenable, and he commits suicide as the result of his unsuccessful repression of his knowledge of Ford's deeds—a public knowledge that must be sequestered until the right moment when the law acts in its own time to disclose what it knows to be already true.

Once the cycle of violence is initiated, Ford, who participates in the investigations of his own crimes, cooperates with the authorities to fulfill the criminal and law's twinned destinies in his virtual suicide, carried out under the aegis of the execution of justice. Ford next kills Johnnie Pappas, the son of a Greek immigrant whom he has befriended and who is initially jailed for the original murder because he has in his possession a marked bill from the stash of money Elmer carried with him at the time of his murder; the real thief, Ford, has paid Pappas with the money, and stages Pappas's suicide in the courthouse jail. Ford explains to Pappas just before killing him the distorted logic of his incarceration, which serves as the means for the law to disavow its own criminality by embodying it in the marginal inhabitants of Central City—prostitutes, Greeks, anyone who is not white and not a "gentleman":

We're living in a funny world, kid, a peculiar civilization. The police are playing crooks in it, and the crooks are doing police duty. The politicians are preachers, and the preachers are politicians. The tax collectors collect for themselves. The Bad People want us to have more dough, and the Good People are fighting to keep it from us. It's not good for us, know what I mean? If we all had all we wanted to eat, we'd crap too much. We'd have inflation in the toilet paper industry. . . . Yeah, Johnnie . . . it's a screwed up, bitched up world, and I'm afraid it's going to stay that way. And I'll tell you why. Because no one, almost no one, sees anything wrong with it. They can't see that things are screwed up, so they're not worried about it. What they're worried about is guys like you. (118)

In Ford's argument, "guys like you . . . [g]uys who know what makes 'em feel good, and aren't going to be talked out of the motion" (118) includes anyone who does not fully participate in a system of exchange of desire and capital that is legitimated within the socioeconomic order as the proper negotiation between the assemblage of drives and affects that constitutes the ego of identity and the law of the collective superego. Displaced onto the cultural other, criminality is a surplus of desire that cannot be expended in the mirrored, paranoiac processes of disclosure and disavowal that undergrid the normality of Central City. It is a surplus located in the split subject of the novel's narrator, one that must be abjected since, in its visibility, it reveals the nature of the desire that properly channeled and commodified, energizes the novel's Manichaean universe.

Ford goes on to kill his fiancée, Amy Stanton, a schoolteacher who recognizes his "sickness" and appears willing to ignore it; like Joyce, she takes masochistic pleasure in Ford's sadism, and like her, Amy must die simply because she knows too much about Ford. In a reduplication of his original plan, he attempts to stage Amy's murder as committed by an itinerant who tries to blackmail Ford and who Ford will then kill on discovering that he "murdered" Amy; the itinerant escapes, though he is gunned down by the police, who assume that any "bum" running down the street with the deputy sheriff running after him yelling "murder" must be guilty. The murders only cease when enough evidence has accrued against Ford to incarcerate him, first in the county jail, then in the panopticon of the state mental asylum; the evidence against him necessarily includes the corpses of his victims who have been indirectly executed by the state as part of the entrapment plan. Temporarily freed because he cannot be forced to confess, Ford is at last confronted by the legal authorities with "the return of the repressed" in the person of Joyce Lakeland, a marginal embodiment of the "living dead" who survives as the surplus or remnant of desire that cannot be fully contained within or abjected by the cultural system of Central City. As such, she is a witness to Ford's criminality that mirrors the criminality of the system in which he serves as both an officer and transgressor of the law. In an act of self-destruction, Ford rushes forward to kill her once again, knowing that he will thereby provide the excuse for his summary execution at the hands of his fellow police officers.

At the conclusion of the novel, the narrator projects a community of desiring subjects: "All of us who started the game with a crooked cue, that wanted so much and got so little, that meant so good and did so bad. All us folks. Me and Joyce Lakeland, and Johnnie Pappas and Bob Maples and big ol' Elmer Conway and little ol' Amy Stanton. All of us" (244). These names comprise the list of those whose deaths Ford is directly or indirectly responsible for, and they are all people who, in his view, bore a surplus of desire in wanting "so much" and getting "so little." Ford feels that all these desiring victims are "asking" him to murder them because they implicitly know of his "sickness" and, in befriending him, disavow it: "All those people. I'd think, why in the hell did they have to do it—I didn't ask 'em to stick their necks out; I'm not begging for friendship. But they *did* give me their friendship and they *did* stick their necks out" (177). In his mind, what they want from him is the response of the law, or more precisely, the response of the law's violence to the excess of their desire for the law to be visited on them. This sadomasochistic excess of criminal desire is merely a redundancy, rather than an aberration, of the desire that runs through the normalized system of disclosure and disavowal that defines the civic operations of Central City. Underlying the social order in Thompson's novel—an order that operates by virtue of a consensual cultural paranoia as the police watch the criminal watching them criminalize him while he observes his victims "asking" for him to lay down the law of masculine violence—is the relation of a collective sadistic superego to a masochistic ego, of the law to desire that, in its properly disciplined forms, constitutes the norm of that order.[18]

As if to explain to himself on the personal level within the manifest cultural system of discipline and punishment, legality and criminality, the narrator constructs what can be construed as a false etiology of his "sickness," his propensity for violence, especially toward women. In other terms, he identifies himself as the symptom of the social body misdiagnosed as psychosomatic rather than physiological. Declaring himself to a split desiring subject positioned between the application and transgression of the law (to Pappas, he says, "You ask me why I stick around, knowing the score. . . . I guess I kind of got a foot on both fences, Johnnie. I planted 'em there and now they've taken root, and I can't move either way and I can't jump. All I can do is wait until I split. Right down the middle" [Thompson, 119]), Ford traces the beginnings of his "sickness" to vaguely remembered sexual experiences with his father's housekeeper, Helene, in childhood, and the discovery that she and his father had been conducting a sadomasochistic affair before he fires Helene after finding her with his son. As a result of this primal trauma, Ford argues in his confession, he has developed a violent hatred for women, all of whom are mere substitutes for "the woman," Helene. An avid reader of his physician father's books on psychology, Ford also claims that the effects of the trauma can be perceived in his paranoia, his overriding belief that "there was a plot against me" (78), that "things were closing in on me" (137), and finally, according to a textbook definition, that as "the subject" he

suffers from strong feelings of guilt . . . combined with a sense of frustration and persecution . . . his behavior appears to be entirely logical. He reasons soundly, even shrewdly. He is completely aware of what he does and why he does it. That was written about a disease, or a condition, rather, called dementia praecox. Schizophrenia, paranoid type. Acute, recurrent, advanced. (218–19)

Ford's first victim, apparently, was a young girl whom he attacked in his adolescence—a crime that had been blamed on his foster brother, whose "accidental" death is quite possibly an act of revenge against the accused molester. Suffering bouts of the "sickness" throughout his life, Ford "manages" it, and his sporadic impotence, with injections prepared from his father's pharmaceutical supply and through his sadistic relations with women until the series of murders beginning with the attempt on Joyce Lakeland's life. Ford's self-diagnosis thus suggests that his story is merely that of a casebook paranoid, suffering from a repressed homoeroticism (the housekeeper, in his memory, positioned as the castrating phallic mother) that unleashes itself in his sadism and violence against women and the masochistic, feminine "killer inside me." [19]

Yet, as I have indicated, because Ford is situated in relation to the law and the community as both desiring subject and enforcer of the law, Thompson's novel works not merely as a portrait of a split, paranoid character. More important, it serves as a critique of a symbolic order in which Ford is tolerated as a kind of symptom that can be "enjoyed" up to the point that his symptomaticity becomes too referential, revealing with too much visibility the necessary relation of dependence between the normal and aberrant that becomes blatantly manifest when the deputy sheriff is the multiple murderer. Perhaps this is why Ford spends much of his confession searching for the motive behind his crimes (a motive, of course, that "fate" provides in retrospect), as if to underscore the inadequacy of a psychological explanation for both his own deeds and the complicitous operations of the novel's cultural regime. As Ford is paranoid about the world closing in on him, so the legal authorities of Central City appear to be paranoid about him, focusing the spreading and contaminatory violence of the town on a single source that must be exorcised. He is an officer of the law whose violent tendencies are condoned as long as they are confined to official business and consonant with a consensually repressed past—for surely in this small town where everybody is "looking awry" at everybody else, no one is really fooled by the ruse of placing the blame for molestation on Ford's foster brother. Ultimately, Ford is Center City's dirty secret, the killer inside *it* whose work is constitutive of law and order.

The embodiment of sadistic desire, both outlaw and lawman, Ford is a mobile, libidinal subject in Central City, a joker and trickster who is allowed to mock public officials and deride conventional forms of expression in the torrent of ridicule he directs at the clichés that serve as the primary means of communication in this spare, yet claustrophobic environment:

"Another thing about the weather," I said. "Everyone talks about it, but no one does anything. But maybe it's better that way. Every cloud has its silver lining, at least that's the way I figure it. I mean, if we didn't have rain we wouldn't have rainbows, now would we?"

"Lou . . ."

"Well," I said, "I guess I'd better shove off. I've got quite a bit of running around to do, and I don't want to rush. Haste makes waste, in my opinion. I like to look before I leap."

That was dragging 'em in by the feet, but I couldn't hold 'em back. Striking at people that way is almost as good as the other, real way. (Thompson, 5)

This form of a sadistic, linguistic "strike" against convention, often accompanied by the laughter that Ford can barely contain when regarding his fellow citizens on the street, is also a form of masochism, "the triumph of the ego over the superego" that is evidenced in the humor of derision and mockery.[20] Just as he occupies both the position of police officer and criminal, and as he embodies both "hard" masculinity (the beater of women) and "soft" masculinity (affecting revulsion to the description of Joyce's "corpse" to the extent that a fellow officer commiserates, "I keep forgetting you've never become hardened to this stuff" [Thompson, 113]), so Ford is at once the town sadist and town masochist, guiltily, yet mockingly seeking out the public suffering and execution he receives as the punishment for his "sickness." Indeed, as with other articulated postmodern identities I have discussed, it is Ford's very mobility that renders him symptomatic of the cultural paranoia of Central City's cultural imaginary as Thompson portrays it, where law and order operate by virtue of a libidinal economy in which normalcy is the mapping or disciplining of abject, outlawed desire.

In *The Killer Inside Me,* Ford thus functions as the switch point between, in Žižek's terms, the "superego" of the law, which Ford represents as an externality to the internal laws of his sickness, and a kind of cultural "id," or the rule of desire that seeks out its paranoid rationale retrospectively in motives, etiologies, fatalities, and historical explanations: as the narrator claims, "There wasn't any other way of being, and that's all any of us are: what we have to be" (185). The novel is a cultural allegory in which "the public guardians of morality, justice, and power are all whitened sepulchres," and that "detonates some myths of small-town America—the benevolent cop, the kindly physician, the free and open country."[21] Published in 1952 by an author who had been a member of the Oklahoma Communist Party and the Federal Writer's Project, and consequently, was thus investigated by the House Committee on Un-American Activities despite his later disenchantment with the CP, *The Killer Inside Me* explores the sociosymbolic logic of a cold war cultural order turned in on itself, situated within the local citizenry of "all of us" rather than remapped on the global displacements of "them." In this logic, the psychopathology of the paranoid criminal is symptomatic of the interiority of cultural paranoia, externalized as the law that negotiates and disavows its sadistic violence in terms of a public code. It is a logic of exchange in which illegal desire, at once invaginated and abjected, is transmuted into desire capitalized and properly deployed: "If we all had all we wanted to eat, we'd crap too much. We'd have inflation in the toilet paper industry," says Ford, indicating that in Central City, the ratio of desire (and of its abjection) is adjusted to the desirable rate of inflation. Finally, it is a logic that legitimates the internalized displacement and debasing of the other in the misogyny and ethnocentricity of the novel's "screwed up world," which appears to be so only in the eyes of the criminal on this side of the law.

■ Men in Black: *Reservoir Dogs*

The Executioner's Song and *The Killer Inside Me* portray the criminal as an agent whose aberrations are symptomatic of a "sick" world from which he is differentiated and individualized either as a random monstrosity or the traumatic, deviant kernel secreted within a normalized social order. In contrast, the criminal band portrayed in Quentin Tarantino's *Reservoir Dogs* (1992), sporting identical black suits and bearing the aliases of a rainbow of colors, represents the corporate identity of cultural paranoia in the spurious play of uniformity and nominal heterogeneity. The film takes place almost entirely in an abandoned warehouse where a group of thieves rendezvous after a botched diamond heist to consider their alternatives, investigate the presence of a police informant in their midst, and torture a captured rookie cop. The plan for the heist calls for a group of professional criminals, strangers to each other and maintaining false identities such that no participant will know the name or history of any other, to join forces on one occasion only and then disperse to parts unknown. The film commences with a scene in a coffee shop during which the collective, prior to the robbery, trade anecdotes and discuss such topics as Madonna's "Like a Virgin" and the plight of waitresses, as if this nomadic gathering of criminals were the weekly local boys' coffee klatch. During the shoot-out that takes place after the attempted robbery, "Mr. Blue" and "Mr. Brown" are killed, along with several police officers and civilians. "Mr. White" arrives first at the rendezvous point with a badly wounded "Mr. Orange," who is really an undercover cop, followed separately by "Mr. Pink," "Mr. Blonde," who has a captured police officer in the trunk of his car, and finally by "Joe," the orchestrator of the robbery, and his son, "Nice-Guy Eddie." Cutting between conversations among the surviving thieves in the warehouse and flashbacks that recall the scene of the bungled robbery and the formation of the band at the behest of Joe, a criminal boss who plays the market ("ride it out like J. P. Morgan," he counsels an associate) and who fluctuates between the roles of godfather, mother, mastermind, and coach in relation to his "boys," *Reservoir Dogs* fabricates a reflexive narrative of conspiratorial causality founded on mistaken identity, comic accident, and sadistic desire run amok. Compared to *The Killer Inside Me* where criminality is interiorized, in this film inhabited almost solely by males, the identity of the corporate man of postmodern nominalism—whether "blue boy" (police officer) or color-coded jewel thief—is externalized in relation to the schizoid economies of homoerotic desire that materially binds a temporary and nomadic band of men on the run.

As John Harvey remarks in his recent cultural history of male fashion, *Men in Black,* the prevalent wearing of black suits or uniforms by Western men suggests

a dominant meaning . . . associated at once with intensity and effacement: with importance, and with the putting on of impersonality. Alone or in ranks, the man of black is an agent of serious power; and of a power claimed over women and the feminine. Black may be a shadow fallen on the feminine part of man.[22]

For Harvey, men's black dress conveys a double logic in which manifest masculinity and the latency of the repressed feminine are conjoined, where both "intensity and effacement" are at play, and where the schizophrenic "key sociological aspect" of wearing black is revealed: "it steps outside, or sidesteps, the established grades of social class, while at the same time, by its gravity, it immediately creates its own dutiful-disciplinary élite" (238).

The inherent contradictions of wearing black that Harvey notes are embodied in the criminal identities of *Reservoir Dogs.* The intensity of the violence that they inflict on their victims and each other, the rampant, over-the-top emotional intensity of their conversations and the relationships they establish in the brief time of the robbery and its aftermath, exist in contrast to the anonymity of their black suits and false names. As Mr. Pink puts it during one shouting and shooting match, "We're all a little emotional here," and the film seems to veer wildly between moments of dissociation in which detachment and anonymity allow for spectacular exhibitions of sadistic machismo, such as when Mr. Blonde cuts off the bound and gagged policeman's ear and douses him with gasoline, and scenes of male intimacy in which, on one occasion, the hardened professional, Mr. White, responds to Mr. Orange, who is dying from a stomach wound and requests to be held, by maternally cradling him and stroking his hair. Amid bantering scenes in which male anal intercourse is the subject of jokes between men "talking like bitches," as Mr. Blonde and Nice-Guy Eddie refer to each other, or in which Joe scolds the collective for their lack of seriousness by likening them to "young broads in a schoolyard," we witness the unfolding of a criminal plot that relies on utter detachment for its deployment and which results in the gory consequences of the extension of phallic power in the film's multiple mutilations and shootings.

The film's "reservoir dogs" are both outside the law and pale of civility in terms of illegal activities and their ultraviolent sadism, yet they are handpicked for the job from among the criminal "dutiful-disciplinary élite." Many of them, like Mr. White, follow a professional code that distinguishes between normalized and aberrant forms of criminality. As a lavatory conversation between Mr. White and Mr. Pink indicates, the "logical" violence of their corporate professionalism is a standard against which is gauged the psychopathic excess of Mr. Blonde, whose random violence during the robbery initiates the unraveling of the plan and the onset of panic, signifying a threat to the band's fragile fraternal and discursive orders:

MR. PINK (toying with his gun): I mean everybody panics, everybody. Things get tense, it's human nature, you panic. I don't care what your name is, you can't help it. Fuck man, you panic on the inside, in your head. Then you give yourself a couple seconds, you get ahold of the situation; you deal with it. What you don't do is start shooting up the place and start killing people.

MR. WHITE (combing his hair): No, what you're 'sposed to do is act like a fucking professional. Psychopath ain't a professional. Can't work with a psychopath, 'cause you just don't know what those sick assholes gonna do next.

The contrived identities of *Reservoir Dogs,* largely articulated through conversations such as these, are mobilities that are negotiated within and between the conflicted strains of impersonality and intimacy, sadistic violence and mortality—the "shadow fallen on the feminine part of man." These affective oppositions link cops and robbers to the criminal "norm" in scenes of wounding and victimization, psychopathic panic and professionalized conformity.

Within a film that comments metafictively on its status as a framing device for a series of recollected and invented narratives that add up to an explanation for the intensities of emotions and bullets exchanged in the warehouse, the norm is represented as a paranoid construct whose assumed universality is contextual, yet infinitely transferable. The logic of professional normalization developed between Mr. White and Mr. Pink occurs in response to the scene of panic initiated by Mr. Blonde as he sprays bullets haphazardly; it occurs between two men who have just attempted a jewel heist and killed a number of people in the process (though as Mr. White claims, he hasn't killed any "real people," just cops), yet the conversation might as easily occur between executives in the corporate bathroom discussing a colleague's hysterical reaction to a sudden drop in the market. The film is comprised of a series of such reflexive mirrorings in which the relationship between cops and robbers, business and criminal professionals, is collapsed as the fragile structure of narrative negotiations between men that preserves a performative social order disintegrates.

Registering the affective panic that attends its recognitions of the frailty and mutability of the nominative performative of the norm, *Reservoir Dogs* portrays relations between men as an assemblage of opposed impulses. Against the chaos of sadistic desire expressing the paranoia of homophobia unleashed by Mr. Blonde, Mr. White and Mr. Pink posit a modular narrative of professionalism that depends on the naturalization of certain speech, dress, and behavior codes that can be deployed in any circumstance, whether the aftermath of a jewel robbery or a meeting of the board. These codes rely on preconceived knowledge and the upholding of paranoid vigilance regarding informational boundaries for their maintenance: the criminals, for example, operate only on a need-to-know basis, which fuels their justified suspicions regarding a mole in their midst. The incompatible arbitrariness and performative contextualism of the codes and the social order to which they refer are embodied in the names both randomly chosen and determinantly conferred by Joe. The disparities inherent in these acts of naming and professional coding inform the film's central contradiction, which can be stated as the inadequacy of performance to desire. On the one hand, there is the free-flowing homoerotic/homophobic libidinality that pursues multiple trajectories across *Reservoir Dogs,* from the intimacy of Mr. White and Mr. Orange, to the mutilation of the "blue boy" by Mr. Blonde, to the oedipal rivalry for Joe's affections between Eddie and Mr. Blonde vocalized in terms of anal aggression. On the other, there is posited a narrative construction that conveys both an adherence to the universality of the norm—the professional rhetoric of men in black suits following the plan of the robbery—and the nominal specificity that subtends the constructed authenticity of the individualized roles, histories, and names of the film's characters viewed in flashback.

In one sequence, the police mole, Mr. Orange, is shown rehearsing his role as an experienced drug dealer, tutored by a fellow undercover cop who urges him to etch in his memory the details of a simulated criminal history by "making them his own." Mr. Orange's teacher demands that he memorize "the commode story," a comic sequence in which the ersatz dealer encounters a group of ersatz federal agents in a bathroom shown in flashback as if it actually happened, thus acquiring the same historical status as the other flashbacks depicting the "real" story behind the selection of the participants in the planned robbery:

MR. ORANGE: What's the commode story?

TUTOR: It's a scene, man, memorize it.

MR. ORANGE: A what?

TUTOR: Look, man, an undercover cop has got to be Marlon Brando, right. To do this job, you got to be a great actor, you got to be naturalistic, you got to be naturalistic as hell. 'Cause if you ain't a great actor, you're a bad actor; a bad actor is bullshit in this job.

MR. ORANGE: (as he's handed a script): Yeah. What is this?

TUTOR: That's an amusing anecdote about a drug dealer.

MR. ORANGE: What?

TUTOR: Something funny that happened to you while you were doing a fucking job.

MR. ORANGE: I got to memorize all this? This is four fuckin' pages long. . . .

TUTOR: Now the thing is, you got to remember all the details; it's the details that sell the story. Now this particular story takes place in a men's room, so you got to know all the details about the men's room. You got to know if they have paper towels or a blower to dry your hands with. You got to know if the stalls ain't got no doors or not. You got to know if they got liquid soap or that pink granulated powdered shit they used to use in high school, remember? You got to know if they have hot water; if it stinks; if some nasty, lowlife, scum-ridden motherfucker sprayed diarrhea all over one of the bowls. You got to know every detail there is to know about this commode. What you got to do, man, is take all them details and make them your own. While you're doing that you got to remember that this story is about you, and about how you perceived the events that went down. The only way to do that, motherfucker, is to keep sayin' it, and sayin' it and sayin' it and sayin' it.

The tutor insists that Mr. Orange immerse himself in the abject details of this contrived story, thereby converting himself into a vehicle of criminal knowledge whose subjectivity is revealed through the repetitive performance of "sayin' it" and the ability to refer to the manufactured details surveyed by his scrupulous and suspicious auditors. The identificatory logic of *Reservoir Dogs* underlying such scenes as this is one in which simulated, discursive formations that "historically" bind the subject to the social collective are pitted against its libidinal impulses; these are expressed through the letting of blood and exchange of bullets that equalize all bodily identities as corpses in the massacre of the film's finale and level all narratives articulated within the film's reflexive frame.

In its portrayal of the relation between the knowing/known (paranoid) subject bound to a criminal social order that mirrors the social as such, and the libidinality through which the contradictions of its bonds are negotiated and subsumed, *Reservoir Dogs* renders a critique of postmodern performativity and the male subjectivities who inhabit the film. The represented corporate system of libidinal exchanges between men—of violence, intimacy, information, blood, and capital—operates by virtue of a performative model in which individual subjects are mobile and anonymous, yet wedded to specific narratives that simulate a historical background that binds them to a social order animated by homophobia and the paranoia of "who knows what?" or "who knows who?" In its cynicism and black humor, the film depicts this system breaking down. The operatic gore of its finale, in which all the principles (save Mr. Pink) are dead on the floor—reminiscent of the massacres of paranoiac revenge tragedies such as those Pynchon parodies in *The Crying of Lot 49*—reveals the fragility of the circuits of information and desire that exist in the huit clos of the warehouse and among the small society of men it contains. These work only by means of a feeble virtuality—an accumulation of simulated narratives and nominal agreements—that collapses in the face of an eruption of the libidinal energies that invigorate the film's social order.

In this collapse, the binary that undergirds this system of capital and corporeal exchange is revealed: control or death; failing domination over discourse and bodies as delineated in the godfatherly conferral of names, the performance of "sayin' it" until it becomes "one's own," Mr. White's attempts to interrogate his colleagues, Mr. Blonde's torturing of the police officer, or acquiescence to the logical ends of such domination in death, where the only intimacy between these funereal men in black is achieved. That the film casts its reflexive survey of the paranoia of male identity in the criminal mode only reinforces the sense that in the social system it portrays, the other of the criminal—in this assemblage of criminals—the cop, is merely positional. The "blue boy" tortured by Mr. Blonde, another man in uniform differentiated only by color, merely occupies the space made necessary for the focalization of the violence that mirrors the contradictions of the phobic/erotic desire that is circulating among all the film's men. As a kind of supplement— the random element that reveals the tenuous contingencies of the criminal/corporate order—Mr. Pink escapes at the film's end with the loot, the only one to survive the murder-suicides of the closing scenes. It is a lucky escape, for being accidentally in the right place at the right time is the only thing that allows Mr. Pink to avoid the hail of bullets around him. But his name, randomly bestowed by Joe and initially rejected by Mr. Pink because of its homosexual connotations, is revealing as the nominal color associated with a desire that both animates and limns the film's paranoid imaginary, and in so doing, illuminates the logic of its orders.

In its depiction of the criminal band, *Reservoir Dogs* anatomizes what can be termed the corporate logic of late capitalism, whose work takes place in this representation as an apocalyptic exchange of desire and capital between anonymous and mobile male subjects bearing simulated histories. Deploying a series of names and symmetries, the film stipulates that the control mechanisms guiding these exchanges are identical whether one is on this or that side of the law. Informational paranoia, discursive mastery, and homophobic sadism conspire in maintaining the fictions and boundaries of the cultural system registered in the codes of professionalism and nominal distinctions between cops and robbers articulated in the warehouse. When these break down, thwarted by the very energies they seek to economize, the violent and deadly ends of the desire on which this system of capital and corporeal exchange is founded are realized. The nomadic running dogs of *Reser-*

voir Dogs, seen twice in the present and the fabricated past, represent in mutual bloody death a leakage in the libidinal reserves of the symbolic order, an eruption of desire that (con)founds it.

In the works explored in this chapter, that hallmark of postmodernity—the compression of time into space—girds narratives in which official and criminal stories intersect, their contingencies and complicities brought into focus, their character-mobilities serving as embodiments of the symmetrical relation between the legal and felonious. The over-voice of *The Executioner's Song* is positioned well outside or beyond the chronotope of Provo. Through this assemblage, Gilmore is conveyed as a historical figure who represents to the social order from which he demands and receives execution a form of reciprocity in which the temporal delay between cause and effect is dissolved, and the distance between the narrative of random aberration and that of historical pattern is closed in terms of vestigial differences and mirroring correspondences. In *The Killer Inside Me,* the story of the individual subject is one of repetition in which the present is a continuous revisiting of the past; but it is also the repressed criminal/manifest legal story of Central City, a space that exists as a timeless, naturalized realm of prejudice and convention. In the confined space of *Reservoir Dogs,* similitude is the order of the day, the only chronology emerging from a network of fabricated histories related in reverse, via flashback. Together, these works can be seen as indicative of a conception of historical process under postmodernity that sustains cultural paranoia—one in which Deleuzian haecceities and reversals of cause and effect (themselves historical symptoms) are *renarrativized* into destinal stories of contemporary fluid subjects anchored within determinate historical orders. In the exit to this study, I consider a work that scrutinizes this conception and offers alternate, if problematic, representations of historicity that limn the complicitous relation I have drawn between multiplicity, haecceity, and paranoia.

Under History: *Underworld*

■ What I have described as cultural paranoia rests on seemingly contra-dictory conceptualizations of temporality and history that coincide in the narratives of paranoia here considered. Haecceitic temporality, or the segmentation of time into dispersed instances whole unto them-selves that randomly intersect and cohere into events, is the material of a conspiratorial, destinal history founded on the retrospective forging of connections between those scattered instances. Such a view of tem-porality both withholds and promises to reveal the one, true, secret history of the real—the latent destiny—that was always there, awaiting discovery by the canny witness, participant, or historian. Postmodern-ist senses of identity as multiple and fluid, both at the periphery and yet the center of disconnected events awaiting amalgamation in a reve-latory history, constitute the agency of cultural paranoia that induces the characters of the assassin, the apocalyptic nomad, the serial killer, or the executor who serve doubly as objects and sources of paranoia in the narratives I've discussed. Whether it is the history of the cold war or the biography in interviews and letters of a capital criminal, history under this rubric is merely the totalized backdrop—a "homogeneous, empty time" that could be characterized as a spatiotemporal collage of particular instances—for the titanic struggle between them and us as these agenting tags become attached to the mobilities of self, party, clan, or nation.[1]

Derrida writes in *Spectres of Marx* that it is this history that con-tinues to inhabit the postmodern, post–cold war West, the avatar of late capitalism and globalization. In this critique of what he calls "anachrony," the "doubtful presence of contemporaneity to itself," Derrida argues that it is impossible to come into contact with the materiality of history as long as we continue to rely on what I have suggested is the temporality of contemporary cultural paranoia: "a general temporality . . . made up of the *successive* linking of presents identical to themselves and contemporary with themselves."[2] Yet, in anachrony, we are haunted by a specter—the ghost of a past that is nonpresent, noncontemporaneous, or the immaterial other of what is present to us that paradoxically conveys the utter materiality of a history that we have sublimated. And for Derrida, it is precisely this haunted anachrony, analogous to Deleuzian haecceity or Lyotardian intensity, that girds our paranoia, for the past, repressed *as* past in the totalized present of our "time out of joint," is experienced as a "spectral *someone* [that] *looks at us*":

We feel ourselves being looked at by it, outside of any synchrony, even before and beyond any look on our part, according to an absolute anteriority . . . and asymmetry, according to an absolutely unmasterable disproportion. Here anachrony makes the law. To feel ourselves seen by a look which it will always be impossible to cross, that is the *visor effect* on the basis of which we inherit from the law. (*Spectres,* 7).

Here, Derrida is analogizing Hamlet's paranoia to that of contemporaneity in articulating a view of the historical utterly dependent on the "spectralizing" of the past in the speculative present for its unfolding *as* history under the law and order of destiny.

The fictions of cultural paranoia I have examined variously convey and critique the anachronistic temporality by which the mutabilities and mobilities of the postmodern identities inhabiting these fictions are ruled. In his compelling assessment of temporality and "commodity culture," and an important contribution to the project of critical postmodernism, John Frow articulates a view of postmodern temporality and history that is neither destinal nor merely disseminated (two seeming opposites that meet in the stories of cultural paranoia), neither eschatological nor haecceitic:

The end of modernity, or the refusal of the simple division in time that the concept works to achieve, is an end of history and the beginning of many histories. This end is radically different from the closure envisaged by Fukuyama: it is neither the climactic self-recognition of spirit in free-market capitalism nor the shattering of the global into a myriad of dispersed and local narratives. It is, precisely, a question of the *linkage* of unequal times in the contingent, shifting, and relatively unstable orderings—political, economic, cultural—which make up our entangled world, and which, while organized as goal-seeking structures, drives toward no predetermined end.[3]

In terms of the discussion of cultural paranoia, this is a revealing but problematic formulation. It suggests that paranoia thrives on "linkage" and the dispersion of "history" into "histories" that, in the work of paranoia, become reconnected into the predestined history that was always there in the first place, scattered in the hidden clues of fragmented histories. Yet this concept of a history that is always in the process of being made from multiple, overlapping contingencies and events taking place within an "unequal" temporal framework offers a redress to the narcissistic rendering of history as latent destiny. To be sure, this conceptualization of history is articulated within the cultural, political, and economic parameters of a postmodernity to which there is no outside or beyond. As Frow asserts, there is no "end" to history conceived in these terms. In this and many other senses, Frow's notion of history on trial (*en proces*) and cultural paranoia can be said to inhabit the same conceptual and social space as contingent modes of working through history and the identifications with the social order symptomatic of this process.

As a novel that renders in contrapuntal terms the trials of contemporary U.S. history, Don DeLillo's *Underworld* provides not an answer or alternative to cultural paranoia that takes us beyond it and, analogously, beyond the cold war world that supposedly stands as its fullest embodiment. Instead, in generating partial linkages between unequal times and contingent histories, *Underworld* shows the extent to which history in these times is a process that is entangled but not whole, narratable but not complete, and entirely dependent on the adjacency and complicity of its competing versions.[4] The sense of history conveyed by DeLillo's knotted fictionalization of the United States during the cold war is that cultural paranoia is not a social disorder, or merely a form of public hysteria framed within cold war politics and correctable by an appeal to historical evidence, but an integral part of what constitutes postmodern history.[5] *Underworld* simply proposes that paranoia is not all of the story: there are other historical processes at work, other kinds of history, that are partially reliant on and yet radical departures from the paranoid view of history that seems so symptomatic of the postmodern condition. As I shall indicate in the brief reading of *Underworld* that concludes this study, for DeLillo, we live within—we have lived through—a history of paranoia, but we are more than just paranoid.

Structurally, the massive assemblage of *Underworld* can be viewed as a historical ruin collapsed around the sundered foundation of a monumental history. The novel is rendered as a series of disconnected and partially connected scenes, sketches, and arrangements that occur sporadically from the 1950s to the 1990s bordered by a prologue (titled "The Triumph of Death," and published in an earlier version as "Pafko at the Wall") and an epilogue (titled "Das Kapital"). DeLillo frames this cold war narrative with, at one end, an account of Bobby Thompson's home run in the 1951 National League play-offs—"the shot heard round the world" that occurred on the same day as the above ground explosion of an atomic bomb by the USSR that commenced the weapons race—and at the other, a surrealistic vision of paranoid identities disseminated into virtual worlds, fulminating the paradox of the scattered, destinal self made global. The novel can be viewed as encapsulating multiple instances of "time out of joint" in threading the myriad, contingent yet "necessary" filiations between unraveling personal destinies and global history seemingly spinning out of control. Constructed as an archive or "arcade," in Walter Benjamin's sense, a "dialectical fairy tale,"[6] *Underworld* conveys the collective fantasies of U.S. national culture during the cold war era, and in skewing the relation between historical agency and historical process, performs an ideological unmasking of them.

The irony of the circumstance in which the assumptions that found such fantasies are largely about history as the site on which the inevitable or accidental collision between national and individual destinies takes place is not missed by DeLillo, who seeks in *Underworld* to show to what degree the formation of postmodern identity (which in the novel's terms, is synchronous with the formation of cold war, national identities) is a forgotten appointment with the real of history. One of the novel's chief actors, Nick Shay, is a waste systems entrepreneur whose job it is to locate sites for the disposal of hazardous waste materials—a global occupation that takes him at the novel's end to a nuclear test site in the former USSR where some of the mock-ups of U.S. suburbs, containing houses still full of canned goods available on U.S. grocery shelves in the 1950s, still stand. Nick is at the site to witness an underground test that will putatively destroy a consignment of plutonium, using radiation, as it were, to obliterate radiation. The paranoid circularity and self-mirroring of this "official" history of cold war waste and its disposal is made adjacent in the novel to Nick's own, disastrous personal history and that of other protagonists. As a teenager growing up during the 1950s in the Bronx, Nick has accidentally shot a man and been convicted of involuntarily manslaughter: *Underworld* thus sporadically traces Nick's story across the cold war as he moves from childhood to middle age. In generating a loose system of disconnected sketches and narratives that bear relation to Nick's story only by virtue of contingency, DeLillo succeeds in making the novel not about Nick or any other character but about history per se as the site where the events of personal lives and those of world historical shifts and movements collide and intersect *both* accidentally and fatally. History is projected as a missed destination in *Underworld,* and it is the multiple senses of history represented in the novel to which we must turn in order to understand how DeLillo renders a view of postmodern identity constructed within historical experience that is other than (just) paranoid.

The prologue of *Underworld* offers a theatricalization of the conflicting senses of history that inform the novel's multiple narratives, but all—no matter how contradictory—reflect identifications between individuals or the crowd and history as the record of collective desire. Beginning with the premise that the temporal coincidence of the two "shots heard round the world" is the manifestation of sheer historical process, as if history momentarily takes off the mask of anonymity in happenstance, the novel proceeds to seek the explanation for this concurrence that signifies the commencement of the cold war, which is to seek the explanation for the presence (or absence) of history as such. This originary or divinatory view of history, which *Underworld* fractures into the manifold historiographies undergirding its scattered narratives, is commented on by DeLillo in an interview. Asked when he first became aware of the coincidence of Bobby Thompson's home run and the explosion of a Soviet nuclear weapon, DeLillo, who here takes on the role of the fortunate author, replies:

I was reading the newspaper one morning in October, 1991, and there was a story about the fortieth anniversary of the legendary ball game between the Giants and Dodgers. . . . I read it and forgot all about it, but several weeks later began to think about it again in a different context—historical. It seemed to be a kind of unrepeatable event, the kind of thing that binds people in a certain way. Not only people who were at the ballpark, but fans in general and even nonfans who were not necessarily interested in the baseball implications. There was the sense, for me, that this was the last such binding event that mainly involved jubilation rather than disaster of some sort. Anyway, I went to the library and found a reel of microfilm for the *New York Times* of the following day, October 4, 1951. I didn't know what I was looking for, but what I found was two headlines, symmetrically matched. It was like fitting together two pieces of ancient pottery. One headline concerned the ballgame, "Giants capture pennant," and so on. The other headline concerned an atomic test that the Soviet Union had set off in Kazhakstan. Very few details were given, but the two bold matching headlines caused a sort of pause in me. There was a strong sense of the power of history, and this is what got me started thinking about the Cold War.[7]

In this comment on the conceptual origins of *Underworld* where his "thinking about the Cold War" begins, DeLillo views the historicity of Thompson's home run as dependent on its nonrepeatability as an event and its capacity to generate an identification between those who have personally witnessed it and those who have merely read or heard about it after the fact. Then, in DeLillo's narrative of the novel's beginnings, a second identification occurs. Inspired by the eschatological sense that this is the last event of its kind, the author searches the historical record for parallels or confirmation, and finds the twinned headlines, "symmetrically matched," which then instills "a strong sense of the power of history."

The novel that follows, *Underworld,* can be understood as an attempt to ask, Where does that power reside? From whence does it come? In DeLillo's anecdote, historicity seems to issue from a combination of unrelated contingencies (Thompson's home run; the nuclear test; the presence or absence of "fans and nonfans"; DeLillo's reading about the fortieth anniversary of the ballgame and his later recollection of a forgetting of that reading; the luck of research) that *become* related through the "power of history," which in this instance is really a form of authorial power, of "fitting [things] together [like] two pieces of ancient pottery." DeLillo, I would argue, is quite conscious of the fact that this perception of history is both exfoliated and deconstructed in the novel's prologue as underlying a version of originary, authorial, destinal history that instantiates the paranoiac binding of selves to nations and stories resulting in the historical identities of the cold war. In this interview and the prologue to *Underworld,* where DeLillo seems to emphasize the fatedness of a kind of conspiracy of people and events that serves as the clearest manifestation of history at work, he simultaneously gestures toward the flimsiness of the foundation on which such conspiracies — and such identities — are constructed: the frailty of perceived symmetries; the inadequacy of memory; the unreliability and spectrality of news, rumor, witnessing. In portraying the contradictions of the authorial, hermeneutic history that purportedly stands at the origin of a novel that theatricalizes the origins of cold war identities and politics, and in depicting the novel's many other forms of history as haunted by the specter of this one, DeLillo effectively reveals the extent of our bondage to a logic of multiplicitous identity parsed through a singular narrative that only becomes "historical" by accident, through the transformation of contingency into fatality.

In *Underworld*, the power of history is both omnipresent and scattered, vestigial. Against the backdrop of a monolithic cold war era, history in *Underworld* is a pastiche of a thousand actualities brought into contact by chance or circumstance, or in the afterglow of coincidence. The novel moves along several "lines of flight": the track of Thompson's home run baseball, grabbed, stolen, and auctioned off until it apparently finds its way into the hands of Nick Shay; the daily progress of the Cuban missile crisis paired with a succession of Lenny Bruce's comedy routines performed during the fateful confrontation between the United States and the Soviet Union; the life and career of Klara Sax, a postmodern artist who has had an affair with Nick during the days of his youth in the Bronx; the path that contaminated waste follows as it is moved to various sites on the planet. The assemblage of narrative tracings that constitute *Underworld* reveal diasporic senses of history that can neither be categorized nor gathered together as a whole history made up of multiple parts.

History in *Underworld* is, for Nick Shay, the "microhistory" of the crowd in an airport:

Coming home, landing at Sky Harbor, I used to wonder how people disperse so quickly from airports . . . people with their separate and unique belongings, the microhistory of toilet articles and intimate garments, the medicines and aspirins and lotions and powders and gels, so incredibly many people intersecting on some hot dry day at the edge of the desert.[8]

Alternatively, history is "the generational tides of beer and shit and cigarettes and peanut shells and disinfectants and pisses in the untold millions" (DeLillo, *Underworld*, 21) layered on the floor of a ballpark men's room. It is the endless procession of the commodities and brand names of U.S. culture: "Johnson & Johnson and Quaker State and RCA Victor and Burlington Mills and Bristol-Meyers and General Motors . . . the venerated emblems of the burgeoning economy, easier to identify than the names of battlefields or dead presidents" (39). History in *Underworld* is, by turns, oral, visual, and written; it is, in its variations, repressed, collective, incremental, apocalyptic, consumable, paranoiac, chaotic. It is "the people's history" as the famed baseball announcer Russ Hodges conceives it, or events as personally experienced and passed onto future generations:

Russ thinks this is another kind of history. He thinks they will carry something out of here that joins them all in a rare way, that binds them to a memory and a protective power. . . . [F]ans at the Polo ground today will be able to tell their grandchildren—they'll be the gassy old men leaning into the next century and trying to convince anyone willing to listen, pressing in with medicine breath, that they were here when it happened. (59–60)

Yet history in the novel is just as much a matter of simulation, or "experience" converted into its own imitations and reproductions, as is the case when Klara Sax views an installation of dozens of television sets stacked on each other in rows, each showing the Zapruder film in endless loops:

Different phases of the sequence showed on different screens and the spectator's eye could jump from Zapruder 239 back to 185. . . . The TV wall was a kind of game board of diagonals and verticals . . . interlocking tarots of elemental fate. . . . She thought to wonder if this home movie was some crude living likeness of the mind's own technology, the sort of death plot that runs in the mind. (495–96)[9]

The representation of history in this scene as the accidental synchronicity of images stands in stark contrast to that which views history as almost an oral materiality—the odor of "medicine breath"—passed down through the generations in patrilineal fashion. It is decidedly an aspect of DeLillo's strategy in the novel to set conflicting nations of history alongside each other, not in order to compare them in terms of accuracy or authenticity, nor to intimate that together they would make the entirety of "History," but to suggest that there is no history as such to be focalized as plots and cabals, only partial and fragmented histories that collide, overlap, and—in utter contradiction—accidentally conspire.

There is one figure of history that predominates in *Underworld:* that of history as litter or waste. At the historic baseball game, historicity and the crowd's identification with the event is marked by trash and "pocket litter" (echoing one of the historical tropes of *Libra*) that rains down from the crowd upon Andy Pafko as he runs into the clubhouse after Thompson's homer,

[the] laundry tickets, envelopes swiped from an office . . . crushed cigarette packs . . . pages from memo pads and pocket calendars . . . snapshots torn to pieces . . . happy garbage now, the fans' intimate wish to be connected to the event, unendably, in the form of pocket litter, personal waste, a thing that carries a shadow identity. (44–45)

For Marvin Lundy, a collector of baseball memorabilia, history is litter recollected, "come to rest" in the home of a souvenir to be found in "The Float," a Pynchonian zone of nomadic bodies and free-floating desire:

All that twilight litter. Maybe some of it was sitting here today, preserved by the stadium sweepers and eventually entering the underground of memory and collection, some kid's airplaned scorecard, a few leaves of toilet tissue unfurled in jubilation from the upper deck, maybe autographed delicately by a player, the scatter of the ball game come to rest all these years later, a continent away. (321)

The figure of history as trash or waste is, for Brian Glassic, Nick's colleague who betrays him in adultery, extended into a metaphor for the telos of Western culture and civilization as he contemplates work at a waste disposal site:

He imagined he was watching the construction of the Great Pyramids of Giza —only this was twenty-five times bigger, with tanker trucks spraying perfumed water on the approach roads. He found the sight inspiring. All this ingenuity and labor, this delicate effort to fit maximum waste into diminishing space. The towers of the World Trade Center were visible in the distance and he sensed a poetic balance between that idea and this one. Bridges, tunnels, scows, tugs, graving docks, container ships, all the great works of transport, trade and linkage were directed in the end to this culminating structure. . . . Brian felt a sting of enlightenment. He looked at all that soaring garbage and knew what his job was all about. Not engineering or transportation or source reduction. He dealt in human behavior, people's habits and impulses, the uncontrollable needs and innocent wishes, maybe their passions, certainly their excesses and indulgences but their kindness too, their generosity, and the question was how to keep this mass metabolism from overwhelming us. (184)

For Glassic, clearly relying on the figural cliché of "the trash heap of history," the transportation and accumulation of waste represents human desire historicized. The "habits and impulses, the uncontrollable needs and innocent wishes" of a million individuals are materially registered in this mass grave of desire's residue from which issues another history, as evidenced in a conversation between Nick and Viktor Maltsev, a cold war Russian historian turned post–cold war nuclear waste disposal specialist:

I tell Viktor there is a curious connection between weapons and waste. I don't know exactly what. . . . He says maybe one is the mystical twin of the other. . . . He says waste is the devil twin. Because waste is the secret history, the under-history, the way archaeologists dig out the history of early cultures, every sort of bone heap and broken tool, literally from under the ground. (791)

Partially echoing the novel's title, history "under the ground" at the nuclear test/disposal site inculcates the mass thanatopic desire that arguably has driven the politics and history of the cold war. At the monumental waste site that Glassic visits, the "mass metabolism" of the heaps of garbage seems to demarcate a contradictory "underhistory" both in the remnants of human contact and "generosity," and the by-products of desire's excesses (ranging from Lundy's career-long pursuit of the mythical baseball to the overproduction of objects and the obscenities of packaging). Like the narrative of Nick's boyhood, interrupted by catastrophe, or the stories of betrayal associated with possession of the one and only home-run baseball, the spectral or underhistory of waste and the pursuit of the objects of desire in *Underworld* runs on a parallel historiographic track to that of the official history of the cold war recorded elsewhere, in the history books.

Indeed, in *Underworld,* underhistory is the only history: the events of the Cuban Missile Crisis are related through a succession of Lenny Bruce routines; the violent racial conflicts of the 1960s and 1970s are symptomatized in the encounters between a white paranoid nun and "Moonman," an African American revolutionary and graffiti artist; the conspiratorial political actions of the FBI during the cold war are represented not through the revelations of declassified files but through De-Lillo's rendition of J. Edgar Hoover's homophobic obsession with cleanliness in his private life. The novel bears the same title in translation of a rediscovered Eisenstein film (*Unterwelt*) suppressed by the Soviet authorities that Klara views on its debut in New York. DeLillo's fictional reconstruction of this putatively lost film portrays the "desiring machine" of the libidinally repressed masses, laboring and struggling for survival, who are "beneath" history, yet whose unrecorded existence is the engine and symptomatic resource of official histories. In writing a novel about cold war America, inspired by the intersection of two historical events that mark its inception, DeLillo replaces history with a patchwork of underhistories that collectively accumulate as massive, monumental desire whose quantifiable metabolism produces qualitative changes that materialize in the events of public history.

It is the relation between history under the ground and the history of the official record—between the history of desire marked by waste and loss, and the history of nation or world—that DeLillo pursues in *Underworld* through a narrative inversion in which official history is represented only indirectly as the symptomatic, destined, yet processional outcome of underhistory. This inverted relation is one in which historical symptomaticity is located in the official version documented in headlines and on the news, while the real history of desiring "underneath" accumulates, transforming the quantity of desire into the qualitative change that is registered *as* history, producing as its residue both waste and event. *Underworld* illustrates both the rift and connection between official histories and underhistory, or the splitting of historical representation from its origins in collective desire; these origins are marked *in* history only by the residue of waste (commodities, bodies, radioactive materials) and the contingency of monumental hoadlines, demarcating occurrence and the conspiracy of events far after the fact. The Benjaminian, symptomatic conceptualization of history revealed in *Underworld* is one in which History, capitalized, is but the semiotic tracing of underhistory's currents.[10] The novel enacts history as a disseminative process through which collective desire is converted into event and transformed into the signs and objects that convey the historical real. It thus signifies the "dis-identification" of history with desire, which as Derrida makes clear, is to bring time out of joint, as the medium of disjunction, back into the picture: the piles of waste where historical material decays in half-life figure the disjunct, temporalized relation between desire and History. In *Underworld*, the representational gap between desire and History is also a temporal one—a delay, shift, or disconnection between competing and partial historical narratives, between the inception of mass desire (always seen in the aftermath as a recognition of fateful contingencies) and its residue.

The complex view of historical process manifested in *Underworld* offers a variance from the "anachrony" of cultural paranoia that, as we have seen in chapter 1, is theorized in postmodern thought as the "zero time" of the utopian libidinal subject. A molecular energy, an intensity moving at random on "the great libidinal skin," this subject is "beyond" history, the transcendent product of late capitalism in that it is instantiated within the dispositif of this epoch, yet is tracked as a sign of "the end of history." As I have claimed throughout, this is also at once the subject of paranoia. In *Underworld*, the epiphanic desire to be at history's end—which for DeLillo, is the "kernel" of the national desire for cold war supremacy and our manifest destiny as arbiter of the "new world order" in the post–cold war era—is historically framed as the impossibility of the subject beyond time, adrift in paranoia. In the novel's final scenes, we witness Sister Edgar, the paranoid nun, surfing the net, visiting the "H-bomb home page" (825), and linking up in cyberspace with "Brother Edgar," the deceased, paranoid director of the FBI:

Here in cyberspace she . . . is not naked exactly but in the open—exposed to every connection you can make on the world wide web.

There is no space or time out here, or in here, wherever she is. There are only connections. Everything is connected. All human knowledge gathered and linked, hyperlinked, this fact referenced to that, a keystroke, a mouse-click, a password—world without end, amen.

But she is in cyberspace, not in heaven, and she feels the grip of systems. . . . She senses the paranoia of the web, the net. There's the perennial threat of virus of course. Sister knows all about contamination and the protective measures they require. This is different—it's a glow, a lustrous rushing force that seems to flow from a billion distant net nodes.

When [she] decide[s] on a whim to visit the H-bomb home page . . . [s]he sees the flash, the thermal pulse. She hears the rumbling, the great gathering force rolling off the 16-bit soundboard. . . . She sees the shock waves and feels the power of false faith, the faith of paranoia. . . .

A click, a hit, and Sister joins the other Edgar. . . . The bulldog fed, J. Edgar Hoover, the Law's debased saint, hyperlinked at last to Sister Edgar—a single fluctuating impulse now, a piece of coded information.

Everything is connected in the end.

Sister and Brother. A fantasy in cyberspace and a way of seeing the other side and a settling of differences that have less to do with gender than with difference itself, all argument, all conflict programmed out. (825–26)

In this vision of digital apotheosis, where everything is exposed and connected, both scattered and linked, arrived at by chance yet fatefully destined, the extremes of the dialectic of cultural paranoia are collapsed into each other. Cyberspace as represented in this passage is a site of sheer, instantaneous connectivity taking place in a dimension beyond space and time. Yet this infinitely open site of pure flow (compare it with Mailer's view of the "landlocked American imagination") is also one of paranoid ultimacy. Here, the multiplicity of available connections, destinations, and personalities is foreclosed by association, by the fact that the content of the net imagined as a space where chance and conspiracy merge is nothing but code, or ciphers available to every possible linkage.[11] In this anachronistic site of indifference (where difference itself has been programmed out), there are no underhistories, no partial, conflicting, deferred narratives where the differences between desire, identity, and event play themselves out. In *Underworld,* DeLillo does not so much posit Sister Edgar's and J. Edgar Hoover's "cute meet" in cyberspace as the future of subjectivity, as he suggests that this is the desired state *of* subjectivity in the end, as the culmination of the novel's cold war. Recalling that in the entry, I stated that one of the reasons for our current fascination with paranoia has to do with a sense that it is the last epistemology, our final purchase on knowledge before it passes away into information, in this scene of perfect mirroring and symmetry, DeLillo posits paranoia as the idealized condition of knowing in the moment when identity has become multiple, virtual, and open to all of the available connections. This is a (non)time and (non)space beyond history; yet pursuing the novel's logic, it is consequence and desideratum of monumental history—the history of all the real and figurative cold wars where the polarities of inside and out side, them and us, accident and fate, manifest and latent destiny, have reigned. In between monumental history and cybernetic posthistory is all the content of *Underworld,* the material underhistories rendered immaterial in cyperspace.

The cyberspace of the novel's closing scenes is, to be sure, a caricature, but one in which, ironically, the connection between paranoia and multiplicity is mapped, where this cybernetic version of postmodern identity is historically booked as result and end of the cold war. In this study of cultural paranoia, I have attempted to show the extent to which contemporary narratives demarcate the linkage between the desire for identificatory mobility and the seemingly contradictory drive for connection—for identification within the cultural imaginary—with national and historical destinies that serve to frame identity as gendered, capitalized, and legal. Yet to trace this linkage is not to sublimate it. We are not "done" with paranoia any more than we are "done" with history, and the critique of cultural paranoia can, by no means, take us beyond it. But in recognizing this connection—admittedly, a recognition that is symptomatic of our condition, and thus, produced by it—the narratives of cultural paranoia enable us also to recognize the nonalignments of material identity: the bodies, desires, and disidentifications with the social order that comprise historical being as such. They thereby allow us to imagine a future for identity within the reach of history, to which we are most bound over as subjects when we most misrecognize it.

Notes

Entry: The Time of Paranoia

1   Gilles Deleuze and Félix Guattari, *A Thousand Plateaus: Capitalism and Schizophrenia*, trans. Brian Massumi (Minneapolis: University of Minnesota Press, 1987), 261.

2   My conceptualization and critique of postmodern temporalities follows in chapter 1, but it is deeply informed throughout the book by Fredric Jameson's notions regarding the processes of commodification, periodicity, space, and the "spatialization of time" (*Postmodernism, or, The Cultural Logic of Late Capitalism* [Durham, N.C.: Duke University Press, 1991], esp. 1–54, 154–80), as well as assessments of the "time-space collapse" coming from studies in critical postmodernism, such as those of John Frow (*Time and Commodity Culture: Essays in Cultural Theory and Postmodernity* [New York: Oxford University Press, 1997]), David Harvey (*The Condition of Postmodernity* [Cambridge, U.K.: Blackwell, 1990]), Peter Osborne (*The Politics of Time: Modernity and the Avant-Garde* [New York: Verso, 1995]), and Eric Alliez (*Capital Times*, trans. Georges van den Abbeele [Minneapolis: University of Minnesota Press, 1996]).

3   Slavoj Žižek, *The Plague of Fantasies* (London: Verso, 1997), 7.

4   Eric L. Santner, *My Own Private Germany: Daniel Paul Schreber's Secret History of Modernity* (Princeton, N.J.: Princeton University Press, 1996), xiii.

1   Postmodernity and the Symptom of Paranoia

1   For assessments of postmodern panic and paranoia, see especially Arthur Kroker, Marilouise Kroker, and David Cook, *Panic Encyclopedia: The Definitive Guide to the Postmodern Scene* (New York: St. Martin's Press, 1989), 13–18, 120–27; and Brian Massumi, *The Politics of Everyday Fear* (Minneapolis: University of Minnesota Press, 1993). The most cogent discussions (and implicit

critiques) of schizophrenia as the dominant postmodern structure of feeling are Fredric Jameson, *Postmodernism, or, The Cultural Logic of Late Capitalism* (Durham, N.C.: Duke University Press, 1991); and David Harvey, *The Condition of Postmodernity* (Cambridge, U.K.: Blackwell, 1990), 53–65. See John Farrell, *Freud's Paranoid Quest: Psychoanalysis and Modern Suspicion* (New York: New York University Press, 1996), for a view of the "paranoid slant" as characteristic of a modernism founded on an "intellectual culture [which] depends fundamentally and without limit upon suspicion of the faculties that make it possible" (213). Farrell's provocative notion of paranoia is essentially neoconservative: for him, modern culture is based on a hermeneutics of suspicion (Marx, Nietzsche, and Freud are the main culprits of the plot) that has crippled the fulfilling of the Enlightenment project, generating, to paraphrase Jürgen Habermas, an "incomplete" modernity. Yet one could argue that Farrell's articulation of the problem of modern paranoia is a paranoiac counterformation to the absent subject of postmodernity to which he does not refer for, implicitly, postmodernity is the "hole" in the incomplete project of modernity.

2   Kroker, Kroker, and Cook, *Panic Encyclopedia*, 18.

3   Eric L. Santner, *My Own Private Germany: Daniel Paul Schreber's Secret History of Modernity* (Princeton, N.J.: Princeton University Press, 1996), xiii. Subsequent references will be cited in the text.

The amount of work that has emerged over the past two decades concerning the cold war and post–cold war eras and their symptoms, ideologies, and effects is prodigious; for my purposes, the most useful and important discussions have appeared in Dana Polan, *Power and Paranoia: History, Narrative, and the American Cinema, 1940–1950* (New York: Columbia University Press, 1986); Stephen J. Whitfield, *The Culture of the Cold War* (Baltimore, Md.: Johns Hopkins University Press, 1991); Michael Rogin, *Ronald Reagan, the Movie, and Other Episodes in Political Demonology* (Berkeley: University of California Press, 1987); Alan Nadel, *Containment Culture: American Narratives, Postmodernism, and the Atomic Age* (Durham, N.C.: Duke University Press, 1995); Thomas Schaub, *American Fiction in the Cold War* (Madison: University of Wisconsin Press, 1991); and Elaine Showalter, *Hysteries: Hysterical Epidemics and Modern Culture* (New York: Columbia University Press, 1997). Frederick Buell, *National Culture and the New Global System* (Baltimore, Md.: Johns Hopkins University Press, 1994), sets U.S. cold war nationalism within the ensuing context of post–cold war globalization. For valuable studies of the relation between Puritanism, the cold war, and U.S. nationalism during the period of national formation, see Donald E. Pease, "National Narratives, Postnational Narration," *Modern Fiction Studies* 43 (1997): 1–23; and Lauren Berlant, *The Anatomy of National Fantasy: Hawthorne, Utopia, and Everyday Life* (Chicago: University of Chicago Press, 1991); Richard Hofstader, "The Paranoid Style in American Politics," in *The Paranoid Style in American Politics and Other Essays* (New York: Knopf, 1966), is a classic essay on the relation between Puritanism, paranoia, and cold war ideology; Sacvan Bercovitch, *The Puritan Origins of the American Self* (New Haven, Conn.: Yale University Press, 1975), furnishes the analysis underlying many explorations of the relation between Puritanism and nationalist ideology; and Eli Sagan, *The Honey and the Hemlock: Democracy and Paranoia in Ancient Athens and Modern America* (New York: Basic Books,

1991), provides a compelling assessment of paranoia, Athenian democracy, and modern U.S. politics. With characteristic brilliance, Avital Ronell articulates a series of associations between apocalypticism and the resurgence of nationalism, especially in her work on the Gulf War in "Support Our Tropes" (in *Finitude's Score: Essays for the End of the Millennium* [Lincoln: University of Nebraska Press, 1994]).

For an analysis of the relation between homophobia, paranoia, and postmodernity, see Thomas B. Byers, "Terminating the Postmodern: Masculinity and Pomophobia," *Modern Fiction Studies* 41 (1994): 5–34; see also Robert J. Corber, *In the Name of National Security: Hitchcock, Homophobia, and the Political Construction of Gender in Postwar America* (Durham, N.C.: Duke University Press, 1993). I rely throughout on the crucial works on masculinity, paranoia, and ideology by Julia Kristeva (*Powers of Horror: An Essay on Abjection* [New York: Columbia University Press, 1982]) and Kaja Silverman (*Male Masculinity at the Margins* [New York: Routledge, 1993]), as well as Freud's founding work on this issue in "Psycho-Analytic Notes upon an Autobiographical Account of a Case of Paranoia (Dementia Paranoides) (1911)," in *Collected Papers*, trans. James Strachey (New York: Basic Books, 1959), 3:390–470. Finally, Timothy Melley's *Empire of Conspiracy: The Culture of Paranoia* (Ithaca, N.Y.: Cornell University Press, 1999), which appeared after work on this book was completed, offers a capacious assessment of contemporary paranoia as motivated by anxieties about human autonomy and individuality.

4   Slavoj Žižek, *Tarrying with the Negative: Kant, Hegel, and the Critique of Ideology* (Durham, N.C.: Duke University Press, 1993), 216. Subsequent references will be cited in the text. Žižek is here summarizing one of the main points of Fredric Jameson's (now) classic discussion of the economic form of postmodern subjectivity in "The Cultural Logic of Late Capitalism" (Jameson, *Postmodernism*, 1–54).

5   Massumi, *Everyday Fear*, 7. In his now classic study of contemporary fiction, Tony Tanner looks at the movement between fixity and form as central to the construction of identity in fiction from the 1950s to 1970s. As Tanner suggests, the dialectic of individual freedom and social paralysis is to be found in U.S. literature at large, but like Richard Poirier before him, Tanner casts the discussion largely within existentialist terms that assume, among other things, that identity and the realm of the social are discrete entities, the former choosing to operate as resistant to or in complicity with the latter. See Tony Tanner, *City of Words: American Fiction, 1950–1970* (New York: Harper and Row, 1971), 3–55. Along somewhat similar lines, Stacey Olster asserts that the reflexive projection of patterns of historical ordering in Norman Mailer, Thomas Pynchon, and John Barth are representative of a "constructionist" response to postwar historical amnesia in the United States and the indeterminacies of the postmodern condition; see *Reminiscence and Re-creation in Contemporary American Fiction* (New York: Cambridge University Press, 1989), 1–12.

6   Freud, "Psycho-Analytic."

7   See Anthony Wilden, *System and Structure: Essays on Communication and Exchange*, 2d ed. (London: Tavistock, 1980), for a somewhat broader conception of cultural paranoia as a fundamental postmodern "epistemological error" that produces "deterministic thinking in biology, elitism in genetics and psycho-

metrics, instincts and intrapsychic conflicts in psychology, the free compe-
tition of the rational subject in economics, and uncritical attempts to apply
the experimental method in the social sciences" (210). Wilden goes on to contend that "in its ideological manifestations . . . the same error feeds pollu-
tion, racism, alienation, exploitation, and ALL OTHER FORMS OF PATHOLOGICAL
COMMUNICATION" (210). For Wilden, at the heart of this error is the confusion
of energy with communication, and it relies on "an overriding commitment to
SYMMETRICAL relationships—such as arms races, corporate mergers, simplis-
tic anti-communism, racism—within which COMPLEMENTARY relationships at
another level—spheres of influence, exploitation of underdeveloped countries,
domestic colonialism, and the like—provide the overall commitment to com-
petitive oppositions" (211). This "ideological paranoia of symmetry (Freud's
reductionist and anti-contextual 'narcissism of minor differences'—Standard
Edition, XVIII, 101) . . . generates further pathological symmetry" (211). It is
no surprise, given these views, that later on in System and Structure Wilden
focuses on Schreber as embodying the "ontological insecurity" that corresponds
with the fundamental "error" that he elucidates throughout this work (cf. 278–
301); I am much indebted to Wilden's groundbreaking interdisciplinary analysis
of (among many other things) cultural paranoia that maps Lacanian psychoanalysis onto economics, communication theory, and social theory.

8   See, for example, Mark Siegel (Pynchon: Creative Paranoia in "Gravity's Rainbow" [Port Washington, N.Y.: Kennikat Press, 1978]), who suggests that paranoia operates not just as a survival mechanism in Pynchon's conspiratorial universe but also as a means of making visible the hidden connections between the
sacred and profane. In contrast, see Leo Bersani's ("Pynchon, Paranoia, and Literature," Representations 25 [1989]: 99–118) compelling antihermeneutic (and
antiredemptive) reading of Gravity's Rainbow, and Ursula K. Heise's (Chronoschisms: Time, Narrative, and Postmodernism [New York: Cambridge University Press, 1997]) more circumspect reading of Pynchon, which views paranoia
as a mode of adequation to postmodern temporality exhibiting the "tension between temporal progression and causal inversion" (181).

9   DeLillo, among others, represents "obviousness," the inverse of hiddenness, as
one of the paradoxical conditions of paranoia. See Patrick O'Donnell, "Obvious
Paranoia: The Politics of Don DeLillo's Running Dog," Centennial Review 34
(1990): 56–72.

10 O. K. Werckmeister (Citadel Culture [Chicago: University of Chicago Press,
1991]), who argues that citadel culture is the "culture of cultural critique, whose
self-reflexive feedback prevents it from extending its universal problem consciousness to its own production and consumption in citadel society. Its built-in
self-critique provides the blind spot for the contradictions of its success" (180).
I can agree with Werckmeister that self-critique is responsible for the paralysis of the citadel or cold war culture that has fostered cultural paranoia only
to the extent that self-critique is limited to hermeneutic, self-reflexive modes
(for example, the mise en abyme of the notions that every form of reference
reveals its own nonreferentiality, that every truth statement is a fiction). Such
concepts, often associated with a reductive version of postmodernity, tend to
nourish cultural paranoia in that the hermeneutic uncertainty that results from
the operations of self-reflexivity fuels a concomitant need for another truth to

deconstruct. A truly radical self-critique would look quite different from this, but a critique of this kind has not been "tried out"—is not operative—in citadel culture.

11 See Jean-François Lyotard, *The Postmodern Condition: A Report on Knowledge,* trans. Geoff Bennington and Brian Massumi (Minneapolis: University of Minnesota Press, 1984), 31–41.

12 Fredric Jameson refers to the spatialization of temporality at several moments in his work, but perhaps most evocatively, and globally, in "The Cultural Logic of Late Capitalism" and *The Seeds of Time* (New York: Columbia University Press, 1994), esp. 20–21. Somewhat differently, Hal Foster (*The Return of the Real* [Cambridge, Mass.: MIT Press, 1996]) views the spatiotemporal compressions of postmodernity that inform cultural paranoia and the formation of the postmodern subject as a series of "splittings":

These are only some of the splittings that occur with a new intensity today: a spatio-temporal splitting, the paradox of immediacy produced through mediation; a moral splitting, the paradox of disgust undercut by fascination, or of sympathy undercut by sadism; and a splitting of the body image, the ecstasy of dispersal rescued by armoring, or the fantasy of disembodiment dispelled by abjection. If a postmodern subject can be posited at all, it is made and unmade in such splittings. Is it any wonder that this subject is often dysfunctional, suspended between obscene proximity and spectacular representation? Is it any wonder then when it does function it is often on automatic, given over to fetishistic responses, to partial recognitions syncopated with complete disavowals: I know about AIDS, but I cannot get it; I know about sexists and racists, but I am not one; I know what the New World Order is, but my paranoia embraces it anyway. (222–23)

13 One of the most illuminating critiques of postmodernity in this regard is that of David Harvey (*Condition of Postmodernity,* 284–307), who, following Jameson, argues that the time-space compressions to be found in postmodern culture (more specifically, the unification of space and the diminution of temporality) are consistent with the globalization of capitalism. The reaction to these compressions, Harvey suggests, is a resurgence of, among other things, nationalism, which depends on the unification of space and historicization of that space under the aegis of an equally unified temporality in the form of a progressive or evolutionary notion of history. Walter Benjamin's "deconstruction" of progressive or evolutionary conceptions of the historical in the *Passagen-Werk* is notable in this regard; see Susan Buck-Morss, *The Dialectics of Seeing: Walter Benjamin and the Arcades Project* (Cambridge, Mass.: MIT Press, 1989), 78–109. In the reaction-formation of cultural paranoia to postmodern time-space compressions that I consider here, the contradictory elision of temporality and projection of an evolutionary historical model are complicit and constitutive.

14 See Peter Sloterdijk, *Critique of Cynical Reason,* trans. Michal Eldred (Minneapolis: University of Minnesota Press, 1987), 76–100. In "Postenlightened Cynicism: Diogenes as Postmodern Intellectual (in *Twilight Memories: Marking Time in a Culture of Amnesia* [New York: Routledge, 1995], 157–74), Andreas Huyssen critiques Sloterdijk's cynicism in terms of its implicit nostalgia for Enlightenment reason and subjectivity. Huyssen notes that Sloterdijk as well as Deleuze and Guattari are in basic disagreement over the status of the postmod-

ern body: "Sloterdijk's concept of a new, kynical subjectivity aims at nothing less than a new, postindustrial reality principle that contrary to the Deluzian schizobody [that is, "the body without organs" of the postsignifying regime] would acknowledge the necessary and productive contradiction between a unified physical body and the processes of psychic deterritorialization" (168). In these debates over the postmodern body and the historicizing of paranoia in relation to the body, my position, as I shall make clear in the readings to follow, is that the Deleuzian "schizobody" is a kind of fantasy projection of, or extrapolation from, the current situation (in which modernity and postmodernity bear the relation, respectively, of remnant and prophecy). In this situation, the omnipresence of paranoia is precisely symptomatic of a refurbished dualism in which there is the phantasmic projection of (to use Donna Haraway's term) the "cyborg body," the mutative body of multiple surfaces—but a projection that is mediated via an outdated, modernistic, signifying, and interpreting consciousness. Paranoia is the attempt, then, to recuperate this dualism or schizophrenia: to recenter the body in the mind.

15 Slavoj Žižek, *The Sublime Object of Ideology* (New York: Verso, 1989), 75. Subsequent references will be cited in the text.

16 Bersani, "Pynchon," 109.

17 In his discussion of colonial power and mimicry, Homi Bhabha ("Signs Taken for Wonders: Questions of Ambivalence and Authority under a Tree outside Delhi, May 1817," in *Race, Writing, and Difference,* ed. Henry Louis Gates Jr. [Chicago: University of Chicago Press, 1986]) makes a similar point about the progression of symptom to sign that is part of the work of "hybridity": "Hybridity is the name of the displacement of value from symbol to sign that causes the dominant discourse to split along the axis of its power to be representation, authoritative. Hybridity represents that ambivalent 'turn' of the discriminated subject into the terrifying, exorbitant object of paranoid classification—a disturbing questioning of the images and presences of authority" (174). Yet, though he sees hybridity as a cultural process taking place under the rubric of an appropriating colonial authority (as I am suggesting that paranoia is symptomatic of, and produced by, anachronistic identity-formations under current conditions), Bhabha wants to save the sign/symptom for the purposes of the subversion of and resistance to colonial authority "hoist by its own petard." Thus, Bhabha writes further on, that "the paranoid threat from the hybrid is finally uncontainable because it breaks down the symmetry and duality of self/Other, inside/outside" (176). However accurate an assessment this may be of paranoia (as manifestation of hybridity, as mimicking resistance) within the historical processes of colonialism, those conditions have changed under, to employ Jameson's epochal phrasing, "the cultural logic of late capitalism" and the postmodernist versions of identity it subsumes: now, I am arguing, paranoia is more often than not the complex symptom of *complicity* between capitalism and the differentials of identity that might include notions of hybridity, pastiche, heterogeneity, etc. It is appropriate to frame Bhabha's work on colonialism—as Abdul JanMohamed has done ("The Economy of Manichean Allegory: The Function of Racial Difference in Colonialist Literature," in *Race, Writing, and Difference,* ed. Henry Louis Gates Jr. [Chicago: University of Chicago Press, 1986], 78–106)—as a practice that historicizes colonialism under the sign of postmodernity.

18 Paul Smith, *Discerning the Subject* (Minneapolis: University of Minnesota Press, 1988), 95. Again, Freud's Schreber case (see "Psycho-Analytic") is the locus classicus for this formulation of paranoia; see also Freud's "A Case of Chronic Paranoia" and "A Case of Paranoia Running Counter to the Psychoanalytic Theory of That Disease," both in *The Standard Edition of the Complete Psychological Works of Sigmund Freud*, trans. James Strachey et al. (London: Hogarth Press, 1953–1974).

19 Julia Kristeva, *Powers of Horror: An Essay on Abjection* (New York: Columbia University Press, 1982), 191.

20 In her Lacanian reading of Hitchcock in "Paranoia and the Film System" (*Screen* 17 [1977]), Jacqueline Rose argues that "the woman is centred in the clinical manifestation of paranoia as position. Paranoia is characterised by a passive homosexual current, and hence a 'feminine' position in both man and woman" (102). Rose traces the trajectory of paranoia as "fixation at the stage of narcissism" (102) from Freud's 1914 paper on narcissism to Lacan's conception of the "imaginary." The notion of "homosexual panic" is, of course, that of Eve Kosofsky Sedgwick (*Epistemology of the Closet* [Berkeley: University of California Press, 1990]), whose reading of Henry James's "The Beast in the Jungle" (182–212) elaborates on the relation between repressed same-sex desire and paranoia.

21 Michael Rogin defines "demonology" as, essentially, a form of paranoia in the terms that I have used. "The demonologist splits the world in two, attributing magical, pervasive power to a conspiratorial center of evil. Fearing chaos and secret penetration, the countersubversive interprets local initiatives as signs of alien power. . . . The countersubversive needs monsters to give shape to his anxieties and to permit him to indulge in forbidden desires. Demonization allows the countersubversive, in the name of battling the subversive, to imitate his enemy" (*Ronald Reagan*, xiii). Rogin comments on President Reagan's defense of his role in the post–Korean conflict film *Prisoner of War* as an example of "the mirroring process [that blends] the subversive into his countersubversive reflection. . . . [T]he movie self, like the countersubversive, points to the definition of identity in doubling and to the absorption of identity in exchange" (40). Peter Sloterdijk, discussing the imaginary differences of the cold war binary, argues that what is "a conflict within the system presents itself in an absurd way as a conflict *between* two systems. . . . By means of a paranoid politics of armament, two real illusory opponents force themselves to maintain an imaginary system difference solidified through self-mystification. In this way, a socialism that does not want to be a capitalism and a capitalism that does not want to be a socialism paralyze each other" (*Critique*, 247), and in so doing, mirror each other. Similarly, Abdul JanMohamed locates cultural paranoia in the "Manichean allegory" of colonialist discourse: "Instead of being an exploration of the racial Other," the projection of the racialized other of the "native" as evil and barbaric is for JanMohamed "essentially specular," a use of the native "as a mirror that reflects the colonialist's self-image" ("Economy," 84). Cultural paranoia, particularly in its self-mirroring aspects, might then be seen as a subset of the larger self/other, subject/object dichotomies that afflict (and sunder) Western philosophy, and "Manichean allegory" as it applies to colonialist discourse might be understood as a localized and historicized manifestation of cultural

paranoia, though it is possible to reverse these equations or generate further subsets depending on where one wants to locate the work of self/other bifurcations. It is my contention here that cultural paranoia operates as something of a floating signifier that has the capacity to locate its operations in whatever split or duality that allows it to shore up the unitary self, whether this representation of identity is categorically essentialized primarily as raced, classed, or gendered. More generally, speaking of identity in categorical terms, however useful it may be for certain kinds of analysis, could be viewed as bearing the "something of the truth" of paranoia, though how to speak otherwise—especially if the root problem is how to understand the other in terms other than those of the self—remains in question.

22 Pease, "National Narratives," 8. I am indebted to Pease's work on nationalism and postnationalism, as well as his conceptions of nation, throughout this chapter and the next.

23 In discussing the space of, as she calls it, the "National Symbolic" as it is manifested in Nathaniel Hawthorne, Lauren Berlant creates the term "mnemotechnique" to stand for the "form or technology of collective identity that harnesses individual and popular fantasy by creating juridically legitimate public memories" (*Anatomy*, 8). Used in this sense, mnemotechnique is a specific, legal/juridical cultural mnemonic that Berlant deploys in order to define the manifestations of the National Symbolic. Berlant's reading of Hawthorne in these terms is compelling, yet I question the homogeneity of *the* National Symbolic or *the* national identity: we may wish to consider instead, particularly under the aegis of postmodernism, a mélange of partial, arbitrarily converging national symbolics that only become capitalized and made singular when one gains ascendancy over the others as the "normal," the "commonsensical." If so, there is no National Symbolic, only its lack as evidenced by the incompleteness of the reigning symbolic at any given moment; this state of affairs, of course, is what fosters paranoia.

24 See Michael André Bernstein, *Foregone Conclusions: Against Apocalyptic History* (Berkeley: University of California Press, 1994) for a forceful exploration of narrative foreshadowing and the elision of the historical in modern and postmodern narratives.

25 This trajectory retracts itself in Stone's *Nixon* (1995), where the "good" and "bad" father are conflated in the single figure of Nixon, who is thus made "historical" as a result of this compression.

26 Stephen Jay Gould, *Wonderful Life: The Burgess Shale and the Nature of History* (New York: W. W. Norton, 1989), 51.

27 For a convincing, if somewhat schematic, discussion of systems and antisystems in contemporary narrative, see Thomas LeClair, *In the Loop: Don DeLillo and the Systems Novel* (Urbana: University of Illinois Press, 1987).

28 Gilles Deleuze and Félix Guattari assiduously avoid the term *postmodern* in their analysis; nevertheless, *A Thousand Plateaus: Capitalism and Schizophrenia*, trans. Brian Massumi (Minneapolis: University of Minnesota Press, 1987), can be considered a key text of postmodernity, even though it does not formulate a version of postmodernism as such. Subsequent references will be cited in the text.

29 While still bearing the marks of the infinite that characterizes the baroque for

Gilles Deleuze (the multilinear system where "everything happens at once" and keeps happening resembling the infinite work of the baroque), the "flows" and "lines of flight" of the multilinear systems of postmodernity operate simultaneously on global and local levels, whereas the "folds" of the baroque are aestheticized and relegated to the interiority of discrete objects: "A fold is always folded within a fold, like a cavern in a cavern. The unit of matter, the smallest element of a labyrinth, is the fold, not the point which is never a part, but the simple extremity of the line. That is why parts of matter are masses or aggregates, as a correlative to elastic compressive force. . . . The model for the sciences of matter is the 'orgami,' . . . or the art of folding paper" (*The Fold: Leibniz and the Baroque,* trans. Tom Conley [Minneapolis: University of Minnesota Press, 1993], 6). The conceptual difference between fold and flow implicitly constitutes, at least for Deleuze across his work, a historical shift within capitalism from more geometric to more unequal, anamorphic systems of exchange.

30   Steven Best and Douglas Kellner, *Postmodern Theory: Critical Interrogations* (New York: Guilford Press, 1991), 154, 157.

31   Jean-François Lyotard, *Libidinal Economy,* trans. Iain Hamilton Grant (Bloomington: Indiana University Press, 1993), 156. Subsequent references will be cited in the text.

32   Cited by translator Iain Hamilton Grant (*Libidinal,* xviii) as occurring in Lyotard's *Peregrinations.*

33   On this triangulation, see Fredric Jameson, *The Political Unconscious: Narrative as a Socially Symbolic Act* (Ithaca, N.Y.: Cornell University Press, 1981), 27.

34   As Vincent B. Leitch has argued, replacing money with credit in the virtualization of surplus value in effect "dissolves" capital; see his *Postmodernism: Local Effects, Global FLows* (Albany: State University of New York Press, 1996), 3–24.

35   In *The Inhuman: Reflections on Time* (trans. Geoffrey Bennington and Rachel Bowlby [Stanford, Calif.: Stanford University Press, 1991]), where he significantly alters his view of temporality from that of *Libidinal Economy,* Lyotard bifurcates temporality into oppositional poles—that of progress and development, and that of a transhistorical, primordial time that recurs via a process of "anamnesis." The "human" is what shuttles between these poles; in my view, the temporal realm manifested through the remembrances of anamnesis is the residue of the atemporal temporality of *Libidinal Economy* (cf. *Inhuman,* 1–5).

36   Jameson, *Seeds,* 15; but of course, as Jameson argues, such seeming incompatibilities are entirely complicit in the production of the consumerist subject.

37   Jacuqes Derrida, *Spectres of Marx: The State of Debt, the Work of Mourning, and the New International,* trans. Peggy Kamuf (New Routledge, 1994), xix. Subsequent references will be cited in the text.

38   For a discussion of the Heideggerian "hauntings" of *Spectres,* see Fredric Jameson, "Marx's Purloined Letter," *New Left Review,* no. 209 (1994): 75–109.

39   See Homi K. Bhabha's "DissemiNation: Time, Narrative, and the Margins of the Modern Nation" (in *Nation and Narration,* ed. Homi K. Bhabha [New York: Routledge, 1990]), where he defines "national time" as a "narrative synchrony . . . a graphically visible position in space . . . a consistent process of surmounting the ghostly time of repetition" (295).

40   Jean Copjec, *Read My Desire: Lacan against the Historicists* (Cambridge, Mass.: MIT Press, 1994), 51.

41   Jacques Derrida, *Given Time 1: Counterfeit Money,* trans. Peggy Kamuf (Chicago: University of Chicago Press, 1992), 40.

2   Head Shots: The Theater of Paranoia

1   Slavoj Žižek, *For They Know Not What They Do: Enjoyment as a Political Factor* (New York: Verso, 1991), 2.

2   DeLillo conveys this sense of moment of the assassination as a quitting point and the origin or site of national trauma in his interview with Anthony DeCurtis ("'An Outside in This Society': An Interview with Don DeLillo," *South Atlantic Quarterly* 89 [1990]): "As the years have flowed away from that point, I think we've all come to feel what's been missing over these past twenty-five years is a sense of manageable reality. Much of that feeling can be traced to that one moment in Dallas. We seem much more aware of elements like randomness and ambiguity and chaos since then" (286). He phrases the matter similarly in the *Rolling Stone* essay ("American Blood: A Journey through the Labyrinth of Dallas and JFK," 8 December 1983) on the assassination that served as the "true beginning" of *Libra:* "What has become unraveled since that afternoon in Dallas is not the plot of course, not the dense mass of characters and events, but the sense of a coherent reality most of us shared. We seem from that moment to have entered a world of randomness and ambiguity, a world totally modern in the way it shades into the century's 'emptiest' literature, the study of what is uncertain and unresolved in our lives, the literature of estrangement and silence" (22).

3   In his Deleuzian reading of the novel, John Johnston ("Superlinear Fiction or Historical Diagram: Don DeLillo's *Libra,*" *Modern Fiction Studies* 40 [1994]) remarks extensively on the nature of the constructed, simulated event as what *Libra* both assembles in its representations of conspiracy and coincidence, and what it critiques in coming to rest on the indeterminacy of the event that founds it as construction (336–39; *Libra,* Johnston contends, thus enacts a deconstruction and concomitant complication of the relation between history (as narrative) and fiction (as narrative). In a different vein, Joseph Kronick's reading via DeMan ("*Libra* and the Assassination of JFK: A Textbook Operation," *Arizona Quarterly* 50 [1994]) argues for the prior textualization of both historical and fictional narratives, but suggests that what distinguishes history as such from any narrative construct is its linguistic materiality, "the materiality of the letter, which prior to any literal or figural meaning is the basis of the meaning-event and the condition, and impossibility, for distinguishing the literal from the figurative" (120). While I am not primarily interested here in viewing *Libra* as differentiating fiction from history, this relation as constructed by the narrative is significant to an understanding of the novel's symptomatic representations of postmodern identity confronting history.

4   DeLillo, "American Blood," 28; and Don DeLillo, *Libra* (1988; reprint, New York: Penguin, 1989), 18. Subsequent references to both will be cited in the text.

5   Cited in DeCurtis, "An outside in This Society," 294.

6   Stephen Bernstein ("*Libra* and the Historical Sublime," *Postmodern Culture* 4, no. 2 [1994]) asserts that rather than "losing" history, *Libra* projects it as a form of the sublime: "DeLillo signifies the operation of history through the sublime at nearly every single step" (paragraph 18); "*Libra's* awesome historical sublime

may simply have its roots in the related sublime of consciousness itself, and the impossibility of understanding the latter is writ large in the impossibility of encompassing the former" (paragraph 24). Along similar lines, Joseph Tabbi (*Postmodern Sublime: Technology and American Writing from Mailer to Cyberpunk* [Ithaca, N.Y.: Cornell University Press, 1995]), in arguing that *Libra* "is not indicative of paranoia" but of DeLillo's "suspicion of orders beyond the visible," suggests that the multiple, but always partial fabrication of selves and plots in the novel represent the "immanent literary meaning in objects and constructed spaces" that exemplifies the "postmodern sublime" (186). My sense of *Libra's* treatment of history and the materiality of the real diverges from this view in that I see "encompassibility" or "immanence" operating in every dimension of the novel as a counterweight to determinacy: each verges toward the other in the dialectic of cultural paranoia.

7 Slavoj Žižek, *Tarrying with the Negative: Kant, Hegel, and the Critique of Ideology* (Durham, N.C.: Duke University Press, 1993), 171.

8 Frank Lentricchia, "*Libra* as Postmodern Critique," *South Atlantic Quarterly* 89 (1990): 439.

9 See Thomas Carmichael ("Lee Harvey Oswald and the Postmodern Subject: History and Intertextuality in Don DeLillo's *Libra*, *The Names*, and *Mao II*," *Contemporary Literature* 34 [1993]), who views Oswald as a postmodern subject emerging "only as an effect of the codes out of which he is articulated, and these codes function in the novel self-consciously as signs of an endlessly disseminating network of intertextual traces" (206).

10 Lentricchia, "Postmodern Critique," 436. Lentricchia argues that *Libra* is not a novel of paranoia because it reflexively registers the degree to which paranoia relies on simulation to achieve its effects. My point throughout, as I've suggested in the first chapter, is that reflexivity does not "save" the text from paranoia, but appositely, that cultural paranoia is a condition that readily enfolds reflexivity as one of its enabling elements.

11 Gilles Deleuze and Félix Guattari, *A Thousand Plateaus: Capitalism and Schizophrenia*, trans. Brian Massumi (Minneapolis: University of Minnesota Press, 1987), 54.

12 Johnston discusses the operation of coincidence in *Libra* in terms similar to my own as a "device" deployed to merge intention with chance ("Superlinear Fiction," 328), the emphasis in the novel thus falling on the construction of accident itself as historical effect. The phrase "orderly disorder" will be recognizable as that of N. Katherine Hayles (*Chaos Bound: Orderly Disorder in Contemporary Literature and Science* [Ithaca, N.Y.: Cornell University Press, 1991]), who employs it to describe the contradictions of represented and perceived postmodern reality as constructed randomness.

13 See, for example, Bill Millard ("The Fable of the Ants: Myopic Interactions in DeLillo's *Libra*," *Postmodern Culture* 4, no. 2 [1994]) who discusses the relation between power and simulacra in *Libra*.

14 In the DeCurtis interview, DeLillo mentions that one of his recurring interests is "a sense of a secret pattern in our lives, a sense of ambiguity" ("An outside in This Society," 295).

15 Ibid., 128.

16 Kronick, "*Libra*," 118.

17   In his study of Schreber, Eric L. Santner (*My Own Private Germany: Daniel Paul Schreber's Secret History of Modernity* [Princeton, N.J.: Princeton University Press, 1996]) argues that what he terms a "*crisis of symbolic investiture*" (26), a condition brought on by a recognition of the insubstantiality of "the exemplary domain of symbolic authority" (32), is symptomatic of modern identity-formations per se. In locating DeLillo's Oswald as the site of such a crisis in postmodernity, I am suggesting that the multiplicity of identity (indicative of the modernist crisis) has come under discipline and, in a sense, been institutionalized; thus, the postmodern version of this crisis as "enjoyed" by Oswald consists of a contradictory desire to relocate a singular identity at the center of the plot while simultaneously maintaining its marginal, nomadic status. In other words, it is as if the Oswald-constructions of *Libra* (and in different ways, those registered by Mailer) accept the wager of the phantasmic foundation of the symbolic order, and in doing so, rematerialize it.

18   Fredric Jameson, *Postmodernism, or, the Cultural Logic of Late Capitalism* (Durham, N.C.: Duke University Press, 1991), 17.

19   Cited in Oliver Stone and Zachary Sklar, *JFK: The Book of the Film* (New York: Applause Books, 1992), 208.

20   In the 1992 television miniseries *Wild Palms*, set in the Los Angeles of the twenty-first century, for which he served as producer, Stone is shown on a talk show bragging about the fact that it turns out he was right about the assassination now, in the future, that the archives have been opened. As I argue throughout the discussion of *JFK*, the "blank parody" exhibited in such maneuvers is fully complicit with Stone's oedipal narratives.

21   Norman K. Denzin, *The Cinematic Society: The Voyeur's Gaze* (London: Sage, 1995), 164.

22   Cited in Stone and Sklar, *JFK*, 383.

23   Cited in ibid., 176. It should be noted parenthetically that at one time, Stone had designed a scene in which the ghost of JFK visits Garrison at home, while he is making a chicken sandwich, moments before Garrison will view the reports of Robert Kennedy's assassination on television.

24   See Robert Burgoyne, "Modernism and the Narration of Nation in JFK," in *The Persistence of History: Cinema, Television, and the Modern Event*, ed. Vivian Sobchek (New York: Routledge, 1996), for an excellent reading of the film as divided between a nostalgia for the lost "national time" that Benedict Anderson depicts as evolutionary and homogeneous (analogous to the narrative parallelism and homogeneity of Stone's cinematic career), and a representation of postassassination time as fragmented, telescoped, and anachronistic.

25   Michael Rogin, "Body and Soul Murder: *JFK*," in *Media Spectacles*, ed. Margorie Garber, Jann Matlock, and Rebecca L. Walkowitz (New York: Routledge, 1993), 10. In this most compelling reading to date of *JFK*, Rogin focuses on the connections made in the film between gay culture and conspiracy, and specifies its oedipality as a reaction to the post–cold war spread of the "homosexual panic" that "organizes *JFK*" (12). As revealing as it is about *JFK*'s sexual politics, Rogin's analysis strikes me as slightly reductive in that homosexual panic becomes the symptom that explains the film, which is to substitute one conspiratorial explanation (the conspiracy in the cultural unconscious against gays) for another (the conspiracy of the military-industrial complex to kill Kennedy). It is this very

logic of substitution on which, I argue, the film grounds its "truthful" assertions. Nevertheless, Rogin makes a number of important connections between Stone's cinematic techniques, "homosexual panic," and Schreber's account of paranoia. See also Denzin's schematic reading of *JFK* as a film about "men watching men make history. . . . The erotics of power: men taking visual, scopic pleasures in the production of rich, thick, audio and visual documents that record the transgressions of others. . . . The paranoid gaze is everywhere" (*Cinematic Society*, 186).

26 See Linda Hutcheon, "The Pastime of Past Time: Fiction, History, Historiographic Metafiction," *Genre* 20 (1987): 285–306, for the initial discussion of this now familiar, widely accepted view of the relation between reflexive fiction and historiography, implicitly contested in this book's exit.

27 Norman Mailer, *Oswald's Tale: An American Mystery* (New York: Random House, 1995), 605–6. Subsequent references will be cited in the text.

28 For an intriguing, if somewhat elliptical, discussion of Mailer's relation to late capitalism and his tendency toward self-commodification in the identifications of textuality and subjectivity, see Richard Godden, *Fictions of Capital: The American Novel from James to Mailer* (New York: Cambridge University Press, 1990), esp. 200–250.

29 A comment Mailer makes in an interview illustrates his concept of character, which I am suggesting is the conflation of subject and object as those terms are expressed in *Oswald's Tale*. "[The process of writing] while interesting in the early stages is not as exciting as the more creative act of allowing your characters to grow. . . . It's when they become almost as complex as one's own personality that the fine excitement begins. Because then they are not really characters any longer—they're beings, which is a distinction I like to make. A character is someone you can grasp as a whole, you have a clear idea of him, but a being is someone whose nature keeps shifting" (cited in Stephen Marcus, "Norman Mailer: An Interview," in *Conversations with Norman Mailer*, ed. J. Michael Lennon [Jackson: University of Mississippi Press, 1988], 91). In *Oswald's Tale*, Mailer constructs Oswald's agency as a dialectic that moves ceaselessly between character and being, between thought and action ("to commit his mind to one action sometimes meant no more than that he was constructing a mental platform which would enable him to spring off in the opposite direction" [560]), until he comes to rest in the historical semiobjectivity of his placement as tragic lone gunman.

30 Mailer's use of the word *dialectic* in an interview illuminates his project to generate the "mystery" of character within a history that is both open to interpretation and determinate in terms of its outcome. Self-schooled in Marx, Mailer says in conversation that "reading *Das Kapital* turned me toward mysticism. It's such a perfect picture of our social machine—if it is a machine—that when you try to understand how such a perfect machine could work, you begin thinking about transcendental machines, and you get into that more mystical of notions, the dialectic" (cited in Charles Monaghan, "Portrait of a Man Reading," in *Conversations with Norman Mailer*, ed. J. Michael Lennon [Jackson: University of Mississippi Press, 1988], 190). The relation between the "mysticism" of the dialectic and the "mystery" of Oswald is intriguing: as Mailer makes clear in further remarks, dialectic for him indicates everything from intertextuality

and the opposition between character and author, to the resistances of the self to historical forces. What these varying senses have in common is their status as ratios by which a process (textual, narratological, identificatory) and its instantiation are measured. For Mailer, I am proposing, such a ratio constitutes the essence of the performative function.

31 J. Hillis Miller, *Ariadne's Thread: Story Lines* (New Haven, Conn.: Yale University Press, 1992), 94.

32 Benedict Anderson, *Imagined Communities: Reflections on the Origin and the Spread of Nationalism*, rev. ed. (New York: Verso, 1989), 24.

33 Cited in John McClure, *Late Imperial Romance* (New York: Verso, 1994), 43.

34 See ibid., esp. 8–29, for an incisive analysis of the genre McClure invents in order to assess the relation between colonialism and the cultural imaginary in the twentieth century.

3 Engendering Paranoia

1 Sigmund Freud, "Psycho-analytic Notes upon an Autobiographical Account of a Case of Paranoia (Dementia Paranoides) (1911)," in *Collected Papers*, trans. James Strachey (New York: Basic Books, 1959), 3: 426.

2 Luce Irigaray, *This Sex Which Is Not One*, trans. Catherine Porter (Ithaca, N.Y.: Cornell University Press, 1985), 172.

3 Eve Kosofsky Sedgwick, *Epistemology of the Closet* (Berkeley: University of California Press, 1990), 187.

4 See Thomas B. Byers, "Terminating the Postmodern: Masculinity and Pomophobia," *Modern Fiction Studies* 41 (1994): 5–34, for an incisive discussion of the relation between male paranoia and the perceived fluidity of identity under postmodernity as represented in the *Terminator* films. In a series of convincing readings, Robert J. Corber (*In the Name of National Security: Hitchcock, Homophobia, and the Political Construction of Gender in Postwar America* [Durham, N.C.: Duke University Press, 1993]) explores the relation between homophobia and cold war culture, which carries over into—and is reinforced by—the "posts" of postmodernity and the post–cold war under which, seemingly, the politics of homophobic paranoia would attenuate. In fact, those politics, both as a reaction to and (to pursue one of my chief arguments) drawing on the alterities of postmodern identity, are as powerful as ever.

5 Teresa Brennan, "The Age of Paranoia," *Paragraph* 14, no. 1 (1991): 26, 28–29. Subsequent references will be cited in the text. The argument in this essay is a condensed version of the one that Brennan makes in her book *History after Lacan* (New York: Routledge, 1993), esp. 19–117. While I find Brennan's work most useful for understanding the relation between paranoia and sexual difference, her insistence on a "transhistorical fantasy" (*History,* 22) that informs the formation of the ego (potentially transcendent by virtue of that transhistoricism) is problematic; equally problematic, for me, is her assertion of a "natural reality" (*History,* 21) that is at the foundation of the real as such, however much the ego may distort it through objectification or attempt to destroy its physical manifestations. But Brennan has done more than any theorist I know to establish the connection between psychotic or neurotic social formations (such as cultural paranoia), sexual difference, and the objectification of women.

6   Brennan's formulation of the child's aggressive relation to its mother is based on a synthesis of the work of Melanie Klein and, more extensively, Julia Kristeva, who in *Revolution in Poetic Language* and *Powers of Horror*, posits a unitary relation between a mother and child before the introduction of language and the splitting of the ego into self and other. Once desire (for the now absent mother), and with it, language, enter the scene, once the child enters the symbolic realm, then the relation to the mother is transformed into one of aggression and abjection as the child both represses what has been lost (the mother and the unitary bond to her) and "recalls" it fragmentarily in poetic language, which contains traces of the mother's semiotic body. See Julia Kristeva, *Revolution in Poetic Language*, trans. Margaret Waller (New York: Columbia University Press, 1984), esp. 19–106, and *The Powers of Horror: An Essay on Abjection* (New York: Columbia University Press, 1982), esp. 32–89. While the readings in this chapter make use, in part, of the Kristevan paradigm, its limitations must be recognized. As Kaja Silverman (*The Acoustic Mirror: The Female Voice in Psychoanalysis and Cinema* [Bloomington: Indiana University Press, 1988]) has argued, Kristeva's notion of "chora" (the acoustic memory of the merging with the mother) is posited in a "highly rationalized language" that acts as a defense against her "desire for the union with the mother" and intimates a contradictory desire for the father and symbolic identity (120). Similarly, Judith Butler (*Gender Trouble: Feminism and the Subversion of Identity* [New York: Routledge, 1990]) suggests that Kristeva's theory "appears to depend upon the stability and reproduction of precisely the paternal law that she seeks to displace" (80). Despite these qualifications, Kristeva's articulation of how the maternal "gets into" language remains most useful for understanding the engendering of cultural paranoia.

7   John Johnston, "Toward the Schizo-Text: Paranoia as Semiotic Regime in *The Crying of Lot 49*," in *New Essays on "The Crying of Lot 49*," ed. Patrick O'Donnell (New York: Cambridge University Press, 1991), 73. Johnston's Deleuzian reading of *The Crying of Lot 49* offers the most satisfying theoretical consideration of the novel's semiotic processes to date, but he stops short of exploring the relation between paranoid sign systems and that which engenders them.

8   Frank Kermode, *The Art of Telling* (Cambridge, Mass.: Harvard University Press, 1984), 83.

9   Cathy N. Davidson, "Oedipa as Androgyne in Thomas Pynchon's *The Crying of Lot 49*," *Contemporary Literature* 18 (1977): 50.

10 Thomas Pynchon, *The Crying of Lot 49* (1966; reprint, New York: Harper and Row, 1986), 181. Subsequent references will be cited in the text.

11 Thomas Schaub, *Pynchon: The Voice of Ambiguity* (Urbana: University of Illinois Press, 1980), provides the fullest discussion of the various modes of ambiguity in Pynchon's fiction.

12 See, however, Pierre-Yeves Petillon, "A Re-cognition of Her Errand into the Wilderness," in *New Essays on "The Crying of Lot 49*," ed. Patrick O'Donnell (New York: Cambridge University Press, 1991), for a reading of *The Crying of Lot 49* as a novel that resonates with the mood and "hum" of the 1950s and beat culture.

13 Anne Mangel's early essay ("Maxwell's Demon, Entropy, Information: *The Crying of Lot 49*," *Triquarterly* 20 [1971]: 194–209) remains one of the best explora-

tions of the complexities of entropy in Pynchon's fiction; for a discussion of the relation between noise, redundancy, and the generation of significance using the double sense of entropy in communications theory and under the second law of thermodynamics, see Anthony Wilden, *System and Structure: Essays on Communication and Exchange*, 2d ed. (London: Tavistock, 1980), 155–90, 395–412.

14 For a compelling look at the relation between loss and metaphor in *The Crying of Lot 49*, see N. Katherine Hayles, "'A Metaphor of God Knows How Many Parts': The Engine That Drives *The Crying of Lot 49*," in *New Essays on "The Crying of Lot 49*," ed. Patrick O'Donnell (New York: Cambridge University Press, 1991).

15 See Jean-Joseph Goux, *Symbolic Economies: Between Marx and Freud*, trans. Jennifer Curtiss Gage (Ithaca, N.Y.: Cornell University Press, 1990). Subsequent references will be cited in the text.

16 For an incisive series of discussions about the relation between masculinity, the nuclear family, and the politics of the Reagan era during which these films were shot and released, see Susan Jeffords, *Hard Bodies: Hollywood Masculinity in the Reagan Era* (New Brunswick, N.J.: Rutgers University Press, 1994).

17 See Tania Modleski, *Loving with a Vengeance: Mass-Produced Fantasies for Women* (New York: Methuen, 1982), 35–58, for an analysis of the genre of popular romance and its depiction/manipulation of "rape-fantasies."

18 For an examination of the elision of subjects and objects, and the status of the object under postmodernity, see Patrick O'Donnell, "American Signatures: Postmodernism, Form, Objects," in *Culture and the Imagination: Proceedings of the Third Stuttgart Seminar in Cultural Studies*, ed. Heide Ziegler (Stuttgart: Metzler, 1995).

19 Julia Kristeva, "Women's Time," in *Feminist Theory: A Critique of Ideology*, ed. Nannerl O. Keohane, Michell Z. Rasaldo, and Barbara C. Gelpi (Chicago: University of Chicago Press, 1982), 46. Subsequent references will be cited in the text. This remarkable early essay of Kristeva's remains one of the richest, most viable accounts of the relation between nationalism, the formation of identity, and what she refers to as "counterinvestments" in the symbolic order, framed within a staging of post–1950s' feminism; it serves as a substrata for much of my commentary on the engendering of paranoia.

20 Diane Johnson, *The Shadow Knows* (New York: Knopf, 1975), 8. Subsequent references will be cited in the text.

21 Arguably, though I do not pursue this line of inquiry here, N. is a negative exemplar of what Elaine Tyler May terms "baby boomer ideology," which underlies a "reproductive consensus" about the formation of the nuclear family and planned production of infant citizens as part of the cold war effort. As a single mother of four children (clearly "badly planned") struggling for an academic career, N. flies in the face of the reproductive consensus that determines her to be a bad mother. See Elaine Tyler May, *Homeward Bound: American Families in the Cold War* (New York: Basic Books, 1988), 135–61.

22 See Barbara Johnson, "Apostrophe, Animation, and Abortion," in *A World of Difference* (Baltimore, Md.: Johns Hopkins University Press, 1987), for a compelling discussion of figural indeterminacy, and the relation between motherhood and death.

23 I use "transparent" in Jean Baudrillard's sense from *The Transparency of Evil*:

Essays on Extreme Phenomena, trans. James Benedict (London: Verso, 1993), which describes his notion that everything in postmodern reality is equally visible or "screenable," and thus undifferentiated. For an incisive comparative study of visuality, transparency, and paranoia in Baudrillard, Lyotard, and Žižek, see Jerry Anne Flieger, "The Listening Eye: Postmodernism, Paranoia, and the Hypervisible," *Diacritics* 26 (1996): 90–109. "Concrete of repression" is from Kathy Acker, *Empire of the Senseless* (New York: Grove Weidenfeld, 1990), 119. Subsequent references will be cited in the text.

24 Kathleen Hulley, "'Transgressing Genre: Kathy Acker's Intertext," in *Intertextuality and Contemporary American Fiction,* ed. Patrick O'Donnell and Robert Con Davis (Baltimore, Md.: Johns Hopkins University Press, 1989), 174–75.

25 This is a play on Kathy Acker's *In Memorium to Identity* (New York: Grove Weidenfeld, 1990), a continuation of the identity dirge of *Empire of the Senseless.*

26 Once more, Johnson's work on the figurative associations between gender identity, monstrosity, maternity, and death illuminates my reading of Acker. See Barbara Johnson, "Apostrophe," and "My Monster/My Self," in *A World of Difference* (Baltimore, Md.: Johns Hopkins University Press, 1987).

27 Gilles Deleuze and Félix Guattari, *A Thousand Plateaus: Capitalism and Schizophrenia,* trans. Brian Massumi (Minneapolis: University of Minnesota Press, 1987), 399.

28 See Slavoj Žižek, "*Cogito:* The Void Called Subject," in *Tarrying with the Negative: Kant, Hegel, and the Critique of Ideology* (Durham, N.C.: Duke University Press, 1993), for a discussion of the contradictory and "ambiguous link between the Symbolic and death" through which identity establishes its ground in an "outpassing" into death through "anticipatory identifications" (76).

29 Donna Haraway, *Simians, Cyborgs, and Women: The Reinvention of Nature* (New York: Routledge, 1991), 154, 181.

30 Judith Roof, *Reproductions of Reproduction: Imagining Symbolic Change* (New York: Routledge, 1996), 15, 16.

31 Meaghan Morris, *The Pirate's Fiancée: Feminism, Reading, Postmodernism* (New York: Verso, 1988), 4.

32 See Roof, *Reproductions of Reproduction.*

33 Žižek, *Tarrying,* 188.

4 Criminality and Paranoia

1 In the more Foucauldian terms of D. A. Miller (*The Novel and the Police* [Berkeley: University of California Press, 1988]), the discipline of the law seeks "to enforce not so much a norm as the normality of normativeness itself. Rather than rendering all its subjects uniformly 'normal,' discipline is interested in putting in place a perceptual grid in which a division between the normal and the deviant inherently imposes itself" (18). In this chapter, I will be exploring, in part, the extent to which the instantiation of normality relies on normative figurations of criminality symptomatic of cultural paranoia.

2 For his articulation of this process of monstration and containment as narrative strategy, see Michel Foucault, ed., *I, Pierre Rivière, Having Slaughtered My Mother, My Sister, and My Brother . . . : A Case of Parricide in the Nine-*

teenth Century, trans. Frank Jellinek (Lincoln: University of Nebraska Press, 1975), 199–211.

3 Michel Foucault, *Discipline and Punish: The Birth of the Prison,* trans. Alan Sheridan (New York: Vintage, 1977), 208.

4 Readings of *The Executioner's Song* have tended to focus around the issue of Gilmore as a victim of the system and the resistant embodiment of dominant ideology, or as a romantic figure who represents defiance of and alienation from the prevailing orders; see, in this regard, David Guest, *Sentenced to Death: The American Novel and Capital Punishment* (Jackson: University Press of Mississippi, 1997), 131–69; and Mark Edmundson, "Romantic Self-Creations: Mailer and Gilmore in *The Executioner's Song,*" *Contemporary Literature* 31 (1990): 434–47.

5 Pierre Bourdieu, *The Logic of Practice,* trans. Richard Nice (Stanford, Calif.: Stanford University Press, 1990), 53. Subsequent references will be cited in the text.

6 Norman Mailer, *The Executioner's Song* (New York: Little, Brown and Co., 1979), 23. Subsequent references will be cited in the text.

7 On probability, chaos, and order in the interrelation between field theory, quantum mechanics, and contemporary fiction, see N. Katherine Hayles, *Chaos Bound: Orderly Disorder in Contemporary Literature and Science* (Ithaca, N.Y.: Cornell University Press, 1991).

8 Once more, see Linda Hutcheon, "The Pastime of Past Time: Fiction, History, Historiographic Metafiction," *Genre* 20 (1987): 285–306, for an elaboration of this term, which in my view, too unproblematically collapses the relation between history and narrative.

9 See Ronald Schleifer, "American Violence: Dreiser, Mailer, and the Nature of Intertextuality," in *Intertextuality and Contemporary American Fiction,* ed. Patrick O'Donnell and Robert Con Davis (Baltimore, Md.: Johns Hopkins University Press, 1989), for a discussion of the novel as a process of "hysterical semiosis" where signs are registered as commodities, and through which, as we have seen in *Oswald's Tale,* "accident" is transformed into "tragedy, pain into a motive for action (murder)," in "a kind of necromancy" (140).

10 Guest, *Sentenced to Death,* 138.

11 Thomas Schaub, *American Fiction in the Cold War* (Madison: University of Wisconsin Press, 1991), 140.

12 Donald E. Pease, *Visionary Compacts: American Renaissance Writings in Cultural Context* (Madison: University of Wisconsin Press, 1987), 30.

13 Gilles Deleuze and Félix Guattari, *A Thousand Plateaus: Capitalism and Schizophrenia,* trans. Brian Massumi (Minneapolis: University of Minnesota Press, 1987), 112.

14 This is clearly another instance of what Žižek, using Wagner's phrase that "the wound is healed only by the spear that smote you," terms "the loop of enjoyment" in post-Kantian subjectivity whereby the threat of dissolution encrypted in otherness (criminality in *The Executioner's Song*) becomes the grounds for reconstituting the self (or community) over against the other. See Slavoj Žižek, *Tarrying with the Negative: Kant, Hegel, and the Critique of Ideology* (Durham, N.C.: Duke University Press, 1993), 165–99.

15 Lynda Zwinger, *Daughters, Fathers, and the Novel: The Sentimental Romance of Heterosexuality* (Madison: University of Wisconsin Press, 1991), 140.

16 Jim Thompson, *The Killer Inside Me* (1952; reprint, New York: Vintage, 1991), 121. Subsequent references will be cited in the text.

17 Here, Thompson reverses the logic of Mailer's territorial paranoia, where since we have run out of room for the expansion of a capacious imaginary, we must turn conspiratorially inward. For Thompson, it is because there is plenty of territory and no "crowd" to "sink into" that the inhabitants of Central City must engage in a continuous operation of disclosure and disavowal in order to remain civilized, a civility that is enforced by the law in distinguishing between legal and criminal activities founded on an identical cultural logic.

18 I rely here and in what follows for the sadomasochistic relation between the law and desire on Gilles Deleuze, *Masochism: Coldness and Cruelty, by Gilles Deleuze, and Venus in Furs, by Leopold von Sacher-Masoch* (New York: Zone Books, 1991), 123–34.

19 For the discussion of "male masochism" that informs my reading of *The Killer Inside Me* at this point and elsewhere, see Kaja Silverman, *Male Subjectivity at the Margins* (New York: Routledge, 1993), 185–213.

20 Deleuze, *Masochism*, 125.

21 Robert Polito, *Savage Art: A Biography of Jim Thompson* (New York: Knopf, 1995), 350.

22 John Harvey, *Men in Black* (Chicago: University of Chicago Press, 1995), 257. Subsequent references will be cited in the text. Interestingly, Harvey chooses as the epigraph for his book the following dialogue from *Reservoir Dogs* in a scene where the group is planning the robbery and discussing their aliases:

MR. PINK: Why can't we pick out our own color.
JOE: I tried that once, it don't work. You get four guys fighting over who's gonna be Mr. Black.

While Harvey does not comment in detail on *Reservoir Dogs* in his book, his use of this passage is suggestive of the way in which the film, as I shall discuss it, negotiates the relation between the uniformity of power signified by the black or blue suit of the corporate citizen and the libidinality expressed in Mr. Pink's existential desire for color choice; the former is categorically disjunctive to the "gay" associations of his arbitrarily imposed alias, yet the two lines of flight are conjoined in the film's logic in which outlawed desire is nominalized and incorporated.

Exit: Under History: *Underworld*

1 The phrase "homogeneous, empty time" is from Walter Benjamin, "Theses on the Philosophy of History," in *Illuminations*, ed. and intro. Hannah Arendt (New York: Schocken Books, 1969), written toward the end of the author's life. Though Benjamin is here critiquing what he considers to be a totalized view of history in favor of an authentic historical materialism, his conception of the historical at this point in his thinking is far less dialectical and far more eschatological than that presented in earlier published portions of the unfinished "Arcades Project."

2   Jacques Derrida, *Spectres of Marx: The State of Debt, the Work of Mourning, and the New International,* trans. Peggy Kamuf (New York: Routledge, 1994), 39, 70. Subsequent references will be cited in the text.

3   John Frow, *Time and Commodity Culture: Essays in Cultural Theory and Post-modernity* (New York: Oxford University Press, 1997), 9–10.

4   It is important to make clear the difference between the historical as Frow conceives it and DeLillo represents it in *Underworld,* and that conveyed by Linda Hutcheon's concept of "historiographic metafiction," or fiction that generates a reflection on the narrative conditions of history. For Frow, it is the linkage between unequal histories that is crucial, not the fictional status of these.

5   For a much-contested discussion of the relation between postmodern identities and public hysteria, see Elaine Showalter, *Hysteries: Hysterical Epidemics and Modern Culture* (New York: Columbia University Press, 1997).

6   Cited in Susan Buck-Morss, *The Dialectics of Seeing: Walter Benjamin and the Arcades Project* (Cambridge, Mass.: MIT Press, 1989), 271.

7   Cited in Gerald Howard, "The American Strangeness: An Interview with Don DeLillo," *Hungry Mind Review,* web edition: http://www.bookwire.com/hmr/hmrinterviews.article$2563.

8   Don DeLillo, *Underworld* (New York: Scribner, 1997), 105. Subsequent references will be cited in the text. In several ways, *Underworld* is a recapitulation of all DeLillo's previous novels: the many representations of crowds and crowd behavior that the novel contains recalls DeLillo's "crowd" novel, *Mao II;* there are several references to the Kennedy assassination and the Zapruder film, evoking *Libra;* the reflections on names and naming to be found throughout the novel bring to mind *The Names.* Although I do not pursue it here, it could be argued that in this manner, *Underworld* generates several parallels between cold war culture and DeLillo's career as a cold war author, an identification between culture and author that resonates in DeLillo's comments, cited previously, about how he found the subject of *Underworld.*

9   I take this scene in the novel as a conscious, if ironic, reference to the notion of pastiche that Fredric Jameson articulates in *Postmodernism, or, the Cultural Logic of Late Capitalism* (Durham, N.C.: Duke University Press, 1991), using as one example the video installations of Nam June Paik:

> In the most interesting postmodern works, however, one can detect a more positive conception of relationship, which restores its proper tension to the notion of difference itself. This new mode of relationship through difference may sometimes be an achieved new and original way of thinking and perceiving; more often it takes the form of an impossible imperative to achieve that new mutation in what can perhaps no longer be called consciousness. I believe that the most striking emblem of this new mode of thinking relationships can be found in the work of Nam June Paik, whose stacked or scattered television screens, positioned at intervals within lush vegetation, or winking down at us from a ceiling of strange new video stars, recapitulate over and over again prearranged sequences or loops of images which return at dysynchronous moments on the various screens. The older aesthetic is then practiced by viewers, who, bewildered by this discontinuous variety, decided to concentrate on a single screen, as though the relatively worthless image sequence to be followed there had some organic value in its own right. The postmodernist viewer, however,

is called upon to do the impossible, namely, to see all the screens at once, in their radical and random difference. (31)

By relating Jameson's postmodern "new mode of thinking relationships" with the Kennedy assassination and Klara's sense that what she is seeing is "the sort of death plot that runs in the mind," DeLillo generates an eerie collusion between postmodernist hermeneutics, the representation of history, and history as such (both accident and plot, as *Libra* suggests) that produces a simulacrum of the mind's techne.

10 The symptomatic conceptualization of history can be contrasted with the asymptomatic version of some new historicisms, which rely for historical veracity on the assumed connectivity of anecdotal knowledge and various forms of scattered information regathered under the principle that everything of historical importance is always already available for manifestation and linkage. For discussions and critiques of these new historicist tendencies, see Carolyn Porter, "Are We Being Historical Yet?" in *The States of Theory: History, Art, and Critical Discourse*, ed. David Carroll (New York: Columbia University Press, 1990); Patrick O'Donnell, "History without Theory: Re-Covering American Literature," *Genre* 22 (1989): 375–93; and Edward Pechter, "The New Historicism and Its Discontents: Politicizing Renaissance Drama," *PMLA* 102 (1987): 292–303.

11 Given this view of cyberspace, is it any accident that the engineers of the Microsoft Windows operating system, as part of an insider's addition to the system's "Control Panel" labeled "Tweak UI," invented a small program called "Paranoia" that allows the user to cover his or her tracks while surfing the net by erasing linkage histories? It is also worth recalling that in the final scene of *Underworld* as I read it, the internet is the invention of the U.S. cold war "military-industrial complex."

Bibliography

Acker, Kathy. *Empire of the Senseless.* New York: Grove Weidenfeld, 1988.
———. *In Memorium to Identity.* New York: Grove Weidenfeld, 1990.
Alliez, Éric. *Capital Times.* Translated by Georges Van Den Abbeele. Minneapolis: University of Minnesota Press, 1996.
Anderson, Benedict. *Imagined Communities: Reflections on the Origin and the Spread of Nationalism.* Rev. ed. New York: Verso, 1989.
Baudrillard, Jean. *The Perfect Crime.* Translated by Chris Turner. New York: Verso, 1996.
———. *The Transparency of Evil: Essays on Extreme Phenomena.* Translated by James Benedict. London: Verso, 1993.
Benjamin, Walter. "Theses on the Philosophy of History." In *Illuminations,* edited and introduced by Hannah Arendt. New York: Schocken Books, 1969.
Bercovitch, Sacvan. *The Puritan Origins of the American Self.* New Haven, Conn.: Yale University Press, 1975.
Berlant, Lauren. *The Anatomy of National Fantasy: Hawthorne, Utopia, and Everyday Life.* Chicago: University of Chicago Press, 1991.
Bernstein, Michael André. *Foregone Conclusions: Against Apocalyptic History.* Berkeley: University of California Press, 1994.
Bernstein, Stephen. "*Libra* and the Historical Sublime." *Postmodern Culture* 4, no. 2 (1994).
Bersani, Leo. "Pynchon, Paranoia, and Literature." *Representations* 25 (1989): 99–118.
Best, Steven, and Douglas Kellner. *Postmodern Theory: Critical Interrogations.* New York: Guilford Press, 1991.
Bhabha, Homi K. "DissemiNation: Time, Narrative, and the Margins of the Modern Nation." In *Nation and Narration,* edited by Homi K. Bhabha. New York: Routledge, 1990.

———. "Signs Taken for Wonders: Questions of Ambivalence and Authority under a Tree outside Delhi, May 1817." In *Race, Writing, and Difference,* edited by Henry Louis Gates Jr. Chicago: University of Chicago Press, 1986.

Bourdieu, Pierre. *The Logic of Practice.* Translated by Richard Nice. Stanford, Calif.: Stanford University Press, 1990.

Brennan, Teresa. "The Age of Paranoia." *Paragraph* 14, no. 1 (1991): 20–45.

———. *History after Lacan.* New York: Routledge, 1993.

Buck-Morss, Susan. *The Dialectics of Seeing: Walter Benjamin and the Arcades Project.* Cambridge, Mass.: MIT Press, 1989.

Buell, Frederick. *National Culture and the New Global System.* Baltimore, Md.: Johns Hopkins University Press, 1994.

Burgoyne, Robert. "Modernism and the Narration of Nation in *JFK.*" In *The Persistence of History: Cinema, Television, and the Modern Event,* edited by Vivian Sobchek. New York: Routledge, 1996.

Butler, Judith. *Gender Trouble: Feminism and the Subversion of Identity.* New York: Routledge, 1990.

Byers, Thomas B. "Terminating the Postmodern: Masculinity and Pomophobia." *Modern Fiction Studies* 41 (1994): 5–34.

Carmichael, Thomas. "Lee Harvey Oswald and the Postmodern Subject: History and Intertextuality in Don DeLillo's *Libra, The Names,* and *Mao II.*" *Contemporary Literature* 34 (1993): 204–18.

Copjec, Jean. *Read My Desire: Lacan against the Historicists.* Cambridge, Mass.: MIT Press, 1994.

Corber, Robert J. *In the Name of National Security: Hitchcock, Homophobia, and the Political Construction of Gender in Postwar America.* Durham, N.C.: Duke University Press, 1993.

Davidson, Cathy N. "Oedipa as Androgyne in Thomas Pynchon's *The Crying of Lot 49.*" *Contemporary Literature* 18 (1977): 38–50.

DeCurtis, Anthony. " 'An Outside in This Society': An Interview with Don DeLillo." *South Atlantic Quarterly* 89 (1990): 281–304.

Deleuze, Gilles. *The Fold: Leibniz and the Baroque.* Translated by Tom Conley. Minneapolis: University of Minnesota Press, 1993.

———. *Masochism: Coldness and Cruelty, by Gilles Deleuze, and Venus in Furs, by Leopold von Sacher-Masoch.* New York: Zone Books, 1991.

Deleuze, Gilles, and Félix Guattari. *A Thousand Plateaus: Capitalism and Schizophrenia.* Translated by Brian Massumi. Minneapolis: University of Minnesota Press, 1987.

DeLillo, Don. "American Blood: A Journey through the Labyrinth of Dallas and JFK." *Rolling Stone,* 8 December 1983, 21–22, 24, 27–28, 74.

———. *Libra.* 1988. Reprint, New York: Penguin, 1989.

———. *Underworld.* New York: Scribner, 1997.

Denzin, Norman K. *The Cinematic Society: The Voyeur's Gaze.* London: Sage, 1995.

Derrida, Jacques. *Given Time 1: Counterfeit Money.* Translated by Peggy Kamuf. Chicago: University of Chicago Press, 1992.

———. *Spectres of Marx: The State of Debt, the Work of Mourning, and the New International.* Translated by Peggy Kamuf. New York: Routledge, 1994.

Edmundson, Mark. "Romantic Self-Creations: Mailer and Gilmore in *The Executioner's Song.*" *Contemporary Literature* 31 (1990): 434–47.

Farrell, John. *Freud's Paranoid Quest: Psychoanalysis and Modern Suspicion.* New York: New York University Press, 1996.

Flieger, Jerry Anne. "The Listening Eye: Postmodernism, Paranoia, and the Hypervisible." *Diacritics* 26 (1996): 90–109.

Foster, Hal. *The Return of the Real.* Cambridge, Mass.: MIT Press, 1996.

Foucault, Michel. *Discipline and Punish: The Birth of the Prison.* Translated by Alan Sheridan. New York: Vintage, 1977.

———, ed. *I, Pierre Rivière, Having Slaughtered My Mother, My Sister, and My Brother . . . . A Case of Parricide in the Nineteenth Century.* Translated by Frank Jellinek. Lincoln: University of Nebraska Press, 1975.

Freud, Sigmund. "A Case of Paranoia Running Counter to the Psychoanalytic Theory of That Disease." In *The Standard Edition of the Complete Psychological Works of Sigmund Freud,* translated by James Strachey et al. Vol. 14. London: Hogarth Press, 1953–1974.

———. "Psycho-analytic Notes upon an Autobiographical Account of a Case of Paranoia (Dementia Paranoides) (1911)." In *Collected Papers,* translated by James Strachey. Vol. 3. New York: Basic Books, 1959.

Frow, John. *Time and Commodity Culture: Essays in Cultural Theory and Postmodernity.* New York: Oxford University Press, 1997.

Godden, Richard. *Fictions of Capital: The American Novel from James to Mailer.* New York: Cambridge University Press, 1990.

Gould, Stephen Jay. *Wonderful Life: The Burgess Shale and the Nature of History.* New York: W. W. Norton, 1989.

Goux, Jean-Joseph. *Symbolic Economies: Between Marx and Freud.* Translated by Jennifer Curtiss Gage. Ithaca, N.Y.: Cornell University Press, 1990.

Guest, David. *Sentenced to Death: The American Novel and Capital Punishment.* Jackson: University Press of Mississippi, 1997.

Haraway, Donna. *Simians, Cyborgs, and Women: The Reinvention of Nature.* New York: Routledge, 1991.

Harvey, David. *The Condition of Postmodernity.* Cambridge, U.K.: Blackwell, 1990.

Harvey, John. *Men in Black.* Chicago: University of Chicago Press, 1995.

Hayles, N. Katherine. *Chaos Bound: Orderly Disorder in Contemporary Literature and Science.* Ithaca, N.Y.: Cornell University Press, 1991.

———. " 'A Metaphor of God Knows How Many Parts': The Engine That Drives *The Crying of Lot 49.*" In *New Essays on "The Crying of Lot 49,"* edited by Patrick O'Donnell. New York: Cambridge University Press, 1991.

Heise, Ursula K. *Chronoschisms: Time, Narrative, and Postmodernism.* New York: Cambridge University Press, 1997.

Hofstader, Richard. "The Paranoid Style in American Politics." In *The Paranoid Style in American Politics and Other Essays.* New York: Knopf, 1966.

Howard, Gerald. "The American Strangeness: An Interview with Don De-

Lillo." *Hungry Mind Review,* web edition: http://www.bookwire.com/hmr/ hmrinterviews.article$2563.

Hulley, Kathleen. "Transgressing Genre: Kathy Acker's Intertext." In *Intertextuality and Contemporary American Fiction,* edited by Patrick O'Donnell and Robert Con Davis. Baltimore, Md.: Johns Hopkins University Press, 1989.

Hutcheon, Linda. "The Pastime of Past Time: Fiction, History, Historiographic Metafiction." *Genre* 20 (1987): 285–306.

Huyssen, Andreas. *Twilight Memories: Marking Time in a Culture of Amnesia.* New York: Routledge, 1995.

Irigaray, Luce. *This Sex Which Is Not One.* Translated by Catherine Porter. Ithaca, N.Y.: Cornell University Press, 1985.

Jameson, Fredric. "Marx's Purloined Letter." *New Left Review,* no. 208 (1994).

———. *The Political Unconscious: Narrative as a Socially Symbolic Act.* Ithaca, N.Y.: Cornell University Press, 1981.

———. *Postmodernism, or, The Cultural Logic of Late Capitalism.* Durham, N.C.: Duke University Press, 1991.

———. *The Seeds of Time.* New York: Columbia University Press, 1994.

JanMohamed, Abdul R. "The Economy of Manichean Allegory: The Function of Racial Difference in Colonialist Literature." In *Race, Writing, and Difference,* edited by Henry Louis Gates Jr. Chicago: University of Chicago Press, 1986.

Jeffords, Susan. *Hard Bodies: Hollywood Masculinity in the Reagan Era.* New Brunswick, N.J.: Rutgers University Press, 1994.

Johnson, Barbara. *A World of Difference.* Baltimore, Md.: Johns Hopkins University Press, 1987.

Johnson, Diane. *The Shadow Knows.* New York: Knopf, 1975.

Johnston, John. "Superlinear Fiction or Historical Diagram: Don DeLillo's *Libra.*" *Modern Fiction Studies* 40 (1994): 319–42.

———. "Toward the Schizo-Text: Paranoia as Semiotic Regime in *The Crying of Lot 49.*" In *New Essays on "The Crying of Lot 49,"* edited by Patrick O'Donnell. New York: Cambridge University Press, 1991.

Kermode, Frank. *The Art of Telling.* Cambridge, Mass.: Harvard University Press, 1984.

Kristeva, Julia. *Powers of Horror: An Essay on Abjection.* New York: Columbia University Press, 1982.

———. *Revolution in Poetic Language.* Translated by Margaret Waller. New York: Columbia University Press, 1984.

———. *Strangers to Ourselves.* Translated by Leon Roudiez. New York: Columbia University Press, 1991.

———. "Women's Time." In *Feminist Theory: A Critique of Ideology,* edited by Nannerl O. Keohane, Michell Z. Rosaldo, and Barbara C. Gelpi. Chicago: University of Chicago Press, 1982.

Kroker, Arthur, Marilouise Kroker, and David Cook. *Panic Encyclopedia: The Definitive Guide to the Postmodern Scene.* New York: St. Martin's Press, 1989.

Kronick, Joseph. *"Libra* and the Assassination of JFK: A Textbook Operation." *Arizona Quarterly* 50 (1994): 109–32.

LeClair, Thomas. *In the Loop: Don DeLillo and the Systems Novel.* Urbana: University of Illinois Press, 1987.

Leitch, Vincent B. *Postmodernism: Local Effects, Global Flows.* Albany: State University of New York Press, 1996.

Lentricchia, Frank. *"Libra* as Postmodern Critique." *South Atlantic Quarterly* 89 (1990): 431–53.

Lyotard, Jean-François. *The Inhuman: Reflections on Time.* Translated by Geoffrey Bennington and Rachel Bowlby. Stanford, Calif.: Stanford University Press, 1991.

———. *Libidinal Economy.* Translated by Iain Hamilton Grant. Bloomington: Indiana University Press, 1993.

———. *The Postmodern Condition: A Report on Knowledge.* Translated by Geoff Bennington and Brian Massumi. Minneapolis: University of Minnesota Press, 1984.

Mailer, Norman. *The Executioner's Song.* New York: Little, Brown and Co., 1979.

———. *Oswald's Tale: An American Mystery.* Now York: Random House, 1995.

Mangel, Anne. "Maxwell's Demon, Entropy, Information: *The Crying of Lot 49.*" *TriQuarterly* 20 (1971): 194–209.

Marcus, Stephen. "Norman Mailer: An Interview." In *Conversations with Norman Mailer,* edited by J. Michael Lennon. Jackson: University of Mississippi Press, 1988.

Massumi, Brian. *The Politics of Everyday Fear.* Minneapolis: University of Minnesota Press, 1993.

May, Elaine Tyler. *Homeward Bound: American Families in the Cold War.* New York: Basic Books, 1988.

McClure, John. *Late Imperial Romance.* New York: Verso, 1994.

Millard, Bill. "The Fable of the Ants: Myopic Interactions in DeLillo's *Libra.*" *Postmodern Culture* 4, no. 2 (1994): http://jefferson.village.virginia.edu/pmc/issue.194/millard.194.html.

Miller, D. A. *The Novel and the Police.* Berkeley: University of California Press, 1988.

Miller, J. Hillis. *Ariadne's Thread: Story Lines.* New Haven, Conn.: Yale University Press, 1992.

Modleski, Tania. *Loving with a Vengeance: Mass-Produced Fantasies for Women.* New York: Methuen, 1982.

Monaghan, Charles. "Portrait of a Man Reading." In *Conversations with Norman Mailer,* edited by J. Michael Lennon. Jackson: University of Mississippi Press, 1988.

Morris, Meaghan. *The Pirate's Fiancée: Feminism, Reading, Postmodernism.* New York: Verso, 1988.

Nadel, Alan. *Containment Culture: American Narratives, Postmodernism, and the Atomic Age.* Durham, N.C.: Duke University Press, 1995.

O'Donnell, Patrick. "American Signatures: Postmodernism, Form, Objects." In

Culture and the Imagination: Proceedings of the Third Stuttgart Seminar in Cultural Studies, edited by Heide Ziegler. Stuttgart: Metzler, 1995.

————. "History without Theory: Re-Covering American Literature." *Genre* 22 (1989): 375–93.

————. "Obvious Paranoia: The Politics of Don DeLillo's *Running Dog*." *Centennial Review* 34 (1990): 56–72.

Olster, Stacey. *Reminiscence and Re-Creation in Contemporary American Fiction*. New York: Cambridge University Press, 1989.

Osborne, Peter. *The Politics of Time: Modernity and Avant-Garde*. New York: Verso, 1995.

Pease, Donald E. "National Narratives, Postnational Narration." *Modern Fiction Studies* 43 (1997): 1–23.

————. *Visionary Compacts: American Renaissance Writings in Cultural Context*. Madison: University of Wisconsin Press, 1987.

Pechter, Edward. "The New Historicism and Its Discontents: Politicizing Renaissance Drama." *PMLA* 102 (1987): 292–303.

Petillon, Pierre-Yeves. "A Re-cognition of Her Errand into the Wilderness." In *New Essays on "The Crying of Lot 49,"* edited by Patrick O'Donnell. New York: Cambridge University Press, 1991.

Polan, Dana. *Power and Paranoia: History, Narrative, and the American Cinema, 1940–1950*. New York: Columbia University Press, 1986.

Polito, Robert. *Savage Art: A Biography of Jim Thompson*. New York: Knopf, 1995.

Porter, Carolyn. "Are We Being Historical Yet?" In *The States of Theory: History, Art, and Critical Discourse*, edited by David Carroll. New York: Columbia University Press, 1990.

Pynchon, Thomas. *The Crying of Lot 49*. 1966. Reprint, New York: Harper and Row, 1986.

Rogin, Michael. "Body and Soul Murder: *JFK*." In *Media Spectacles*, edited by Margorie Garber, Jann Matlock, and Rebecca L. Walkowitz. New York: Routledge, 1993.

————. *Ronald Reagan, the Movie, and Other Episodes in Political Demonology*. Berkeley: University of California Press, 1987.

Ronell, Avital. *Finitude's Score: Essays for the End of the Millennium*. Lincoln: University of Nebraska Press, 1994.

Roof, Judith. *Reproductions of Reproduction: Imaging Symbolic Change*. New York: Routledge, 1996.

Rose, Jacqueline. "Paranoia and the Film System." *Screen* 17 (1977): 85–104.

Sagan, Eli. *The Honey and the Hemlock: Democracy and Paranoia in Ancient Athens and Modern America*. New York: Basic Books, 1991.

Santner, Eric L. *My Own Private Germany: Daniel Paul Schreber's Secret History of Modernity*. Princeton, N.J.: Princeton University Press, 1996.

Schaub, Thomas. *American Fiction in the Cold War*. Madison: University of Wisconsin Press, 1991.

————. *Pynchon: The Voice of Ambiguity*. Urbana: University of Illinois Press, 1980.

Schleifer, Ronald. "American Violence: Dreiser, Mailer, and the Nature of Intertextuality." In *Intertextuality and Contemporary American Fiction,* edited by Patrick O'Donnell and Robert Con Davis. Baltimore, Md.: Johns Hopkins University Press, 1989.

Sedgwick, Eve Kosofsky. *Epistemology of the Closet.* Berkeley: University of California Press, 1990.

Seltzer, Mark. *Serial Killers: Death and Life in America's Wound Culture.* New York: Routledge, 1998.

Showalter, Elaine. *Hysteries: Hysterical Epidemics and Modern Culture.* New York: Columbia University Press, 1997.

Siegel, Mark. *Pynchon: Creative Paranoia in "Gravity's Rainbow."* Port Washington, N.Y.: Kennikat Press, 1978.

Silverman, Kaja. *The Acoustic Mirror: The Female Voice in Psychoanalysis and Cinema.* Bloomington: Indiana University Press, 1988.

———. *Male Subjectivity at the Margins.* New York: Routledge, 1993.

Sloterdijk, Peter. *Critique of Cynical Reason.* Translated by Michal Eldred. Minneapolis: University of Minnesota Press, 1987.

Smith, Paul. *Discerning the Subject.* Minneapolis: University of Minnesota Press, 1988.

Stone, Oliver, and Zachary Sklar. *JFK: The Book of the Film.* New York: Applause Books, 1992.

Stone, Oliver, dir. *JFK.* Warner Brothers, 1991.

Tabbi, Joseph. *Postmodern Sublime: Technology and American Writing from Mailer to Cyberpunk.* Ithaca, N.Y.: Cornell University Press, 1995.

Tanner, Tony. *City of Words: American Fiction, 1950–1970.* New York: Harper and Row, 1971.

Tarrantino, Quentin, dir. *Reservoir Dogs.* Miramax, 1992.

Thompson, Jim. *The Killer Inside Me.* 1952. Reprint, New York: Vintage, 1991.

Werckmeister, Otto Karl. *Citadel Culture.* Chicago: University of Chicago Press, 1991.

Whitfield, Stephen J. *The Culture of the Cold War.* Baltimore, Md.: Johns Hopkins University Press, 1991.

Wilden, Anthony. *System and Structure: Essays on Communication and Exchange.* 2d ed. London: Tavistock, 1980.

Žižek, Slavoj. *For They Know Not What They Do: Enjoyment as a Political Factor.* New York: Verso, 1991.

———. *Metastases of Enjoyment: Six Essays on Women and Causality.* New York: Verso, 1994.

———. *The Plague of Fantasies.* London: Verso, 1997.

———. *The Sublime Object of Ideology.* New York: Verso, 1989.

———. *Tarrying with the Negative: Kant, Hegel, and the Critique of Ideology.* Durham, N.C.: Duke University Press, 1993.

Zwinger, Lynda. *Daughters, Fathers, and the Novel: The Sentimental Romance of Heterosexuality.* Madison: University of Wisconsin Press, 1991.

Index

■ Patrick O'Donnell is Professor and Chair of the Department
of English at Michigan State University. He is the author of *Echo
Chambers: Figuring Voice in Modern Narrative; Passionate
Doubts: Designs of Interpretation in Contemporary American
Fiction;* and *John Hawkes.* The former editor of *MFS: Modern
Fiction Studies,* he has also edited *New Essays on "The Crying of
Lot 49"* and (with Robert Con Davis) *Intertextuality and
Contemporary American Fiction.*

Library of Congress Cataloging-in-Publication Data
O'Donnell, Patrick, 1948–
Latent destinies : cultural paranoia and contemporary U.S.
narrative / Patrick O'Donnell.
p. cm. — (New Americanists)
Includes bibliographical references and index.
ISBN 0-8223-2558-6 (alk. paper)
ISBN 0-8223-2587-x (pbk. : alk. paper)
1. American fiction—20th century—History and criticism.
2. Paranoia in literature. 3. Literature and society—United
states—History—20th century. 4. Motion pictures—United
States—History and criticism. 5. Postmodernism—United
States. 6. Narration (Rhetoric) I. Series.
PS374.P35 O36   2000
700'.1'030973—dc21   00-026812